*For Bob
 and for Herman,
without you, it would never have been.*

*Sincere thanks, too,
 to Lori and Don,
   librarians par excellence at Wittenberg University
 and to Bonnie, a truly understanding editor.*

Contents

Why Consider Opposing Viewpoints?

> *"It is better to debate a question without settling it than to settle a question without debating it."*
>
> Joseph Joubert (1754-1824)

The Importance of Examining Opposing Viewpoints

The purpose of the Opposing Viewpoints Series, and this book in particular, is to present balanced, and often difficult to find, opposing points of view on complex and sensitive issues.

Probably the best way to become informed is to analyze the positions of those who are regarded as experts and well studied on issues. It is important to consider every variety of opinion in an attempt to determine the truth. Opinions from the mainstream of society should be examined. But also important are opinions that are considered radical, reactionary, or minority as well as those stigmatized by some other uncomplimentary label. An important lesson of history is the eventual acceptance of many unpopular and even despised opinions. The ideas of Socrates, Jesus, and Galileo are good examples of this.

Readers will approach this book with their own opinions on the issues debated within it. However, to have a good grasp of one's own viewpoint, it is necessary to understand the arguments of those with whom one disagrees. It can be said that those who do not completely understand their adversary's point of view do not fully understand their own.

A persuasive case for considering opposing viewpoints has been presented by John Stuart Mill in his work *On Liberty*. When examining controversial issues it may be helpful to reflect on this suggestion:

The only way in which a human being can make some approach to knowing the whole of a subject, is by hearing what can be said about it by persons of every variety of opinion, and studying all modes in which it can be looked at by every character of mind. No wise man ever acquired his wisdom in any mode but this.

Analyzing Sources of Information

The Opposing Viewpoints Series includes diverse materials taken from magazines, journals, books, and newspapers, as well as statements and position papers from a wide range of individuals, organizations, and governments. This broad spectrum of sources helps to develop patterns of thinking which are open to the consideration of a variety of opinions.

Pitfalls to Avoid

A pitfall to avoid in considering opposing points of view is that of regarding one's own opinion as being common sense and the most rational stance, and the point of view of others as being only opinion and naturally wrong. It may be that another's opinion is correct and one's own is in error.

Another pitfall to avoid is that of closing one's mind to the opinions of those with whom one disagrees. The best way to approach a dialogue is to make one's primary purpose that of understanding the mind and arguments of the other person and not that of enlightening him or her with one's own solutions. More can be learned by listening than speaking.

It is my hope that after reading this book the reader will have a deeper understanding of the issues debated and will appreciate the complexity of even seemingly simple issues on which good and honest people disagree. This awareness is particularly important in a democratic society such as ours where people enter into public debate to determine the common good. Those with whom one disagrees should not necessarily be regarded as enemies, but perhaps simply as people who suggest different paths to a common goal.

Developing Basic Reading and Thinking Skills

In this book, carefully edited opposing viewpoints are purposely placed back to back to create a running debate; each viewpoint is preceded by a short quotation that best expresses the author's main argument. This format instantly plunges the reader into the midst of a controversial issue and greatly aids that reader in mastering the basic skill of recognizing an author's point of view.

A number of basic skills for critical thinking are practiced in the activities that appear throughout the books in the series. Some of the skills are:

9

Evaluating Sources of Information. The ability to choose from among alternative sources the most reliable and accurate source in relation to a given subject.

Separating Fact from Opinion. The ability to make the basic distinction between factual statements (those that can be demonstrated or verified empirically) and statements of opinion (those that are beliefs or attitudes that cannot be proved).

Identifying Stereotypes. The ability to identify oversimplified, exaggerated descriptions (favorable or unfavorable) about people and insulting statements about racial, religious, or national groups, based upon misinformation or lack of information.

Recognizing Ethnocentrism. The ability to recognize attitudes or opinions that express the view that one's own race, culture, or group is inherently superior, or those attitudes that judge another culture or group in terms of one's own.

It is important to consider opposing viewpoints and equally important to be able to critically analyze those viewpoints. The activities in this book are designed to help the reader master these thinking skills. Statements are taken from the book's viewpoints and the reader is asked to analyze them. This technique aids the reader in developing skills that not only can be applied to the viewpoints in this book, but also to situations where opinionated spokespersons comment on controversial issues. Although the activities are helpful to the solitary reader, they are most useful when the reader can benefit from the interaction of group discussion.

Using this book and others in the series should help readers develop basic reading and thinking skills. These skills should improve the reader's ability to understand what is read. Readers should be better able to separate fact from opinion, substance from rhetoric, and become better consumers of information in our media-centered culture.

This volume of the Opposing Viewpoints Series does not advocate a particular point of view. Quite the contrary! The very nature of the book leaves it to the reader to formulate the opinions he or she finds most suitable. My purpose as publisher is to see that this is made possible by offering a wide range of viewpoints that are fairly presented.

David L. Bender
Publisher

Introduction

"Uncritical adulation and [equally uncritical] lambasting . . . are both unhistorical, in the sense that they select from the often cloudy record of Columbus's actual motives and deeds what suits the researcher's twentieth century purposes. That sort of history caricatures the complexity of human reality by turning Columbus into either a bloody ogre or a plaster saint."

William Hardy McNeill

Though his landing was not at the spot that he had proposed to the Spanish sovereigns, Columbus's arrival at Guanahaní was to have consequences far more significant and far-reaching than the discovery of a western trade route to India. Perhaps the most significant consequence of Columbus's voyage was the unleashing of a set of extraordinary forces of change. As Columbus strode ashore to meet the friendly, generous natives, he inaugurated a series of exchanges between the two worlds. From that moment on, neither world was ever the same.

Historian Alfred W. Crosby Jr. calls this process the Columbian exchange. Crosby notes that some catalysts, like the potato, were humble, while others, like religion, were more profound. The Smithsonian Institution selected five catalysts, which it called "seeds," for its 1992 exhibit, Seeds of Change: disease, the horse, corn, the potato, and sugar. As the exhibit pointed out, the exchange was not one-way. While sugar and the horse were brought to the Americas, corn and the potato were taken to Europe and Africa. Diseases sought out victims in both hemispheres. Each of these seeds, once transplanted, had far-reaching, often contradictory, consequences.

At first an agent of Spanish conquest, horses became a catalyst for change in Indian culture. By giving the Plains Indians increased mobility, the horse brought tribes into increased contact—both peaceful and warlike—with each other and with encroaching whites. Moreover, it influenced virtually every dimension of Plains culture, from hunting and transportation to concepts of wealth and courage, to marriage customs and funeral traditions.

Disease, too, brought major changes in both hemispheres after

11

Columbus's voyages. Smallpox, especially, among the diseases endemic in Europe but unknown in the Americas, ravaged the native American population, producing as much as a 90 percent population loss in the first century after contact. Some tribes, like the Mandan, became virtually extinct. Though the disease was not introduced intentionally, it became an unexpected ally of the conquest. Cortés's victory at Tenochtitlan can be credited largely to the effects of smallpox. Moreover, throughout the Americas, European disease, terrifyingly inexplicable, withstood Indian medical practices and swept through populations lacking immunity. In the process, political structures of Indian society were destroyed as leaders succumbed and processes of orderly succession were disrupted by death. Often, native religious practices were undermined as Indians saw practitioners of the new religion seemingly invulnerable to the disease. It would have seemed little solace to those decimated by smallpox to have learned that Columbus's sailors almost certainly took syphilis with them back to Europe.

Food

Food seems a more benevolent seed of change. For Europe and Africa, the Americas provided a cornucopia of new foods. Among the over three hundred food crops cultivated by the American Indians were peanuts, beans, squash, sweet potatoes, pumpkins, papayas, manioc (cassava or tapioca), guavas, avocados, pineapples, tomatoes, chili peppers, cocoa, sunflowers, and the two "miracle crops" corn and potatoes. Despite initial European objections to foods from the New World (for example, that they were not mentioned in the Bible; thus, they were "fruits of the Devil") hunger was a strong impetus for acceptance. The major New World crops, especially corn and the potato, provided a greater number of calories per acre than did the Old World wheat, barley, rice, or rye. Other foods, like many varieties of beans, became known as the "poor man's meat," providing a source of protein for those who could not afford to own livestock.

In contrast to most of these crops, sugar brought controversial change. Growing and processing sugar is labor-intensive, and, when the native labor pool declined from disease and harsh treatment, alternative sources were needed: indentured servants and slaves from Africa. In addition, the environment was greatly affected by sugar: widespread deforestation occurred to provide fuel for the boiling houses. By the eighteenth century, sugar cane was the most important cash crop in tropical America. The Americas became an integral part of the world economy, largely because of the sugar trade. The sugar colonies bought slaves from Africa, manufactured goods and luxuries for Europe, and harvested basic foods and lumber from North America. In return,

Two eras of exploration merge into a single moment: Replicas of Columbus's ships arrive off Florida's Cape Canaveral as the space shuttle Endeavor *awaits its maiden launch into the new world of outer space.*

they exported sugar, rum, and molasses. The sugar industry of the Americas inaugurated a global economy in which decisions made on one continent had consequences for several others. It is this interconnectedness that the Smithsonian claimed was Columbus's greatest legacy. In 1492 the world was round. After 1492 the world was one.

Others, however, take issue with efforts to make these changes the focus of Columbus's reevaluation. Bill Bigelow, coordinator of the Rethinking Columbus Project of the Network of Educators on Central America, criticizes the Smithsonian exhibit and other such evaluations as neutral, passionless, and pro-capitalist. He argues that they are also dangerous because they

> steer people away from critical analyses of today's Columbuses, today's empires, today's slaveries. . . . The encounter/exchange mythmakers are no more willing to condemn the brutality and degradation of Spanish imperialism than are the writers of Columbus children's biographies. . . . This failure to take on the imperialists of 500 years ago discourages people from recognizing and denouncing imperial features in our own society. Criticizing a long-ago social system built on controlling other people's land and resources, accompanied at home by vast inequalities of wealth and power, could and should spawn a similar critique of contemporary U.S. society.

Bigelow believes the Seeds of Change exhibit was just another attempt to neutralize the real legacy of Columbus: death, slavery, and brutality.

Bigelow believes that affixing blame is necessary for society to learn the lessons of the past and to make good choices for the future. Doing so is difficult, if not impossible. Who, for example, is to blame for the human degradation resulting from the sugar economy? Columbus? The crown who wanted to hold Hispaniola after gold-seeking Spaniards chose to abandon it? The friars who asked permission to import slaves? The second sons of the Irish aristocracy who owned plantations? The eighteenth-century English, who used increasing quantities of sugar in their coffee, cocoa, and tea? We—as we continue to support labor conditions in the sugar fields that are still appalling today? Christopher Columbus was no saint, but to affix blame to consequences he could not have foreseen and to attitudes he could not have envisioned adopting seems somewhat pointless.

Today, the world is even more closely linked than it became in October 1492. This, then, may be the most significant result of Columbus's voyages—not that he discovered a "a new world" but rather that, from his time on, two "old worlds" merged into one.

In this new world we must learn the intricacies of living interrelated lives. Today, many local decisions have global consequences. For example, the cutting of Amazonian rain forests, while providing additional land for farming and profit, has exacerbated global warming. As we voyage into the future, we need be ever more conscious that the world—perhaps the universe—is one, and that we must be responsible for it.

14

CHAPTER 1

Christopher Columbus Evaluated

Chapter Preface

Christopher Columbus was a complex and contradictory man. For example, he often demonstrated petty selfishness, as when he appropriated the reward promised to the sailor who first sighted land. Yet he could also devote himself unselfishly to a larger cause, such as his goal to finance the recapture of Jerusalem. Although he never married his mistress Beatriz, mother of his younger son Ferdinand, most likely because she was of humble birth and might hinder his ambitions, he provided an annuity for her for a while and, in his last will, said "she weighs heavily on my conscience." On the one hand, he could dream great dreams, assimilate the knowledge of navigators and geographers, and plan the westward route across the Ocean Sea. On the other, he was a terrible colonial administrator, unable to make firm decisions or to choose the right subordinates. And while he had advocates at court, he was less than adept at building support for his actions. For example, after some of the colonists at Santo Domingo had mutinied and reported back to the monarchs on his failings, Columbus was arrested and sent back to Spain in chains by Francisco de Bobadilla, who had been sent by the crown to restore order.

Because the consequences of Columbus's career are neither black nor white, evaluations of his impact—both historical and modern—are sharply polarized, as the viewpoints in this chapter attest. Pope Pius IX wanted to make him a saint; Russell Means, a Native American activist, charges that Columbus "makes Hitler look like a juvenile delinquent." While these characterizations are drawn from different centuries, divergent viewpoints about Christopher Columbus have been present almost from the moment of his first appearance at Ferdinand and Isabella's court. The truth lies somewhere in the middle; Columbus was neither virtue nor vice incarnate. As the historian William Hardy McNeill has written:

> Uncritical adulation and [equally uncritical] lambasting . . . are both unhistorical, in the sense that they select from the often cloudy record of Columbus's actual motives and deeds what suits the researcher's . . . purposes. That sort of history caricatures the complexity of human reality by turning Columbus into either a bloody ogre or a plaster saint.

As the quincentennial of Columbus's first voyage comes to an end, it is perhaps inevitable that sharply polarized opinions about

Columbus and his legacy once more appear, as they did in 1792 and 1892. Each writer seems to find his own Christopher Columbus. Contradictory analyses of Columbus have been proffered by Arabs and Jews, environmentalists and entrepreneurs, Christian conservatives and Christian radicals, amateur archeologists and professional naval officers, scholars and newspaper reporters, and senators and schoolchildren. These analyses confirm that each individual, viewing a single person or event through his or her own perspective on the world, will interpret things differently.

This, in the long run, may be the value of recurring examinations of Columbus: We may realize that divergent opinions are attributable to our own assumptions, society, and values, more than they are to the historical reality of Columbus.

VIEWPOINT 1

"The whole history of the Americas stems from the Four Voyages of Columbus; and as the Greek city-states looked back to the deathless gods as their founders, so today a score of independent nations and dominions unite in homage to Christopher the stout-hearted son of Genoa."

Columbus Was a Hero

Samuel Eliot Morison

Adm. Samuel Eliot Morison won a Pulitzer prize for *Admiral of the Ocean Sea: A Life of Christopher Columbus*. An avid sailor, Morison undertook an expedition in 1939 to sail a 147-foot yacht, *Capitana*, to the New World, following Columbus's route as closely as possible. His explanation: "You cannot write a story out of these fifteenth and sixteenth century narratives that means anything to a modern reader, merely by studying them in a library with the aid of maps." Thus, written by an author immersed in the practical difficulties of sailing the Atlantic, *Admiral of the Ocean Sea* has been, since its publication in 1942, the definitive biography against which other Columbus scholars are measured. Morison's other books include *The Two Ocean War: A Short History of the United States Navy in the Second World War* and *John Paul Jones: A Sailor's Biography*. Morison was professor emeritus of history at Harvard University. His fascination with, and admiration of, Columbus was profound. While his biography does not ignore Columbus's flaws, it tends to demonstrate his epic dimensions.

18

As you read, consider the following questions:

1. How does Morison evaluate Columbus's place in history?
2. What traits of Columbus does the author find admirable?
3. If an epic is defined as a story of the founding of a nation or race, in what way(s) does Morison cast Columbus as an epic hero?

———————————

Let us pause and find out if we can what manner of man was this Columbus at the dangerous age of thirty—dangerous that is in youthful ambition, to ideals and visions, the age that makes others settle down, drains the fire from ardent youth, turns men into tabby cats content to sit by the fire. Hear what was said about Columbus by men who knew him, and whose lives crossed his.

No description of Columbus at this precise period exists; we have to work back from what people said of him after the great achievement. Oviedo, who witnessed the Admiral's triumphant entry into Barcelona in 1493, says this of him in a work that was printed forty years later: "A man of honest parents and life, of good stature and appearance, taller than the average and strongly limbed: the eyes lively and other parts of the face of good proportion, the hair very red, and the face somewhat ruddy and freckled; fair in speech, tactful and of a great creative talent; a nice Latinist and most learned cosmographer; gracious when he wished to be, irascible when annoyed."

Columbus Described by His Son

Ferdinand Columbus, who was with his father constantly between the ages of twelve and eighteen, has this description in his biography:

The Admiral was a well built man of more than medium stature, long visaged with cheeks somewhat high, but neither fat nor thin. He had an aquiline nose and his eyes were light in color; his complexion too was light, but kindling to a vivid red. In youth his hair was blond, but when he came to his thirtieth year it all turned white. In eating and drinking and the adornment of his person he was always continent and modest. Among strangers his conversation was affable, and with members of his household very pleasant, but with a modest and pleasing dignity. In matters of religion he was so strict that for fasting and saying all the canonical offices he might have been taken for a member of a religious order. And he was so great an enemy to cursing and swearing, that I swear I never heard him utter any other oath than "by San Fernando!" and when he was most angry with any-

19

one, his reprimand was to say, "May God take you!" for doing or saying that. And when he had to write anything, he would not try the pen without first writing these words, *Jesus cum Maria sit nobis in via* [Jesus and Mary be with us on the way], and in such fair letters that he might have gained his bread by them alone.

Las Casas' View of Columbus

Las Casas, who saw the Admiral in Hispaniola in 1500, and whose father and uncle had been shipmates and colonists under him, amplifies Ferdinand's description in the *Historia de las Indias*:

As regards his exterior person and bodily disposition, he was more than middling tall; face long and giving an air of authority; aquiline nose, blue eyes, complexion light and tending to bright red; beard and hair red when young but very soon turned gray from his labors; he was affable and cheerful in speaking, . . . eloquent and boastful in his negotiations; he was serious in moderation, affable with strangers, and with members of his household gentle and pleasant, with modest gravity and discreet conversation; and so could easily incite those who saw him to love him. In fine, he was most impressive in his port and countenance, a person of great state and authority and worthy of all reverence. He was sober and moderate in eating, drinking, clothing and footwear; it was commonly said that he spoke cheerfully in familiar conversation, or with indignation when he gave reproof or was angry with somebody: "May God take you, don't you agree to this and that?" or "Why have you done this and that?" In matters of the Christian religion, without doubt he was a Catholic and of great devotion; for in everything he did and said or sought to begin, he always interposed "In the name of the Holy Trinity I will do this," or "launch this" or "this will come to pass." In whatever letter or other thing he wrote, he put at the head "Jesus and Mary be with us on the way.". . .

He observed the fasts of the Church most faithfully, confessed and made communion often, read the canonical offices like a churchman or member of a religious order, hated blasphemy and profane swearing, was most devoted to Our Lady and to the seraphic father St. Francis; seemed very grateful to God for benefits received from the divine hand, wherefore, as in the proverb, he hourly admitted that God had conferred upon him great mercies, as upon David. When gold or precious things were brought to him, he entered his cabin, knelt down, summoned the bystanders, and said, "Let us give thanks to Our Lord that he has thought us worthy to discover so many good things." He was extraordinarily zealous for the divine service; he desired and was eager for the conversion of these people [the Indians], and that in every region the faith of Jesus Christ be planted and enhanced. . . .

He was a gentleman of great force of spirit, of lofty thoughts, naturally inclined (from what one may gather of his life, deeds, writings and conversation) to undertake worthy deeds and signal enterprises; patient and long-suffering (as later shall appear), and a forgiver of injuries, and wished nothing more than that those who offended against him should recognize their errors, and that the delinquents be reconciled with him; most constant and endowed with forbearance in the hardships and adversities which were always occurring and which were incredible and infinite; ever holding great confidence in divine providence. And verily, from what I have heard from him and from my own father, who was with him when he returned to colonize Hispaniola in 1493, and from others who accompanied and served him, he held and always kept on terms of intimate fidelity and devotion to the Sovereigns.

Judging Columbus

So Columbus appeared to those who knew him, and who took pains to study his character and set it down a few years after his death. The reader will have ample opportunity to judge the Discoverer's character for himself. Physical courage, which the early historians took for granted, he will find in plenty; and untiring persistence and unbreakable will. Certain defects will appear, especially lack of due appreciation for the labors of his subordinates; unwillingness to admit his shortcomings as a colonizer; a tendency to complain and be sorry for himself whenever the Sovereigns, owing to these shortcomings, withdrew some measure of their trust in him. These were the defects of the qualities that made him a great historical figure. For he was not, like a Washington, a Cromwell or a Bolivar, an instrument chosen by multitudes to express their wills and lead a cause; Columbus was a Man with a Mission, and such men are apt to be unreasonable and even disagreeable to those who cannot see the mission. There was no psalm-singing New Model, no Spirit of '76, no Army of Liberation with drums and trumpets behind Columbus. He was Man alone with God against human stupidity and depravity, against greedy conquistadors, cowardly seamen, even against nature and the sea.

Always with God, though; in that his biographers were right; for God is with men who for a good cause put their trust in Him. Men may doubt this, but there can be no doubt that the faith of Columbus was genuine and sincere, and that his frequent communion with forces unseen was a vital element in his achievement. It gave him confidence in his destiny, assurance that his performance would be equal to the promise of his name. This conviction that God destined him to be an instrument for spread-

A New Age of Hope

Christopher Columbus belonged to an age that was past, yet he became the sign and symbol of [a] new age of hope, glory and accomplishment. His medieval faith impelled him to a modern solution: expansion. If the Turk could not be pried loose from the Holy Sepulchre by ordinary means, let Europe seek new means overseas; and he, Christopher the Christ-bearer, would be the humble yet proud instrument of Europe's regeneration. So it turned out, although not as he anticipated. The First Voyage to America that he accomplished with a maximum of faith and a minimum of technique, a bare sufficiency of equipment and a superabundance of stout-heartedness, gave Europe new confidence in herself, more than doubled the area of Christianity, enlarged indefinitely the scope for human thought and speculation, and "led the way to those fields of freedom which, planted with great seed, have now sprung up to the fructification of the world."

In his faith, his deductive methods of reasoning, his unquestioning acceptance of the current ethics, Columbus was a man of the Middle Ages, and in the best sense. In his readiness to translate thought into action, in lively curiosity and accurate observation of natural phenomena, in his joyous sense of adventure and desire to win wealth and recognition, he was a modern man. This dualism makes the character and career of Columbus a puzzle to the dull-witted, a delight to the discerning. It unlocks most of the so-called Columbus "mysteries," "questions" and "problems," which were neither mysteries, questions nor problems to his contemporaries, but recent creations of dull pedants without faith who never tasted the joy of sea adventure.

Samuel Eliot Morison, *Admiral of the Ocean Sea*, 1942.

---

ing the faith was far more potent than the desire to win glory, wealth and worldly honors, to which he was certainly far from indifferent. . . .

America would eventually have been discovered if the Great Enterprise of Columbus had been rejected; yet who can predict what would have been the outcome? The voyage that took him to "The Indies" and home was no blind chance, but the creation of his own brain and soul, long studied, carefully planned, repeatedly urged on indifferent princes, and carried through by virtue of his courage, sea-knowledge and indomitable will. No later voyage could ever have such spectacular results, and Columbus's fame would have been secure had he retired from the sea in 1493. Yet a lofty ambition to explore further, to organize the territories won for Castile, and to complete the circuit of the globe, sent him thrice more to America. These voyages, even more than the first, proved him to be the greatest navigator of his age, and enabled him to train the captains and pilots who were to display the banners of Spain off every American cape and island between Fifty North and Fifty South. The ease with which he dissipated the unknown terrors of the Ocean, the skill with which he found his way out and home, again and again, led thousands of men from every Western European nation into maritime adventure and exploration. And if Columbus was a failure as a colonial administrator, it was partly because his conception of a colony transcended the desire of his followers to impart, and the capacity of natives to receive, the institutions and culture of Renaissance Europe.

Columbus had a proud, passionate and sensitive nature that suffered deeply from the contempt to which he was early subjected, and the envy, disloyalty, ingratitude and injustice which he met as a discoverer. He wrote so freely out of the abundance of his complaint, as to give the impression that his life was more full of woe than of weal. That impression is false. As with other mariners, a month at sea healed the wounds of a year ashore, and a fair wind blew away the memory of foul weather. Command of a tall and gallant ship speeding over blue water before a fresh trade wind, shaping her course for some new and marvelous land where gold is abundant and the women are kind, is a mariner's dream of the good life. Columbus had a Hellenic sense of wonder at the new and strange, combined with an artist's appreciation of natural beauty; and his voyages to this strange new world brought him to some of the most gorgeous coastlines on the earth's surface. Moreover, Columbus had a deep conviction of the immanence, the sovereignty and the infinite wisdom of God, which transcended all his suffering, and enhanced all his triumphs. Waste no pity on the Admiral of the Ocean Sea! He enjoyed long stretches of pure delight such as only a seaman may know, and moments of high, proud exultation that only a discoverer can experience.

One only wishes that the Admiral might have been afforded the sense of fulfillment that would have come from foreseeing all that flowed from his discoveries; that would have turned all the sorrows of his last years to joy. The whole history of the Americas stems from the Four Voyages of Columbus; and as the Greek city-states looked back to the deathless gods as their founders, so today a score of independent nations and dominions unite in homage to Christopher the stout-hearted son of Genoa, who carried Christian civilization across the Ocean Sea.

VIEWPOINT 2

"Hardly a name in profane history is more august than his. Hardly another character in the world's record has made so little of its opportunities."

Columbus Was a Pitiable Man

Justin Winsor

Justin Winsor was one of the first historians to write that Columbus was a flawed person, not an epic hero. In his biography, *Christopher Columbus and How He Received and Imparted the Spirit of Discovery*, Winsor took a far more critical look at Columbus than was customary at the time. Although Winsor acknowledges Columbus's courage and accepts the importance of his discovery, he attacks the explorer's behavior and morality for such actions as usurping the lookout's credit for sighting land and thus stealing his legitimate reward. Winsor himself became the center of a firestorm of criticism from those who preferred the heroic Columbus. Typical of such critics was Chauncey DePew, president of the New York Central Railroad, speaking at Columbus Day ceremonies in 1892: "If there is anything which I detest more than another, it is that spirit of critical historical inquiry which doubts everything; that modern spirit which destroys all the illusions and all the heroes which have been the inspiration of patriotism through all the centuries."

As you read, consider the following questions:

1. Why does Winsor call Columbus "pitiable"?
2. How does the author refute other historians' views of Columbus in order to establish his own position?
3. In what ways, according to Winsor, did Columbus fall far short of being a hero? In Winsor's view, was Columbus a good man?

No man craves more than Columbus to be judged with all the palliations demanded of a difference of his own age and ours. No child of any age ever did less to improve his contemporaries, and few ever did more to prepare the way for such improvements. The age created him and the age left him. There is no more conspicuous example in history of a man showing the path and losing it.

It is by no means sure, with all our boast of benevolent progress, that atrocities not much short of those which we ascribe to Columbus and his compeers may not at any time disgrace the coming as they have blackened the past years of the nineteenth century. This fact gives us the right to judge the infirmities of man in any age from the high vantage-ground of the best emotions of all the centuries. In the application of such perennial justice Columbus must inevitably suffer. The degradation of the times ceases to be an excuse when the man to be judged stands on the pinnacle of the ages. The biographer cannot forget, indeed, that Columbus is a portrait set in the surroundings of his times; but it is equally his duty at the same time to judge the paths which he trod by the scale of an eternal nobleness.

Columbus Did Not Change World History

The very domination of this man in the history of two hemispheres warrants us in estimating him by an austere sense of occasions lost and of opportunities embraced. The really great man is superior to his age, and anticipates its future; not as a sudden apparition, but as the embodiment of a long growth of ideas of which he is the inheritor and the capable exemplar. . . . It is extremely doubtful if any instance can be found of a great idea changing the world's history, which has been created by any single man. None such was created by Columbus. There are always forerunners whose agency is postponed because the times are not propitious. A masterful thought has often a long pedigree, starting from a remote antiquity, but it will be dormant till it is environed by the circumstances suited to fructify it. This was just the destiny of the intuition which began with Aristotle and came down to Columbus. To make his first voyage partook of foolhardiness, as many a looker-on reasonably declared. It was none the less foolhardy when it was done. If he had reached the opulent and powerful kings of the Orient, his little cockboats and their brave souls might have fared hard for their intrusion. His blunder in geography very likely saved him from annihilation.

The character of Columbus has been variously drawn, almost always with a violent projection of the limner's own personality.

We find [William H.] Prescott contending that "whatever the defects of Columbus's mental constitution, the finger of the historian will find it difficult to point to a single blemish in his moral character." It is certainly difficult to point to a more flagrant disregard of truth than when we find Prescott further saying, "Whether we contemplate his character in its public or private relations, in all its features it wears the same noble aspects. It was in perfect harmony with the grandeur of his plans, and with results more stupendous than those which Heaven has permitted any other mortal to achieve." It is very striking to find Prescott, after thus speaking of his private as well as public character, and forgetting the remorse of Columbus for the social wrongs he had committed, append in a footnote to this very passage a reference to his "illegitimate" son. It seems to mark an obdurate purpose to disguise the truth. This is also nowhere more patent than in the palliating hero-worship of [Washington] Irving, with his constant effort to save a world's exemplar for the world's admiration, and more for the world's sake than for Columbus's. . . . The Admiral was certainly not destitute of keen observation of nature, but unfortunately this quality was not infrequently prostituted to ignoble purposes. . . . It would have been better for the fame of Columbus if he had kept this scientific survey in its purity. It was simply, for instance, a vitiated desire to astound that made him mingle theological and physical theories about the land of Paradise. Such jugglery was promptly weighed in Spain and Italy by Peter Martyr and others as the wild, disjointed effusions of an overwrought mind, and "the reflex of a false erudition," as [Alexander von] Humboldt expresses it. It was palpably by another effort, of a like kind, that he seized upon the views of the fathers of the Church that the earthly Paradise lay in the extreme Orient, and he was quite as audacious when he exacted the oath on the Cuban coast, to make it appear by it that he had really reached the outermost parts of Asia.

Humboldt seeks to explain this errant habit by calling it "the sudden movement of his ardent and passionate soul; the disarrangement of ideas which were the effect of an incoherent method and of the extreme rapidity of his reading; while all was increased by his misfortunes and religious mysticism." Such an explanation hardly relieves the subject of it from blunter imputations. This urgency for some responsive wonderment at every experience appears constantly in the journal of Columbus's first voyage, as, for instance, when he makes every harbor exceed in beauty the last he had seen. This was the commonplace exaggeration which in our day is confined to the calls of speculating land companies. The fact was that Humboldt transferred to his hero something of the superlative love of nature that he himself had experienced in the same regions; but there was all the difference between him and Columbus that there is between a genuine love of nature and a commercial use of it. Whenever Columbus could divert his mind from a purpose to make the Indies a paying investment, we find some signs of an insight that shows either observation of his own or the garnering of it from others, as, for example, when he remarks on the decrease of rain in the Canaries and the Azores which followed upon the felling of trees, and when he conjectures that the elongated shape of the islands of the Antilles on the lines of the parallels was due to the strength of the equatorial current. . . .

Columbus Erratic Throughout His Life

The mental hallucinations of Columbus, so patent in his last years, were not beyond recognition at a much earlier age, and those who would get the true import of his character must trace these sorrowful manifestations to their beginnings, and distinguish accurately between Columbus when his purpose was lofty and unselfish and himself again when he became mercenary and erratic. . . .

That Columbus was a devout Catholic, according to the Catholicism of his epoch, does not admit of question, but when tried by any test that finds the perennial in holy acts, Columbus fails to bear the examination. He had nothing of the generous and noble spirit of a conjoint lover of man and of God, as the higher spirits of all times have developed it. There was no all-loving Deity in his conception. His Lord was one in whose name it was convenient to practice enormities. He shared this subterfuge with Isabella and the rest. We need to think on what Las Casas could be among his contemporaries, if we hesitate to apply the conceptions of an everlasting humanity.

The mines which Columbus went to seek were hard to find. The people he went to save to Christ were easy to exterminate. He mourned bitterly that his own efforts were ill requited. He had no pity for the misery of others, except they be his dependents and co-sharers of his purposes. He found a policy worth commemorating in slitting the noses and tearing off the ears of a naked heathen. He vindicates his excess by impressing upon the world that a man setting out to conquer the Indies must not be judged by the amenities of life which belong to a quiet rule in established countries. Yet, with a chance to establish a humane life among peoples ready to be moulded to good purposes, he sought from the very first to organize among them the inherited evils of "established countries." He talked a great deal about making converts of the poor souls, while the very first sight which he had of them prompted him to consign them to the slave-mart, just as if the first step to Christianize was the step which unmans.

Columbus's Cruelties to the Natives

The first vicar apostolic sent to teach the faith in Santo Domingo returned to Spain, no longer able to remain, powerless, in sight of the cruelties practiced by Columbus. Isabella prevented the selling of the natives as slaves in Spain, when Columbus had dispatched thither five shiploads. Las Casas tells us that in 1494-96 Columbus was generally hated in Española for his odiousness and injustice, and that the Admiral's policy with the natives killed a third of them in those two years. The Franciscans, when they arrived at the island, found the colonists exuberant that they had been relieved of the rule which Columbus had instituted; and the Benedictines and Dominicans added their testimony to the same effect.

The very first words, as has been said, that he used, in conveying to expectant Europe the wonders of his discovery, suggested a scheme of enslaving the strange people. He had already made the voyage that of a kidnapper, by entrapping nine of the unsuspecting natives.

On his second voyage he sent home a vessel-load of slaves, on the pretense of converting them, but his sovereigns intimated to him that it would cost less to convert them in their own homes. Then he thought of the righteous alternative of sending some to Spain to be sold to buy provisions to support those who would convert others in their homes. The monarchs were perhaps dazed at this sophistry; and Columbus again sent home four vessels laden with reeking cargoes of flesh. When he returned to Spain, in 1496, to circumvent his enemies, he once more sought in his turn, and by his reasoning, to cheat the devil of heathen souls by sending other cargoes. At last the line was drawn. It was not to save their souls, but to punish them for daring to war against the Spaniards, that they should be made to endure such horrors.

It is to Columbus, also, that we trace the beginning of that monstrous guilt which Spanish law sanctioned under the name of *repartimientos*, and by which to every colonist, and even to the vilest, absolute power was given over as many natives as his means and rank entitled him to hold. Las Casas tells us that Ferdinand could hardly have had a conception of the enormities of the system. If so, it was because he winked out of sight the testimony of observers, while he listened to the tales prompted of greed, rapine, and cruelty. The value of the system to force heathen out of hell, and at the same time to replenish his treasury, was the side of it presented to Ferdinand's mind by such as had access to his person. In 1501, we find the Dominicans entering their protest, and by this Ferdinand was moved to take the counsel of men learned in the law and in what passed in those days for Christian ethics. This court of appeal approved these necessary efforts, as was claimed, to increase those who were new to the faith, and to reward those who supported it.

The Bloody Trail of Conquest

It lies within our comfortable liberal tradition that we don't like events to be depicted in stark colors. We like shadings. We particularly don't like things or people to be written up as all bad. Everything has its nuances, we claim. Only fanatics and extremists fail to see that.

Mankind and womankind, sitting (still rather well-fed) in their (still rather well-heated) rooms, feel a considerable tenderness toward themselves.

Upperdog, mostly white, mankind, that is. And throughout its bloody history, mankind has labelled as fanatics, agitators, and troublemakers all those who have felt less tender and rosy about the world.

Well, fanatical and extreme as it may be, I find it very hard to think of any shadings or nuances in a character portrait of Christopher Columbus.

Grant him the originality and fierce ambition needed to set that western course. But what else is there to say? Here was a man greedy in large ways, and in small ways—to the point where he took for himself the reward for first sighting land from the Pinta lookout. Cruel in petty things, as when he set a dying monkey with two paws cut off to fight a wild pig; cruel on a continental scale, as when he set in motion what de las Casas called "the beginning of the bloody trail of conquest across the Americas."

Hans Konig, *Columbus: His Enterprise*, 1991.

Peter Martyr expressed the comforting sentiments of the age: "National right and that of the Church concede personal liberty to man. State policy, however, demurs. Custom repels the idea. Long experience shows that slavery is necessary to prevent those returning to their idolatry and error whom the Church has once gained." All professed servants of the Church, with a few exceptions like Las Casas, ranged themselves with Columbus on the side of such specious thoughts; and Las Casas, in recognizing this fact, asks what we could expect of an old sailor and fighter like Columbus, when the wisest and most respectable of the priesthood backed him in his views. It was indeed the misery of Columbus to miss the opportunity of being wiser than his fellows, the occasion always sought by a commanding spirit, and it was offered to him almost as to no other.

There was no restraining the evil. The cupidity of the colonists overcame all obstacles. The Queen was beguiled into giving equivocal instructions to Ovando, who succeeded to Bobadilla, and out of them by interpretation grew an increase of the monstrous evil. In 1503, every atrocity had reached a legal recognition. Labor was forced; the slaves were carried whither the colonists willed; and for eight months at least in every year, families were at pleasure disrupted without mercy. One feels some satisfaction in seeing Columbus himself at last, in a letter to Diego, December 1, 1504, shudder at the atrocities of Ovando. When one sees the utter annihilation of the whole race of the Antilles, a thing clearly assured at the date of the death of Columbus, one wishes that that dismal death-bed in Valladolid could have had its gloom illumined by a consciousness that the hand which lifted the banner of Spain and of Christ at San Salvador had done something to stay the misery which cupidity and perverted piety had put in course. When a man seeks to find and parades reasons for committing a crime, it is to stifle his conscience. Columbus passed years in doing it. . . .

Columbus as Mercenary

The downfall of Columbus began when he wrested from the reluctant monarchs what he called his privileges, and when he insisted upon riches as the accompaniment of such state and consequence as those privileges might entail. The terms were granted, so far as the King was concerned, simply to put a stop to importunities, for he never anticipated being called upon to confirm them. The insistency of Columbus in this respect is in strange contrast to the satisfaction which the captains of Prince Henry, Da Gama and the rest, were content to find in the unpolluted triumphs of science. The mercenary Columbus . . . was wont to say that gold gave the soul its flight to paradise. Perhaps he referred to the masses which could be bought, or to the alms which could propitiate Heaven. He might better have remembered the words of warning given to Baruch: "Seekest thou great things for thyself? Seek them not. For, saith the Lord, thy life will I give unto them for a prey in all places whither thou goest." And a prey in all places he became. . . .

If Columbus had found riches in the New World as easily as he anticipated, it is possible that such affluence would have moulded his character in other ways for good or for evil. He soon found himself confronting a difficult task, to satisfy with insufficient means a craving which his exaggerations had established. This led him to spare no device, at whatever sacrifice of the natives, to produce the coveted gold, and it was an ingenious mockery that induced him to deck his captives with golden chains and parade them through the Spanish towns. . . .

Ambition Defiled Purpose

When we view the character of Columbus in its influence upon the minds of men, we find some strange anomalies. Before his passion was tainted with the ambition of wealth and its consequence, and while he was urging the acceptance of his views for their own sake, it is very evident that he impressed others in a way that never happened after he had secured his privileges. It is after this turning-point of his life that we begin to see his falsities and indiscretions, or at least to find record of them. The incident of the moving light in the night before his first landfall is a striking instance of his daring disregard of all the qualities that help a commander in his dominance over his men. It needs little discrimination to discern the utter deceitfulness of that pretense. A noble desire to win the loftiest honors of the discovery did not satisfy a mean, insatiable greed. He blunted every sentiment of generosity when he deprived a poor sailor of his pecuniary reward. That there was no actual light to be seen is apparent from the distance that the discoverers sailed before they saw land, since if the light had been ahead they would not have gone on, and if it had been abeam they would not have left it. The evidence is that of himself and a thrall and he kept it secret at the time. The author of the *Historie* sees the difficulty, and attempts to vaporize the whole story by saying that the light was spiritual, and not physical. Navarete passes it by as a thing necessary, for the fame of Columbus, to be ignored.

A second instance of Columbus's luckless impotence, at a time when an honorable man would have relied upon his character, was the attempt to make it appear that he had reached the coast of Asia by imposing an oath on his men to that effect, in penalty of having their tongues wrenched out if they recanted. One can hardly conceive a more debasing exercise of power.

His insistence upon territorial power was the serious mistake of his life. He thought, in making an agreement with his sovereigns to become a viceroy, that he was securing an honor; he was in truth pledging his happiness and beggaring his life. He sought to attain that which the fates had unfitted him for, and the Spanish monarchs, in an evil day, which was in due time their regret, submitted to his hallucinated dictation. No man every evinced less capacity for ruling a colony.

The most sorrowful of all the phases of Columbus's character is that hapless collapse, when he abandoned all faith in the natural world, and his premonitions of it, and threw himself headlong into the vortex of what he called inspiration.

Everything in his scientific argument had been logical. It produced the reliance which comes of wisdom. It was a manly show of an incisive reason. If he had rested here his claims for honor, he would have ranked with the great seers of the universe, with Copernicus and the rest. His successful suit with the Spanish sovereigns turned his head, and his degradation began when he debased a noble purpose to the level of mercenary claims. He relied, during his first voyage, more on chicanery in controlling his crew than upon the dignity of his aim and the natural command inherent in a lofty spirit. This deceit was the beginning of his decadence, which ended in a sad self-aggrandizement, when he felt himself no longer an instrument of intuition to probe the secrets of the earth, but a possessor of miraculous inspiration. The man who had been self-contained became a thrall to a fevered hallucination.

The earnest mental study which had sustained his inquisitive spirit through long years of dealings with the great physical problems of the earth was forgotten. He hopelessly began to accredit to Divinity the measure of his own fallibility. "God made me," he says, "the messenger of the new heaven and the new earth, of which He spoke in the Apocalypse by St. John, after having spoken of it by the mouth of Isaiah, and He showed me the spot where to find it." He no longer thought it the views of Aristotle which guided him. The Greek might be pardoned for his ignorance of the intervening America. It was mere sacrilege to impute such ignorance to the Divine wisdom. . . .

We have seen a pitiable man meet a pitiable death. Hardly a name in profane history is more august than his. Hardly another character in the world's record has made so little of its opportunities. His discovery was a blunder; his blunder was a new world; the New World is his monument! Its discoverer might have been its father; he proved to be its despoiler. He might have given its young days such a benignity as the world likes to associate with a maker; he left it a legacy of devastation and crime. He might have been an unselfish promoter of geographical science; he proved a rabid seeker for gold and a viceroyalty. He might have won converts to the fold of Christ by the kindness of his spirit; he gained the execrations of the good angels. He might, like Las Casas, have rebuked the fiendishness of his contemporaries; he set them an example of perverted belief. The triumph of Barcelona led down to the ignominy of Valladolid, with every step in the degradation palpable and resultant.

VIEWPOINT 3

"Columbus is one of us. . . . The Catholic faith superlatively inspired the enterprise and its execution."

Columbus Is a Christian Hero: A Catholic View in 1892

Pope Leo XIII

As the quadricentennial of Columbus's first voyage approached in 1892, Pope Leo XIII sent a letter to the bishops of Spain, Italy, and North and South America. In it he reviewed the life and accomplishments of Christopher Columbus, especially his part in spreading Christianity to the New World. The pope decreed that on October 12, 1892, or on the first Sunday thereafter, a special mass be said in honor of Columbus.

As you read, consider the following questions:

1. How does Pope Leo describe American Indians before Columbus's voyage?
2. What, according to the pope, sets Columbus apart from other explorers of his time?
3. How does Pope Leo's assessment of Columbus compare to Morison's in Viewpoint 1?

While we see on all sides the preparations that are eagerly being made for the celebration of the Columbian quadri-centenary feasts in memory of a man most illustrious, and deserving of

Christianity and all cultured humanity, we hear with great pleasure that the United States has, among other nations, entered this competition of praise in such a manner as befits both the vastness and richness of the country and the memory of the man so great as he to whom these honors are being shown. . . . It is a testimony of honor and gratitude to that immortal man of whom we have spoken, who, desirous of finding a road by which the light and truth and all the adornments of civil culture might be carried to the most distant parts of the world, could neither be deterred by dangers nor wearied by labors, until, having in a certain manner renewed the bonds between two parts of the human race so long separated, he bestowed upon both such great benefits that he in justice must be said to have few equals or a superior. . . .

From the end of the fifteenth century, since a man from Liguria first landed, under the auspices of God, on the transatlantic shores, humanity has been strongly inclined to celebrate with gratitude the recollection of this event. It would certainly not be an easy matter to find a more worthy cause to touch [humanity's] hearts and to inflame their zeal. The event, in effect, is such in itself that no other epoch has seen a grander and more beautiful one accomplished by man.

As to who accomplished it, there are few who can be compared to him in greatness of soul and genius. By his work a new world flashed forth from the unexplored ocean, thousands upon thousands of mortals were returned to the common society of the human race, led from their barbarous life to peacefulness and civilization, and, which is of much more importance, recalled from perdition to eternal life by the bestowal of the gifts which Jesus Christ brought to the world.

Europe, astonished alike by the novelty and the prodigiousness of this unexpected event, understood little by little, in due course of time, what she owed to Columbus, when, by sending colonies to America, by frequent communications, by exchange of services, by the resources confided to the sea and received in return, there was discovered an accession of the most favorable nature possible to the knowledge of nature, to the reciprocal abundance of riches, with the result that the prestige of Europe increased enormously.

Therefore, it would not be fitting, amid these numerous testimonials on honor, and in these concerts of felicitations, that the Church should maintain complete silence, since, in accordance with her character and her institution, she willingly approves and endeavors to favor all that appears, wherever it is, to be worthy of honor and praise. Undoubtedly, she receives particular and supreme honors to the virtues pre-eminent in regard to morality, inasmuch as they are united to the eternal salvation of souls; nevertheless, she does not despise the rest, neither does she abstain from esteeming them as they deserve; it is even her habit to favor with all her power and to always have in honor those who have well merited of human society and who have passed to posterity.

Certainly, God is admirable in His saints, but the vestiges of His divine virtues appear as imprinted in those in whom shines a superior force of soul and mind, for this elevation of heart and this spark of genius could only come from God, their author and protector.

It is in addition an entirely special reason for which we believe we should commemorate in a grateful spirit this immortal event. It is that Columbus is one of us. When one considers with what motive above all he undertook the plan of exploring the dark sea, and with what object he endeavored to realize this plan, one can not doubt that the Catholic faith superlatively inspired the enterprise and its execution, so that by this title, also, humanity is not a little indebted to the Church.

There are without doubt many men of hardihood and full of experience who, before Christopher Columbus and after him, explored with persevering efforts unknown lands across seas still more unknown. Their memory is celebrated, and will be so by the renown and the recollection of their good deeds, seeing that they have extended the frontiers of science and of civilization, and that not at the price of slight efforts, but with an exalted ardor of spirit, and often through extreme perils. It is not the less true that there is a great difference between them and him of whom we speak.

Columbus's Grand Objective

The eminently distinctive point in Columbus is, that in crossing the immense expanses of the ocean he followed an object more grand and more elevated than the others. This does not say, doubtless, that he was not in any way influenced by the very praiseworthy desire to be master of science, to well deserve the approval of society, or that he despised the glory whose stimulant is ordinarily more sensitive to elevated minds, or that he was not at all looking to his own personal interests. But above all these human reasons, that of religion was uppermost by a great deal in him, and it was this, without any doubt, which sustained his spirit and his will, and which frequently, in the midst of extreme difficulties, filled him with consolation. He learned in reality that his plan, his resolution profoundly carved in his heart, was to open access to the gospel in new lands and in new seas.

This may seem hardly probable to those who, concentrating all their care, all their thoughts, in the present nature of things, as it is perceived by the senses, refuse to look upon greater benefits. But, on the other hand, it is the characteristic of eminent minds to prefer to elevate themselves higher, for they are better disposed than all others to seize the impulses and the inspirations of the divine faith. Certainly, Columbus had united the study of nature to the study of religion, and he had conformed his mind to the precepts intimately drawn from the Catholic faith.

It is thus that, having learned by astronomy and ancient documents that beyond the limits of the known world there were, in addition, toward the west, large tracts of territory unexplored up to that time by anybody, he considered in his mind the immense multitude of those who were plunged in lamentable darkness, subject to insensate rites and to the superstitions of senseless divinities. He considered that they miserably led a savage life, with ferocious customs; that, more miserably still, they were wanting in all notion of the most important things, and that they were plunged in ignorance of the only true God.

Thus, in considering this in himself, he aimed first of all to propagate the name of Christianity and the benefits of Christian charity in the West. As a fact, as soon as he presented himself to the sovereigns of Spain, Ferdinand and Isabella, he explained the cause for which they were not to fear taking a warm interest in the enterprise, as their glory would increase to the point of becoming immortal if they decided to carry the name and the doctrine of Jesus Christ into such distant regions. And when, not long afterward, his prayers were granted, he called to witness that he wished to obtain from God that these sovereigns, sustained by His help and His mercy, should persevere in causing the gospel to penetrate upon new shores and in new lands. . . .

If Columbus also asks of Ferdinand and Isabella to permit only Catholic Christians to go to the New World, there to accelerate trade with the natives, he supports this motive by the fact that by his enterprise and efforts he has not sought for anything else than the glory and the development of the Christian religion.

This was what was perfectly known to Isabella, who, better than any other person, had penetrated the mind of such a great man; much more, it appears that this same plan was fully adopted by this very pious woman of great heart and manly mind. She bore witness, in effect, of Columbus, that in courageously giving himself up to the vast ocean, he realized, for the divine glory, a most signal enterprise; and to Columbus himself, when he had happily returned, she wrote that she esteemed as having been highly employed the resources which she had consecrated and which she would still consecrate to the expeditions in the Indies, in view of the fact that the propagation of Catholicism would result from them.

Also, if he had not inspired himself from a cause superior to human interests, where then would he have drawn the constancy

36

and the strength of soul to support what he was obliged to the end to endure and to submit to; that is to say, the unpropitious advice of the learned people, the repulses of princes, the tempests of the furious ocean, the continual watches, during which he more than once risked losing his sight.

To that add the combats sustained against the barbarians; the infidelities of his friends, of his companions; the villainous conspiracies, the perfidiousness of the envious, the calumnies of the traducers, the chains with which, after all, though innocent, he was loaded. It was inevitable that a man overwhelmed with a burden of trials so great and so intense would have succumbed had he not sustained himself by the consciousness of fulfilling a very noble enterprise, which he conjectured would be glorious for the Christian name and salutary for an infinite multitude. . . .

The Importance of Columbus

Let's not forget the fact that what Christopher Columbus accomplished was probably the most important thing that happened to the world since the birth of Christ.

Frank Donatelli, Chairman, the Christopher Columbus Quincentenary Jubilee Commission, 1991.

To call the Indian race to Christianity, this was, without doubt, the mission and the work of the Church in this mission. From the beginning, she continued to fulfill it with an uninterrupted course of charity, and she still continues it, having advanced herself recently so far as the extremities of Patagonia.

Thus, when compelled by the Portuguese, by the Genoese, to leave without having obtained any result, he went to Spain. He matured the grand plan of the projected discovery in the midst of the walls of a convent, with the knowledge of and with the advice of a monk of the Order of St. Francis d'Assisi, after seven years had revolved. When at last he goes to dare the ocean, he takes care that the expedition shall comply with the acts of spiritual expiation; he prays to the Queen of Heaven to assist the enterprise and to direct its course, and before giving the order to make sail he invokes the august divine Trinity. Then, once fairly at sea, while the waters agitate themselves, while the crew murmurs, he maintains, under God's care, a calm constancy of mind.

His plan manifests itself in the very names which he imposes on the new islands, and each time that he is called upon to land upon one of them he worships the Almighty God, and only takes possession of it in the name of Jesus Christ. At whatever coast he approaches he has nothing more as his first idea than the planting on the shore of the sacred sign of the cross; and the divine name of the Redeemer, which he had sung so frequently on the open sea to the sound of the murmuring waves—he is the first to make it reverberate in the new islands in the same way. When he institutes the Spanish colony he causes it to be commenced by the construction of a temple, where he first provides that the popular fêtes shall be celebrated by august ceremonies.

Here, then, is what Columbus aimed at and what he accomplished when he went in search, over so great an expanse of sea and of land, of regions up to that time unexplored and uncultivated, but whose civilization, renown, and riches were to rapidly attain that immense development which we see to-day.

In all this, the magnitude of the event, the efficacy and the variety of the benefits which have resulted from it, tend assuredly to celebrate he, who was the author of it, by a grateful remembrance and by all sorts of testimonials of honor; but, in the first place, we must recognize and venerate particularly the divine project, to which the discoverer of the New World was subservient and which he knowingly obeyed.

In order to celebrate worthily and in a manner suitable to the truth of the facts the solemn anniversary of Columbus, the sacredness of religion must be united to the splendor of the civil pomp.

VIEWPOINT 4

"It is widely accepted today that Columbus had serious moral flaws and that the Christianity brought to these shores was often tarnished by human weakness."

Columbus's Role in Christianity Should Be Reassessed: Views from 1992

Jack Wintz

Jack Wintz is a Franciscan priest, ordained in 1963. Having received his M.A. in English literature from Xavier University in Cincinnati, Ohio, Wintz taught English in the United States and the Philippines. The following viewpoint presents two of five interviews Wintz conducted with American Catholics of varying backgrounds about Columbus for the *St. Anthony Messenger*.

As you read, consider the following questions:

1. The pastoral letter *Heritage and Hope* points out that evangelization in the Americas has brought mixed results, some "harsh and painful," others "humanizing." How does each respondent personally reconcile these contradictions?
2. How does each respondent evaluate historical events and their impact on modern society? How might their backgrounds influence their observations?

No responsible person I know is lobbying for a triumphalistic celebration as the best way for the Church to observe the 500th anniversary of the arrival of Christopher Columbus and Christianity to our shores.

It is widely accepted today that Columbus had serious moral flaws and that the Christianity brought to these shores was often tarnished by human weakness and sin. The quincentenary has stirred up a lot of discussion, controversy and even demonstrations from Native Americans and other groups. Yet the debate has been helpful. It has led many to a more balanced assessment of the past 500 years. . . .

In weighing its own evangelizing efforts, for example, the Catholic Church has come to recognize its failures as well as successes. In *Heritage and Hope*, a pastoral letter on the Fifth Centenary of Evangelization of the Americas, the U.S. bishops confess: "As Church, we often have been unconscious and insensitive to the mistreatment of our Native American brothers and sisters and have at times reflected the racism of the dominant culture of which we have been a part. In this quincentennial year, we extend our apology to the Native peoples. . . ."

The bishops go on to describe the "harsh and painful" encounter between the Christian colonizers and the indigenous peoples, which led to the "death of millions" from diseases brought from Europe to which the Native peoples had no immunity. "Added to that," the bishops note, "were the cultural oppression, the injustices, the disrespect for Native ways and traditions that must be acknowledged and lamented. The great waves of European colonization were accompanied by destruction of Native American civilization, the violent usurpation of their lands, and the brutalization of their inhabitants."

The bishops likewise regret the failure of missionaries "to see in the Natives the workings of the same God that they espoused." Indigenous religious values were often destroyed, as Native peoples were "forced to become European at the same time they became Christian." The bishops recall as well the evils of the "slave trade," stating that "the injustice done to the African peoples was profound and deplorable."

At the same time, the bishops believe that an exclusively negative picture is "not an accurate interpretation of the past." There have been inspiring examples of missionaries who brought a "humanizing presence in the midst of colonization," and, what is more, "the gospel did in fact take root."

Other voices remind us that, indeed, the gift of faith did come to the Americas despite the human weakness and mistakes involved. Internationally-known peacemaker and Brazilian bishop Dom Helder Camara recently shared the same conviction: "The important thing," he told the *Pax Christi USA Newsletter*, "is that while Columbus's arrival brought many problems, it also brought a great favor, the privilege of faith. For me this is very important."

A New Evangelization

Evangelization always occurs in a process of encounter between a given historical society and the Christian message. Puebla, in 1979, correctly traced for us the path of any evangelization worthy of the name:

The church has been acquiring an increasingly clear and deep realization that evangelization is its fundamental mission; and that it cannot possibly carry out this mission without an ongoing effort to know the real situation and to adapt the gospel message to today's human beings in a dynamic, attractive and convincing way.

Leonardo Boff, in *The Voice of the Victims*, 1990.

In calling for a "new evangelization," Pope John Paul II and others are not calling the Christian community to an all-out bashing of past efforts. They urge us, rather, to learn from the lights and shadows of our past 500 years *so as to evangelize better*.

In this spirit, *St. Anthony Messenger* interviewed five American Catholics from varied backgrounds and sought their views on how best to use the "teaching moment" provided by the quincentenary.

Marie Therese Archambault

A Native American, Marie Therese Archambault was born at Fort Yates, North Dakota, on the Standing Rock Reservation. She is a member of the Hunkpapa tribe of the Sioux nation. All her schooling—elementary through high school—was received in Catholic Mission schools on the Standing Rock, Pine Ridge and Rosebud Indian Reservations of North and South Dakota.

Presently based in Denver, Sister Marie Therese teaches religious studies at Regis University and is active in Native lay ministry development. She is often asked to speak on Native American issues and has recently been appointed Native urban ministry coordinator for the national Tekakwitha Conference, a Catholic Native American organization named after Blessed Kateri Tekakwitha.

"Difficult" is a word Sister Marie Therese uses to describe the question of how Catholics should commemorate the quincentenary. "How can I celebrate this event," she asks, "in view of the history of the Catholic Church's participation in the destruction of Native cultures—in the very act of evangelizing *in the name of Jesus Christ!*"

She's been grappling with that question for the past year now. "As a Native person, at first, I wanted nothing to do with the quincentenary. Then, as a Catholic, I could say: 'Well, all right . . . but don't celebrate. Just commemorate. Do penance!' Finally, there is a conciliatory stage in which I can say, 'Hey, let's work together on this.' It won't be easy, but we have to work together at healing the memories of what happened to us in this country. Let's grieve and go on."

And as for Christopher Columbus, Sister Marie Therese can only talk of pain. "As Native children, we were taught that he was our cultural hero too," she says. "It was only well into my adulthood that we began to look at our own great persons as heroes. Until I read portions of Columbus's log, as recorded in Howard Zinn's book, *The People's History*, I had no sense of who Columbus was. But after learning more of what he actually wrote down, I realize that he was deeply formed by the European mentality of his day. He thought he was better than the Arawak people he encountered in the West Indies and that he had the right to enslave them—and enslave them he did.

"The Arawaks welcomed him—and, in return, he thought only of how easy it would be to dominate and enslave them, in the name of his sovereigns and Christ! How can we evaluate a man with this frame of mind? Sure, he was a man of his culture and could have acted in no other way. But some people have lived with the negative results of Columbus's frame of mind until today. These are the indigenous peoples of this hemisphere.

"Columbus's arrival here unleashed waves of cultural, spiritual destruction on the indigenous peoples of this land. I have experienced the effects of this destruction in my life, in my family, my friends and members of my tribe." The best she can say about Columbus is that he symbolizes a certain "daring seamanship and adventure," qualities which, she hopes, might inspire us to make "adventurous" voyages from the oppression of the past.

As Sister Marie Therese tries to weigh Christianity's successes and failures over the last 500 years, she can only comment: "Great success? No. Complete failure? No. Maybe it's more like this: At the deepest level of cultural identity, Native people and the larger Catholic Church, in great part, passed each other like ships in the night. . . . I'm amazed after 500 years how little has been accomplished in terms of *real dialogue* between the Catholic Church and us Native Catholics. . . . This important part of evangelization work has never been done. Maybe now it will begin.

"I must be honest and say that there are a number of Native

people who are good Catholics. On occasion, you might hear them thank God for their Catholic faith," Sister Marie Therese affirms. Yet, from her years of living in Europe, especially in Italy and Germany, she has come to see that Native Americans don't feel the same kind of identity with Catholic tradition as do their fellow Catholics of European extraction. European Catholics have a stronger link to that Catholic identity and history because they are familiar with its manifestation in European Church architecture, art, museum pieces and so forth.

A Clash of Cultures

We know that the arrival of the Spanish and Portuguese produced not a meeting, but a clash of cultures, a relationship of domination and destruction. The Pontifical Commission for Justice and Peace's document *The Church and Racism* (1989) recognizes the facts with precision:

> The first great wave of European colonization was indeed accompanied by a massive destruction of the pre-Columbian civilizations and a brutal subjugation of their populations. . . . Soldiers and traders killed to establish themselves; in order to profit from the labour of the indigenous population and, later, of the blacks, they reduce them to slavery.

The idea of evangelizing cultures in Latin America only makes sense in relation to this trauma, and therefore from a perspective of liberation, that is, starting from the restoration, recognition and promotion of the cultures of the dominated.

Leonardo Boff, in *The Voice of the Victims*, 1990.

This "lack of identification" on the part of many Native Americans helps explain why "they are willing to let others take over and lead them in the Church," she says. "Somehow, we do not trust ourselves, or envision ourselves in leadership positions in the Church. . . . We do not sense that it is really *our* Church.

"On the other hand, if you test the depth of this Native faith, you would probably find that, in many cases, it is profound as well as simple. Native people pray easily," she asserts, but active participation and Native leadership do not come so easily.

Sister Marie Therese believes that the 500th anniversary is "a great teaching moment for us Natives and non-Natives alike. . . . I believe we can learn humility. We can learn the true love of Christ in the form of respect, dialogue, listening and taking 'unimportant' people seriously in the Church.

"We can relearn a more balanced view of our American history. We can learn to work together in a new way as partners. We can find our way into the next century as a multicultural 'people church' which will truly express *catholicity* by its very diversity and universality.

"In this future Church, my Native relatives and Native people will be at home—and be themselves. They will be free to pray as they know best, dance the round dance, and sing out about being *Native and Catholic* in the Catholic Church. I hope and pray that in this next 500 years the face of 'Christ, the Native American' will emerge in us—and we will experience ourselves as equal persons who find a real home in the Church.". . .

Maria Luisa Gastón

Maria Luisa Gastón was born in Cuba, one of the first islands visited in 1492 by Christopher Columbus on his first voyage. She came to the United States at age 15. For several years Gastón was a religious educator in the Archdiocese of Miami and was involved in Hispanic ministry on both local and national levels. [In 1990,] she moved to Washington, D.C., to become national coordinator for the U.S. Bishops' Committee for the Observance of the Fifth Centenary of Evangelization in the Americas.

By blood, Gastón's ancestry goes back to Spain, but she says, "I feel African roots in me—in my culture as a Cuban. I'm Caribbean; I feel a lot in common with the whole Caribbean community. There are African roots embedded in the Cuban community." In similar ways, she feels she can identify with indigenous and *mestizo* elements in her cultural background.

She believes the quincentenary is an event that should be commemorated "from a multicultural perspective. . . . The quincentenary is an opportunity for Catholics to recognize that their Church today is the fruit of various strands of evangelization and of various groups."

After two years of reading about Christopher Columbus from all sides, Gastón confides that she "swings back and forth" from the anti-Columbus perspective to the pro-Columbus perspective. "Some blame him for all the bad that has happened since 1492 and others with all the good! He's not to be blamed for either.

"I think he was a great man in some ways: He was visionary and daring . . . and had the guts to convince others about undertaking the voyage. At La Rábida, the Franciscan monastery in the South of Spain, he spent months praying and reflecting on what he was doing. He found motivation in the pages of Scripture. You can't take that from him." Gastón showed me photos she had taken on a recent trip to Spain. One was of a painting showing Christopher Columbus and crew receiving holy Communion from the friars before embarking on their journey. "Even in my most 'indigenous' moments," she adds, "I don't see Columbus as someone planning to murder Native peoples.

"At the same time, neither can one gloss over the fact that he was ambitious and wanted glory and power and money. I don't think he was a saint. I see him as a person of mixed motives—a person whose life was not integrated and who had areas in his life that were not evangelized."

In Gastón's view, the story of the evangelization of the Americas is one of success and failure, and both need to be recognized. "We've learned that never again can Christianity be linked with conquest. Evangelization has to be a free offer. We've progressed as human beings," she asserts. "The very fact that we can look back today and criticize ourselves is a success."

Also, as we look back, she says, we see that "the seeds of faith *were sown,* and many have been faithful to the gospel over the centuries. The gift of faith has affected our society in many ways, for example, through education, hospital work and service to the poor."

But there are things to deplore. "We need to atone for disregarding that which was humanly and spiritually good in the indigenous cultures," she believes, and for the times we have failed to be "prophetic in denouncing instances of oppression and discrimination."

Gastón suggests that we should use this "teachable moment" to "rediscover our own Church histories . . . to sit down with each other and dialogue across cultural and racial lines. It's a time to tell each other our stories . . . to heal our divisions and affirm our faith."

Chapter 2

The Conquistadors

Chapter Preface

However Columbus's impact on the Americas is evaluated, almost all historians agree that he pursued three goals that influenced those who followed him: God, gold, and glory.

Columbus's religious goals were clear. He wanted to help regain Jerusalem for Christianity. He also wanted to bring Christianity to the Indians in his new-found Eden. Columbus's missionary efforts were based on his notion that the natives lacked religion. This is made clear in his log on November 11, 1492:

> I see and know that these people have no religion whatever, nor are they idolaters. . . . Your Highnesses must resolve to make them Christians. I believe that if this effort commences, in a short time a multitude of peoples will be converted to our Holy Faith.

His search for gold is also firmly documented. As revealed in his log, time after time he is lured on to explore yet another island on the rumor of gold. With gold, Columbus could fulfill his promise to the crown, finance the recapture of Jerusalem, become wealthy, and provide a measure of prestige for his family.

Glory, too, consumed him. The agreement between Columbus and the monarchs, known as the Capitulations of Santa Fe and signed on April 17, 1492, established this motive. Since, throughout the document, Columbus is referred to as Don Cristobal Colón, it is obvious that he had already been advanced to a noble's status. In addition, the monarchs promised him the rank of admiral for life, the title to be passed in perpetuity to his heirs. He was to be viceroy and governor general in all islands and mainlands he might discover. Finally, of all wealth "whether pearls, precious stones, gold, silver, spices . . . which may be bought, bartered, discovered, acquired and obtained," the sovereigns agreed to grant Columbus "the tenth part of the whole," after expenses, reserving the other nine parts for themselves.

John Noble Wilford, author of *The Mysterious History of Columbus*, analyzes the significance of this agreement:

> Beyond its authorization of royal support, the document's significance lies in the insight it affords into Columbus's paramount interests and intentions. He had struck a business deal. He can be seen here as a grasping merchant with an eye to securing a monopoly on the riches he expected to find in lands he intended to exploit, much as he had witnessed the Portuguese doing on the African coast. An exploitative attitude

toward America and native Americans was thus fixed at the outset. And this attitude was normal for the times. Exploration, more often than not, is motivated not by scientific and geographic curiosity but by the quest for wealth and power; it would be anachronistic to believe it otherwise in a society two centuries before the Scientific Revolution.

The Spanish conquistadors who followed Columbus shared these three pursuits. God, gold and glory—in varying proportions—sent Cortés and Pizarro, Balboa and de Soto, Alvarado and Zarate to New Spain and Peru, to the Orinoco and the Pacific. Many of these men were attempting to escape the grinding poverty in Spain. Out of this struggle against poverty came one of the most enduring images of the New World—a land of opportunity, a place of new beginnings.

The examination of the conquistadors in this chapter is not meant to excoriate the Spaniards nor to contribute to the Black Legend. Rather it is to note that the Spanish conquistadors, in their contacts with the native peoples of the Americas, established patterns of behavior and demonstrated attitudes that others would later adopt. After all, they were the first; by the time of the English settlement at Jamestown in 1607, the Spaniards had been conquerors and colonists for over a century.

One of the attitudes the Spaniards held was an absolute belief in the superiority of their culture. Spaniards, flush from victory against the Moors who had occupied Spain for centuries, were militant Christians who had warred with the infidel and were now determined to make new converts in the Americas. This determination was reinforced when native religious practices horrified the conquistadors. Soldiers with Cortés in the conquest of New Spain were repulsed and terrified by the ritual sacrifice and cannibalism practiced by the Aztecs. When Cortés's efforts to sway the natives from these practices failed, the Spaniards became convinced they needed to eradicate them by military means.

Nevertheless, some Spaniards could not completely condemn native American culture and religion. Many of the conquistadors were awed by the size and sophistication of the cities in Mexico and Peru. Spanish soldiers, most from the Spanish provinces, had never seen cities such as Tenochtitlan, which easily rivaled—or surpassed—the mini-metropolises of Paris or London. Bernal Díaz, a soldier in Cortés's army, describes Mexico's capital city as if he's fallen into a magical kingdom. An intricate system of lakes and causeways linked elegant palaces and imposing temples. Stalls of skilled craftsmen—jewelers and goldsmiths and featherworkers—dotted the thoroughfares. Zoos, aviaries, and gardens provided recreation for the nobles. Throughout the city, entertainers—stiltwalkers, clowns, and dancers—plied their trades. Even the market was more than a match for the best the

world had to offer: "Some of our soldiers who had been in
. . . Constantinople, in Rome, and all over Italy, said that they had
never seen a market so well laid out, so large, so orderly, and so
full of people." Many of the conquerors must have felt like country bumpkins. In the face of such opulence and sophistication, it
must have been difficult for simple men from Spanish provinces
to maintain their previously unquestioned sense of superiority to
the natives.

A similar discrepancy may be seen in the attitudes of the
missionaries who accompanied the conquest. While it is true that
some priests zealously consigned precious native documents and
artifacts to the flames as works of the Devil, others, like Toribio
Motolinia, carefully described and documented native culture.
And while some priests overlooked the cruel treatment of the Indians by soldiers and colonists, others, like Bartolomé de las
Casas, became strong and outspoken advocates of humane treatment of the Indians.

Despite these sympathetic responses to native culture, the
Spaniards quickly worked to establish military dominance. Although their military superiority probably could not have been
achieved without the unintentional ally of communicable disease,
especially smallpox, Spanish military technology—ships that
used sails as well as oars, arquebuses, cannon, metal armor and
swords—was formidable. Effective, too, were their four-footed
compatriots—the mastiffs and the horses.

Yet another pattern of behavior established by the Spanish conquistadors was the exploitation of the land. While most Indian
tribes held reverence for nature and lived in harmony with it, the
Spaniards sought to extract nature's riches: gold in Mexico, pearls
at the mouth of the Orinoco, and silver at Potosi. The Indians
marveled at this strange longing for riches. The Aztecs observed
the Spanish response to gifts of gold:

> And when they were given these presents, the Spaniards burst
> into smiles; their eyes shone with pleasure; they were delighted
> by them. They picked up the gold and fingered it like monkeys;
> they seemed to be transported by joy, as if their hearts were illu-
> mined and made new. The truth is that they longed and lusted
> for gold. Their bodies swelled with greed, and their hunger was
> ravenous; they hungered like pigs for that gold.

When exploitation of the land's mineral resources became less
profitable, plantations were established, especially in the
Caribbean and in Brazil. The "white gold," sugar, became an additional source of wealth. To the European, land was to be
worked and made to yield a profit.

One of the ironies for many of the conquistadors was that they
died without wealth or prestige. Bernal Díaz died poor, aware
that he had been treated unfairly by his leaders. Hernando de

Soto, explorer of Florida, Georgia, and Alabama, died of a fever. His body was thrown into the Mississippi to prevent capture by the Indians. Panfilo de Narváez, leader of an expedition to Florida, drowned. Pedro de Alvarado, who saw active duty in Mexico and Guatemala, was crushed by a horse. Pedro de Valdivia, conqueror of Chile, was eaten by cannibals. And Diego de Orgaz, leader of an expedition to the Amazon, was probably poisoned while being shipped back to Spain under arrest. One can hope that in these travails, and lacking gold or glory, the conquistadors at least had their God.

VIEWPOINT 1

"[The conquistador] is a Spaniard, the product of the conquering and mystical Spain of the sixteenth century, made in its image, and reflecting the somber glory of its contradictory passions."

The Conquistadors' Motives Were Pure

Jean Descola

Jean Descola, a Parisian by birth, clearly is a Hispanophile. Unlike many English writers, he is far more sympathetic to the conquistadors, perhaps because Spain was never a national enemy to the French to the same degree it was to the English and Dutch. Much of Descola's writing has been on Spain and Latin America. *Les Conquistadors*, from which the following viewpoint is excerpted, won a major French literary prize, Le Grand Prix d'Histoire.

As you read, consider the following questions:

1. How does Descola use quotations of other writers on Spain to build his case? How does he deal with those critical of the conquistadors?
2. According to the author, what trait must be understood if one is to understand Spanish character? Is this trait tempered in any way?
3. How did conquistadors use religion to advance their goals? Did this make them hypocrites?
4. What was the impact on Spain of the influx of wealth from the New World?
5. Did most conquistadors personally benefit from their activities?

51

The Conquistador resembles no one but himself. He is a Spaniard, the product of the conquering and mystical Spain of the sixteenth century, made in its image, and reflecting the somber glory of its contradictory passions. He carries in himself, with a sort of terrible ingenuity, the whole of Spain. He *is* Spain. And just as we cannot define in one word, or reduce to a single formula, the historic face of Charles V's Spain, so we must consider successively the various aspects of the Conquistador, so that a true portrait may emerge, one removed both from the "black legend" and from the romantic image.

Neither Saints nor Bandits

Here are a few judgments on the Conquistadors. Heinrich Heine was categorical: "They were bandits," he said. Angel Canivet claims that they conquered "by spontaneous necessity, by virtue of a natural impulse toward independence, without other purpose than to reveal the grandeur which hid itself beneath their apparent smallness." Maurice Legendre says: "Spain, by its Conquistadors, was going to seek outside, by sheer energy, the strength which at home she had only potentially and which it was essential for her to realize in order to maintain her independence." Salvador de Madariaga finds in them "the typically Spanish trait: the coexistence of contrary tendencies."

Each of these opinions, even that of Heine, who detested Spain and understood her little, has its share of the truth. Bandits at certain times—crises of panic and greed—the Conquistadors never lost their sense of grandeur. This was one of their contradictions. But the most striking was to have so closely associated the religion of self and the love of country.

The people of Spain, whatever may be her political regime, are the least possible "community-minded." They do not believe in the "collective soul," that invention of sociologists, useful sometimes as a propaganda theme but as sterile as it is theoretical. How could a collection of individuals form a single individual, at least without denying the personal soul? Deny the soul! An old proverb says that every Spaniard *"tiene su alma en su almario"*: a play on words, meaning that he keeps his soul in his closet; it is his own property, a secret thing. Pride and privation: that was the Spaniard of the sixteenth century. . . .

Although fiercely individualistic, the Conquistadors were no less ardently patriotic. Every Spaniard carried in his heart a fragment of Spain and very often bathed it in his solitary tears. Andalusia had provided the first sailors, and Castile the majority of the soldiers. Columbus's sailors were almost all from Palos and

Moguer, and the captains of the conquest came from Estremadura. Francisco Pizarro had recruited his companions at Trujillo, his native village; Cortés was from Medellín, Balboa from Jerez de los Caballeros, Valdivia from Villanueva de la Serena. They must have dreamed constantly of their *casa solariega* and the herd at the bottom of the field tilled by the elder brother. Manor houses with nail-studded doors, or huts of slate—the thought evokes them both. That sunburned landscape of Estremadura, with its wide and melancholy horizons, haunted the Conquistadors, and to their conquests they gave the names of home: Medellín, Guadalajara, Trujillo, Cáceres, Badajoz, and countless Santiagos. This was the compensation of these voluntary exiles, who were so attached to their homeland that one might have been able, it seems, by scratching the soles of their shoes, to find a scrap of the red clay of the Tierra de Baros.

Under the King's Eye

This Conquistador, brightly daring, taking possession of scraps of empire as he galloped along, and listening to nothing but the promptings of his own heart. . . . His plume could be seen on the narrow roads of the Andes, in the vast grasslands, by the edges of leaden lakes and upon the lava flows, and advancing by night along the rims of craters, white in the moonlight. Could nothing stop him but the fear of God? Yes, the fear of the king, for the Conquistador was not the soldier of God alone. He was the liegeman of the Spanish monarch, and his motto was that of Spain: *un monarca, un imperio, y una espada* (one monarch, one realm, and one sword). There was only one who tried to escape from royal tutelage—Gonzalo Pizarro, and he died under the executioner's ax. He who had no fear of cannibals trembled at the thought of incurring the king's wrath. Six thousand miles from Valladolid, his heart froze at the thought of displeasing Charles V. The receipt of a dispatch bearing the royal seal immediately aroused his anxiety. At a single word from the king, he did not hesitate to cross deserts, mountains, and oceans, to take orders, report, or sometimes to give himself up to justice. All, even the greatest, made this humiliating journey. Columbus (three times), Cortés, the Pizarro brothers. . . . The knee had to be bent before the Caesarian monarch if the sheet of parchment legalizing the enterprise was to be secured.

Not a caravel ever left a Spanish port in a westerly direction without a representative of the king aboard. When Columbus left for his first voyage in 1492—for the unknown, moreover—Rodrigo de Escobedo and Sánchez de Segovia, Royal Notary and Comptroller respectively, had been forced upon him. "Master after God," the Admiral of the Ocean Sea saw the king come between himself and God. Thenceforward, the two faces could make only one. Intoxicated as they were by sudden fortune, the Conquistadors never omitted to put aside a fifth part of their booty for the royal treasury. And if any man swindled the accounts, it was at his own risk and peril: all knew that the garrote awaited the man who took it into his head to defraud the king of his share. . . .

The Romantics

"Weary of carrying their lofty miseries," "intoxicated by a heroic and brutal dream," "hoping for epic tomorrows": such was the way in which José Maria de Heredia, a Cuban descendant of the Conquistadors . . . , pictured his ancestors steering for Cipango in search of the "fabulous metal." This is the Conquistador adorned with all the romantic accessories; nothing is missing, neither violence nor insupportable pride nor the mirage of gold nor the confusion of instinct and imagination. Another feature common to the romantics was stoicism, sometimes theatrical but most often silent. Arrogant and dignified while they paced up and down the *plazuela* of their native towns, draped in their ragged capes, waiting for adventure, the Conquistadors were even more so when in the very midst of the adventure.

Romantics, indeed, with all the credulity and artless wonder that is associated with the word. Into the extravagant pact they had made with fortune the Conquistadors had brought the passionate quest for risk and the intense curiosity that always made of them something more than old campaigners. In this respect, however, they differ from the romantics, the eternally unsatisfied. The Conquistadors were overwhelmed. For once, the imagination had to admit itself surpassed by reality. No adventurer had ever known such adventure as this, and no actor had ever performed on such a stage. This splendid prize, outstretched beneath their gaze and within their reach, seemed the more beautiful to the conquerors even as the tropical sun burned into their brains. What matter? Atahualpa's treasure and the magnificence of Mexican possessions were not mirages. The enchanted forest emerged from legend to become the tangible virgin forest of America, bathed in twilight shadows. Amadis of Gaul had turned into Pedro de Alvarado; Bernal Díaz del Castillo was about to rewrite a chivalrous novel. With eyes wide open, the Conquistadors lived in a lucid and endless delirium. . . .

Under the Pretense of Religion

"*So color de religión—van a buscar plata y oro—del encubierto tesoro . . .*": "Under the pretense of religion, they went in search of silver and gold and of hidden treasure." These harsh words of

Cortés' Actions Were Justified

[Cortés] had set out with a score of ships and a handful of men towards an unknown shore. His intention, like that of Balboa, had been to found a modest colony and amass a modest fortune. Even in his broadest imaginings he had not envisaged the discovery of a vast kingdom, its monuments certainly as imposing as those of Europe, ruled by an Emperor more wealthy, more powerful and more feared than his own. He had suddenly been confronted with an unexpected and monumental task, for which he was wretchedly provided. He had been required, with puny and contemptible means, to surmount a whole cordillera of setbacks and obstacles, to overthrow that Emperor and conquer that kingdom. It was a challenge to his courage, his manhood, his intelligence, his pride as a Spaniard and as an individual. And he had won through. . . .

Everything he had done was justified. He had attempted to act, according to his lights, with justice and with a reasonable moderation. He had brought light to the heathen. He had introduced the civilization of Spain and Europe to a backward and barbarous continent. He had put his own mark and that of the imperial *raza* on a huge segment of the globe. He had placed his brand on Time itself.

And yet, what else did he feel on that stormy August night, in that stinking square, with the wounds in his head and hand aching, as he attempted to envisage the gigantic measure of what he had brought into existence and what he had destroyed? That day a vast and ancient ordering of human life had largely passed away, and a vast new ordering of human life had taken its place. The thought was exciting—and melancholy. Perhaps that was the symbolic moment when the profound melancholy of Spain and the ineradicable melancholy of Mexico fused together to constitute one of the basic traits of the new breed of men that was henceforward to arise.

Jon Manchip White, *Cortés and the Downfall of the Aztec Empire*, 1971.

Lope de Vega in his play *El Nuevo Mundo* call for comment, if not for correction. Certainly the injustices and the crimes committed in the name of religion revolt the heart as well as the conscience. Certainly the Conquistadors used the instruments of the Faith to further their ventures. Thus Ovando, when fighting in Cuba, had given the signal to an ambush by placing his hand on his cross of the Knights of Alcántara, while Valverde warned Pizarro's soldiers that the moment of attack had come by waving the Bible at Atahualpa. The system of *requerimiento* inflicted on the primitive people, the mass baptisms, the conversions *in extremis* that preceded strangulation, the expiatory stake, and the massacres that ended in the *Te Deum* seem to justify the words of one Indian, exhorted by a monk to die in the Christian faith: "Are there Spaniards in your Paradise? Then I prefer to die a heathen!" Who would dream of denying that the ceremonial of the liturgy often took on the appearance of a funeral procession? But Lope de Vega was wrong on one point: the violent acts of the Conquistadors—abduction, robberies, assassinations—though sometimes performed "in the name of" religion, were never "under the pretense of" religion.

The Conquistadors were sincere. The legality of the enterprise was guaranteed them by pontifical bulls. They had been given to understand that they were leaving for a crusade—the one against Islam having ended but recently—and that after the Jew and the Mohammedan, it was now a question of converting the Heathen. They had been born into a hatred and terror of heresy. They had wept with delight at the capture of Granada, trembled before the Inquisition, and shuddered at the very name of Luther. While still children, they had often spat at the passing of a Moor or set fire to the booth of a Jew. Spain in the sixteenth century was nothing but a vast monastery, noisy with orisons and bells. They had grown up in the shadow of cathedrals and breathed the odor of incense from their earliest years, while the first words they had uttered had been the names of the saints.

A Fanatical Spirit

The Conquistadors, although for the most part illiterate, had had no need of letters to feel the same fanatical spirit as did the horsemen of the Prophet when they invaded the old Greco-Latin world, or the Crusaders when they spread over the Syrian plains, or their own fathers at the reconquest of Granada. They had been told—they had been convinced—that millions of Indians would burn forever in Hell if they, the Conquistadors, did not bring them the Faith. They believed this quite simply. Religion was for them not a pretext but a banner. The existence of God in three persons, the immortality of the soul, sin, the Last Judgment—it never occurred to any one of them to dispute these facts or even to discuss them. These men of war and passion had retained the faith of little children. Their confessions were sincere, they participated in the Mass not only in the flesh but also in the spirit. The worst of them died in penitence. Pierced by arrows, or with a sword blade in the throat, or tied to the stake under torture, they called loudly for the last rites. *So color de religión.* . . . What an error! No ulterior motive colored the faith of the Conquistadors. They remained men of the Middle Ages. Religious hypocrisy had not yet been invented; it was to turn up later, covering iniquity with its black cloak. The hypocrite is a creature of the seventeenth century.

The Conquistadors believed in God fiercely and unreservedly. But they believed also—above all else!—in the Devil. Now, the

New World was the empire of the Devil, a Devil with multiform face, always hideous. The somber Mexican divinities, Huitzilopochtli (the Sorcerer-Hummingbird) and Tezcatlipoca (the Smoking Mirror), the horrible Kinich Kakmo of the Mayas, the Peruvian Viracocha who symbolized boiling lava, the sinister totems of the Araucanians and Diaguites. . . . Why, the medieval demon with short horns, lustful eye, and a tail that was curled like a vine shoot seemed a "good devil" besides such as these! Spaniards who in Estremaduran twilights had taken the flight of a bat for the passing of the Evil One were naturally terrified before these monsters of stone, with bared fangs and gleaming eyes, that seemed to come to fantastic life as night fell. How could they have watched an Aztec ceremony without nausea? The black-robed priests with matted hair, burrowing with their knives in the breasts of their victims, the human skulls piled up at the feet of the teocallis, the cannibal feasts around statues spattered with putrid blood, and the charnel-house stench which all the perfumes of Mexico were never able to hide. . . .

Conquistadors Were Individuals

It is impossible to universalize and to portray a typical conquistador, the archetype as it were. They were men of differing temperaments who did their deeds in very different circumstances. A Cortés is not like . . . a Valdivia . . . or a Jiménez de Quesada. . . .

Let us avoid oversimplification and also the conviction that they were a gang of thugs, looking only for gold, blood, and women. . . .

They were individualists, and they will continue to be such as long as they are Spaniards. . . . They were religious, without being sacristans. . . . Fortitude they had in the face of adversity and suffering, and it was necessary to ensure the goals to which they were committed. They suffered almost beyond the power of words to describe, and they resigned themselves and never allowed themselves to drift toward despair or self-destruction. . . . There is no need to bring forward examples of rashness and daring in speaking of these men. . . . Honor and fame motivated one and all. . . .

Francisco Morales Padrón, *The Spanish Conquistadors: Men or Devils?* 1960.

Such things froze the spirits of the Conquistadors, surpassing the nightmares of their childhoods. Satan himself was there, and his worship was celebrated among the dismembered corpses. His maleficent power was honored. He was no longer, as in Spain, the familiar accomplice that could be driven off by a flick of the finger, or the shameful specter slipping furtively through one's conscience but put to flight by a sprinkling of holy water. He was enthroned. Carved in granite, incrusted with precious stones and encircled with golden serpents, he was the superb incarnation of Evil. He glorified sin. Nothing was lacking in this perfect representation of Hell, not even the pots in which certain tribes of the Colombian jungle cooked their enemies alive. This indeed was Satan himself, adorned with all his lugubrious attractions.

Why, therefore, should we be astonished at the reactions of the Spaniards? In the depths of the Indian sanctuaries they could see the Prince of Darkness standing in all his macabre splendor. Looking heavenward, they could distinguish the silvery figure of Saint James galloping across the clouds. The conflict between the true and the false, between good and evil, was manifest in this double apparition. The problem was simple and their duty was clear. The Indians were possessed of the Devil, who had to be exorcised, first by destroying the material evidence of Devil worship. This is why the conquerors, activated by the same blind zeal as early Christians when they shattered the Roman statues, overturned the pre-Columbian idols and burned the ritual articles and the manuscripts that transmitted the sacred tradition—in short, showed a holy ardor to abolish the very memory of the heathen liturgy. This they counted as pious work and a salutary need.

Iconoclasts? Vandals? These epithets would have scandalized the Conquistadors. Who would have applied such words except the agents of Satan who served a vile master? But the Conquistadors did not limit themselves to casting down the idols. In order that the exorcism be fully effective, it was not enough to drive away the demons; it was proper also to set up in their places the symbols of the True Faith. Just as holy medals were laid upon flesh that was eaten away with ulcers, the soldiers of Charles V planted crosses on the tops of the teocallis or at crossroads. On the stones that were still spattered with blood from the sacrificial tables, they raised altars to Our Lady of Guadalupe. Tolerance was not for them. Others would follow who would use gentler methods. No one doubts that these booted and armored Christians often lacked the Christian spirit and that charity was almost always missing from their pitiless fervor; but their Faith and their good faith were whole. More even than the love of God and of one's neighbor, the horror of Beelzebub explains certain of the Conquistadors' attitudes, though of course it is understood that to explain is not to absolve.

The Conquistadors never ceased to oscillate between the opposing poles of idealism and realism. . . .

The Death of the Conquistadors

One last look at the Conquistadors. We know now how and why they lived. But how did they die? In opulence and glory?

One imagines sumptuous places of retirement, or at least comfortable ones, for the captains of the conquest who had returned home with their fortunes made. They would restore the family *solar*, and those who were literate would write their memoirs. Those who were nostalgic for power would hold some honorary position at court; and as for the soldiers—those without rank—they would return to their villages in La Mancha and Estremadura. They would be rich and would buy land, and in the course of endless social gatherings they would relate their campaigns, telling the stories of the Caribbean, of treasure and princesses. They would willingly show their enormous scars, for such wounds were not to be seen every day. Think of it! Scimitars of sharpened obsidian, and darts poisoned with the juice of the manchineel tree! And they would blow out great clouds of smoke from their pipes of Mexican tobacco. . . .

But the reality was quite different. The majority of the Conquistadors died while still in action, by accident, sickness, or violence. Those who survived ended their days in oblivion and, some of them, in poverty. That so melancholy and wretched a fate should have distinguished these enterprises, which at the beginning had been so full of promise, seems scarcely credible. Yet examples abound, and here are some of them, chosen from the most illustrious.

First the Discoverer himself, Christopher Columbus: he died at Valladolid, cast out by the king whose glory he had made. Juan de la Cosa, the father of Atlantic pilots, died riddled with arrows. Núñez de Balboa was beheaded, on his father-in-law's orders. Díaz de Solís was stoned to death. Nicuesa was lost at sea. Ponce de León died of an arrow in the heart. Hernandez de Córdoba was mortally wounded by Indians. Hernando de Soto was carried off by fever. Pedro de Alvarado was crushed by a horse. Juan de Escalante was killed by the natives of Vera Cruz. Hernán Cortés died poor and alone in an Andalusian village. Pánfilo de Narváez was drowned. Pedro de Valdivia was devoured by cannibals. Bastidas was stabbed by one of his own lieutenants. Diego de Ordaz died of sunstroke. Pedro de Mendoza died at sea.

And what happened to the Conquistadors of Peru? Hernando Pizarro ordered Almagro garroted; the latter's son assassinated Francisco Pizarro; Vaca de Castro had the younger Almagro beheaded; and Gonzalo Pizarro, before being condemned to death by Gasca, killed Nunez de Vela. Fifty captains were hanged. Not one of those who governed Peru during a quarter of a century, except Gasca, died other than by violence.

We know now that the alliance of Spain and the New World was sealed with blood. We know, too, that those who profited greatly by the venture were not legion. Is it true, then, that wealth acquired by violence never brings happiness and that there is a curse on gold acquired unjustly? A shadow passes over the flamboyant façade of the temple of Mammon: is it the disheveled figure of the goddess Nemesis? The drama is ended. The curtain falls slowly on a pyramid of corpses, as in the last act of a Shakespearean tragedy. It is finished, but another play is about to begin. What is its prologue? The difficult day of the conquest has just ended in a blaze of gold and blood. *Oro y sangre*—a funereal apotheosis! Night descends upon the battlefield of the Conquistadors, and silence follows. But at dawn, into the shadows that slowly pale, phantoms slip one by one. Then day is here, and the morning light falls gradually upon these new beings, lighting their resolute features with its silver gleam. They wear neither helmet nor breastplate, but robes of monkish homespun or the sober doublets of men of law. They carry no swords, but in their hands is the mason's trowel or the ivory staff of the alcalde or the cavalier's lance. At first there are only a few, but soon a numberless crowd emerges from the shadows. They gather up the dead and bury them. The battlefield has become a cemetery. Then, in serried ranks, elbow to elbow, like the Spartan phalanxes, they move off westward. These are the colonists.

VIEWPOINT 2

"Never have the Indians in all the Indies committed any act against the Spanish Christians, until those Christians have first and many times committed countless cruel aggressions against them. . . . For in the beginning the Indians regarded the Spaniards as angels from Heaven."

The Conquistadors Were Murderers

Bartolomé de las Casas

Bartolomé de las Casas, born in 1474, became known as an advocate of Indian rights. In 1492 las Casas was beginning legal and theological studies at the University of Salamanca. His father and uncle accompanied Columbus on the second voyage. The younger las Casas went to the New World originally as a colonist. He knew personally many of the leaders of the conquest—Cortés, Pizarro, and Alvarado, and accompanied Diego Velásquez and Panfilo de Narváez in the "pacification" of Cuba in 1512. Renouncing his possessions and slaves, las Casas was ordained. He spent most of the rest of his life—from 1514 on—defending the Indians against extermination. In addition to writing the *Apologetic History of the Indies* and the *General History of the Indies*, las Casas systematically collected manuscripts, letters, and official documents referring to the conquest of America. Without him, we would not have Columbus's ships' logs, for he preserved a transcript of those documents in his archives. He returned to Madrid for the last time in 1547. One of his last public acts was a debate in Vallodolid with Ginés de Sepúlveda in 1550 over whether the conquest of Indian lands and the war against the Indians were justified. Las Casas vehemently argued no. Las Casas died in 1566, writing in defense of the Indians until the very last.

As you read, consider the following questions:

1. The viewpoint begins almost like a history but quickly shifts to a more personal style. How soon does this shift occur? What textual evidence is there of this change?
2. According to las Casas, was Spanish cruelty the exception or the normal behavior for colonists and conquerors?
3. What, according to this viewpoint, motivated the Spaniards? What were the major negative consequences of their behavior?
4. Why would enemies of Spain capitalize on las Casas's descriptions? How could they be adopted for propaganda purposes?

The Indies were discovered in the year one thousand four hundred and ninety-two. In the following year a great many Spaniards went there with the intention of settling the land. Thus, forty-nine years have passed since the first settlers penetrated the land, the first so-claimed being the large and most happy isle called Hispaniola, which is six hundred leagues in circumference. Around it in all directions are many other islands, some very big, others very small, and all of them were, as we saw with our own eyes, densely populated with native peoples called Indians. This large island was perhaps the most densely populated place in the world. There must be close to two hundred leagues of land on this island, and the seacoast has been explored for more than ten thousand leagues, and each day more of it is being explored. And all the land so far discovered is a beehive of people; it is as though God had crowded into these lands the great majority of mankind.

A Description of the Indians

And of all the infinite universe of humanity, these people are the most guileless, the most devoid of wickedness and duplicity, the most obedient and faithful to their native masters and to the Spanish Christians whom they serve. They are by nature the most humble, patient, and peaceable, holding no grudges, free from embroilments, neither excitable nor quarrelsome. These people are the most devoid of rancors, hatreds, or desire for vengeance of any people in the world. And because they are so weak and complaisant, they are less able to endure heavy labor and soon die of no matter what malady. The sons of nobles among us, brought up in the enjoyments of life's refinements, are no more delicate than are these Indians, even those among them who are of the lowest rank of laborers. They are also poor people, for they not only possess little but have no desire to possess worldly goods. For this reason they are not arrogant, embittered, or greedy. Their repasts are such that the food of the holy fathers in the desert can scarcely be more parsimonious, scanty, and poor. As to their dress, they are generally naked, with only their pudenda covered somewhat. And when they cover their shoulders it is with a square cloth no more than two varas in size. They have no beds, but sleep on a kind of matting or else in a kind of suspended net called *hamacas*. They are very clean in their persons, with alert, intelligent minds, docile and open to doctrine, very apt to receive our holy Catholic faith, to be endowed with virtuous customs, and to behave in a godly fashion. And once they begin to hear the tidings of the Faith, they are so insistent on knowing more and on taking the sacraments of the Church and on observing the divine cult that, truly, the missionaries who are here need to be endowed by God with great patience in order to cope with such eagerness. Some of the secular Spaniards who have been here for many years say that the goodness of the Indians is undeniable and that if this gifted people could be brought to know the one true God they would be the most fortunate people in the world.

Ravening Wild Beasts

Yet into this sheepfold, into this land of meek outcasts there came some Spaniards who immediately behaved like ravening wild beasts, wolves, tigers, or lions that had been starved for many days. And Spaniards have behaved in no other way during the past forty years, down to the present time, for they are still acting like ravening beasts, killing, terrorizing, afflicting, torturing, and destroying the native peoples, doing all this with the strangest and most varied new methods of cruelty, never seen or heard of before, and to such a degree that this Island of Hispaniola, once so populous (having a population that I estimated to be more than three millions), has now a population of barely two hundred persons.

The island of Cuba is nearly as long as the distance between Valladolid and Rome; it is now almost completely depopulated. San Juan and Jamaica are two of the largest, most productive and attractive islands; both are now deserted and devastated. On the northern side of Cuba and Hispaniola lie the neighboring Lucayos comprising more than sixty islands including those called *Gigantes*, beside numerous other islands, some small some large.

The least felicitous of them were more fertile and beautiful than the gardens of the King of Seville. They have the healthiest lands in the world, where lived more than five hundred thousand souls; they are now deserted, inhabited by not a single living creature. All the people were slain or died after being taken into captivity and brought to the Island of Hispaniola to be sold as slaves. When the Spaniards saw that some of these had escaped, they sent a ship to find them, and it voyaged for three years among the islands searching for those who had escaped being slaughtered, for a good Christian had helped them escape, taking pity on them and had won them over to Christ; of these there were eleven persons and these I saw.

Cruelty and Inhumanity

And now that all true Christians may be mov'd with the greater compassion towards the poor creatures, that their losses may appeare the more deplorable, that they may with a greater indignation detest the ambition, cruelty, and covetousness, of the *Spaniards*, to those which I have abovesaid, I will also adde this for a truth, that, from the time *America* was first discovered unto this present, the *Indians* never were the men that ever shewed the least disaffection, or offer'd the least injury to the *Spaniards*, but rather ador'd them as Angels of immortality come to visit them from Heaven, till their owne actions betrayd them to a far worse censure.

This I will also adde, that from the beginning to this day, the *Spaniards* were never any more mindful to spread the Gospel among them, as if they had been dogs; but on the contrary forbid religious persons to exercise their dutie, deferring them by many afflictions and persecutions from preaching and teaching among them, for that they thought would have hindered them in getting their Gold, and kept the people from their labours. Neither had they any more knowledge of the God of Heaven, as to say whether he were of wood, brasse, or iron, than they had above a hundred years before. *New Spaine* being onely excepted, whither the Religious persons had most liberty to go: So that they all dy'd without Faith or Sacraments, to the willing destruction of their souls.

Bartolomé de las Casas, *Tears of the Indians,* 1656.

More than thirty other islands in the vicinity of San Juan are for the most part and for the same reason depopulated, and the land laid waste. On these islands I estimate there are 2,100 leagues of land that have been ruined and depopulated, empty of people.

As for the vast mainland, which is ten times larger than all Spain, even including Aragon and Portugal, containing more land than the distance between Seville and Jerusalem, or more than two thousand leagues, we are sure that our Spaniards, with their cruel and abominable acts, have devastated the land and exterminated the rational people who fully inhabited it. We can estimate very surely and truthfully that in the forty years that have passed, with the infernal actions of the Christians, there have been unjustly slain more than twelve million men, women, and children. In truth, I believe without trying to deceive myself that the number of the slain is more like fifteen million.

The common ways mainly employed by the Spaniards who call themselves Christian and who have gone there to extirpate those pitiful nations and wipe them off the earth is by unjustly waging cruel and bloody wars. Then, when they have slain all those who fought for their lives or to escape the tortures they would have to endure, that is to say, when they have slain all the native rulers and young men (since the Spaniards usually spare only the women and children, who are subjected to the hardest and bitterest servitude ever suffered by man or beast), they enslave any survivors. With these infernal methods of tyranny they debase and weaken countless numbers of those pitiful Indian nations.

A Wish for Gold

Their reason for killing and destroying such an infinite number of souls is that the Christians have an ultimate aim, which is to acquire gold, and to swell themselves with riches in a very brief time and thus rise to a high estate disproportionate to their merits. It should be kept in mind that their insatiable greed and ambition, the greatest ever seen in the world, is the cause of their villainies. And also, those lands are so rich and felicitous, the native peoples so meek and patient, so easy to subject, that our Spaniards have no more consideration for them than beasts. And I say this from my own knowledge of the acts I witnessed. But I should not say "than beasts" for, thanks be to God, they have treated beasts with some respect; I should say instead like excrement on the public squares. And thus they have deprived the Indians of their lives and souls, for the millions I mentioned have died without the Faith and without the benefit of the sacraments. This is a well-known and proven fact which even the tyrant Governors, themselves killers, know and admit. And never have the Indians in all the Indies committed any act against the Spanish Christians, until those Christians have first and many times committed countless cruel aggressions against them or against neighboring nations. For in the beginning the Indians regarded the Spaniards as angels from Heaven. Only after the Spaniards had used violence against them, killing, robbing, torturing, did the Indians ever rise up against them.

On the Island Hispaniola was where the Spaniards first landed, as I have said. Here those Christians perpetrated their first ravages and oppressions against the native peoples. This was the first land in the New World to be destroyed and depopulated by the Christians, and here they began their subjection of the women and children, taking them away from the Indians to use them and ill use them, eating the food they provided with their sweat and toil. The Spaniards did not content themselves with what the Indians gave them of their own free will, according to their ability, which was always too little to satisfy enormous appetites, for a Christian eats and consumes in one day an amount of food that would suffice to feed three houses inhabited by ten Indians for one month. And they committed other acts of force and violence and oppression which made the Indians realize that these men had not come from Heaven. And some of the Indians concealed their foods while others concealed their wives and children and still others fled to the mountains to avoid the terrible transactions of the Christians.

And the Christians attacked them with buffets and beatings, until finally they laid hands on the nobles of the villages. Then they behaved with such temerity and shamelessness that the most powerful ruler of the islands had to see his own wife raped by a Christian officer.

From that time onward the Indians began to seek ways to throw the Christians out of their lands. They took up arms, but their weapons were very weak and of little service in offense and still less in defense. (Because of this, the wars of the Indians against each other are little more than games played by children.) And the Christians, with their horses and swords and pikes began to carry out massacres and strange cruelties against them. They attacked the towns and spared neither the children nor the aged nor pregnant women nor women in childbed, not only stabbing them and dismembering them but cutting them to pieces as if dealing with sheep in the slaughter house. They laid bets as to who, with one stroke of the sword, could split a man in two or could cut off his head or spill out his entrails with a single stroke of the pike. They took infants from their mothers' breasts, snatching them by the legs and pitching them headfirst against the crags or snatched them by the arms and threw them into the rivers, roaring with laughter and saying as the babies fell into the water, "Boil there, you offspring of the devil!" Other infants they put to the sword along with their mothers and anyone else who happened to be nearby. They made some low wide gallows on which the hanged victim's feet almost touched the ground, stringing up their victims in lots of thirteen, in memory of Our Redeemer and His twelve Apostles, then set burning wood at their feet and thus burned them alive. To others they attached

66

straw or wrapped their whole bodies in straw and set them afire. With still others, all those they wanted to capture alive, they cut off their hands and hung them round the victim's neck, saying, "Go now, carry the message," meaning, Take the news to the Indians who have fled to the mountains. They usually dealt with the chieftains and nobles in the following way: they made a grid of rods which they placed on forked sticks, then lashed the victims to the grid and lighted a smoldering fire underneath, so that little by little, as those captives screamed in despair and torment, their souls would leave them.

Incredible Brutality

I once saw this, when there were four or five nobles lashed on grids and burning; I seem even to recall that there were two or three pairs of grids where others were burning, and because they uttered such loud screams that they disturbed the captain's sleep, he ordered them to be strangled. And the constable, who was worse than an executioner, did not want to obey that order (and I know the name of that constable and know his relatives in Seville), but instead put a stick over the victims' tongues, so they could not make a sound, and he stirred up the fire, but not too much, so that they roasted slowly, as he liked. I saw all these things I have described, and countless others.

And because all the people who could do so fled to the mountains to escape these inhuman, ruthless, and ferocious acts, the Spanish captains, enemies of the human race, pursued them with the fierce dogs they kept which attacked the Indians, tearing them to pieces and devouring them. And because on few and far between occasions, the Indians justifiably killed some Christians, the Spaniards made a rule among themselves that for every Christian slain by the Indians, they would slay a hundred Indians. . . .

Wicked and Cruel by Nature

Among the noteworthy outrages they committed was the one they perpetrated against a cacique, a very important noble, by name Hatuey, who had come to Cuba from Hispaniola with many of his people, to flee the calamities and inhuman acts of the Christians. When he was told by certain Indians that the Christians were now coming to Cuba, he assembled as many of his followers as he could and said this to them: "Now you must know that they are saying the Christians are coming here, and you know by experience how they put So and So and So and So, and other nobles to an end. And now they are coming from Haiti (which is Hispaniola) to do the same here. Do you know why they do this?" The Indians replied: "We do not know. But it may be that they are by nature wicked and cruel." And he told them:

"No, they do not act only because of that, but because they have a God they greatly worship and they want us to worship that God, and that is why they struggle with us and subject us and kill us."

Bathing Horses' Mouths in Blood

Between the Maya and the Aztec empires was a third civilization con-quered by the Spaniards. In what is now Colombia, the natives de-fended against the Conquistadors led by Balthasar Maldonado. When he proposed peace in 1541, Tundama, the leader of the Chibcha, re-fused to comply. This excerpt is taken from Tundama's speech.

I am not so barbarous, famous Spaniard, not to believe peace to be the centre on which the bounds of this world depend; but do not think I'm unaware that the bland words with which you offer it to me are much belied by your harsh behaviour.

Who will say that Tundama should give to the vassal the tribute due to the king? I cannot serve someone who serves his king so badly. According to your own accounts of the King of Spain's clemency, it is not credible that he should send you to kill and rob us so.

More barbarian than the Panches and the Muzos, you bathe your horses' mouths in our blood, which they drink out of hunger and thirst and which you spill to display your cruelty. You desecrate the sanctuaries of our gods and sack the houses of men who haven't of-fended you. Who would choose to undergo these insults, being not insensitive? Who would omit to rid himself of such harassment, even at the cost of his life?

You well know that my people were bred with no fewer natural privileges than yours. We now know that you are not immortal or descended from the sun. Since your people refuse tax and tyranny you cannot be surprised that mine do, with determination.

Do not take as examples the Zipas, killed sooner through your treachery or their bad government, or because they fought with less right, than because of the valour you claim for yourselves.

Note well the survivors who await you, to undeceive you that vic-tory is always yours.

Tundama, quoted in Miguel Leon-Portilla, *Image of the New World*, 1979.

He had a basket full of gold and jewels and he said: "You see their God here, the God of the Christians. If you agree to it, let us dance for this God, who knows, it may please the God of the Christians and then they will do us no harm." And his followers said, all together, "Yes, that is good, that is good!" And they danced round the basket of gold until they fell down exhausted. Then their chief, the cacique Hatuey, said to them: "See here, if we keep this basket of gold they will take it from us and will end up by killing us. So let us cast away the basket into the river." They all agreed to do this, and they flung the basket of gold into the river that was nearby.

This cacique, Hatuey, was constantly fleeing before the Christians from the time they arrived on the island of Cuba, since he knew them and of what they were capable. Now and then they encountered him and he defended himself, but they finally killed him. And they did this for the sole reason that he had fled from those cruel and wicked Christians and had defended himself against them. And when they had captured him and as many of his followers as they could, they burned them all at the stake.

When tied to the stake, the cacique Hatuey was told by a Franciscan friar who was present, an artless rascal, something about the God of the Christians and of the articles of the Faith. And he was told what he could do in the brief time that remained to him, in order to be saved and go to Heaven. The cacique, who had never heard any of this before, and was told he would go to Inferno where if he did not adopt the Christian Faith, he would suffer eternal torment, asked the Franciscan friar if Christians all went to Heaven. When told that they did he said he would prefer to go to Hell. Such is the fame and honor that God and our Faith have earned through the Christians who have gone out to the Indies.

"They sacrificed all our men in this way, eating their legs and arms, offering their hearts and blood to their idols."

The Conquistadors Fought in Self-Defense

Bernal Díaz del Castillo

Bernal Díaz del Castillo, the last survivor of the Conquest of Mexico, died on his estate in Guatemala at the age of eighty-nine. He was over seventy when he began *The Conquest of New Spain*, written in part to counter errors of other historians. His first-person account is a soldier's vivid recollection, the "story of myself and my comrades, all true conquerors, who served His Majesty in the discovery, conquest, pacification, and settlement of the provinces of New Spain." In his account of the battle for Tenochtitlan, or Mexico City, the conquistador comes off as a far more vulnerable human being than is usually depicted.

As you read, consider the following questions:

1. In the author's opinion, do the Mexicans appear to be victims of the conquistadors?
2. What elements of the author's narrative reveal his opinion of the conquistadors?
3. What elements of Mexican society are revealed in this viewpoint?
4. How does Díaz characterize Cortés?

Seeing that it was impossible to fill in every channel and gap that we captured in the daytime and that the Mexicans reopened and refortified each night, and that all of us together fighting, filling in, and keeping watch was very hard labour, Cortes decided to hold consultations with the captains and soldiers in his camp, and wrote to us in Alvarado's camp, and to those in Sandoval's, to learn the opinion of us all. . . .

Cortes listened to our opinions and the reasons with which we supported them. But the sole outcome of all this discussion was that next day we were to advance with all possible strength from all three camps, horsemen, crossbowmen, musketeers, and soldiers, and push forward into the great market square of Tlatelolco. When all was ready in the three camps, and warnings had been sent to our Tlascalan allies, the men of Texcoco, and those of the other towns who had recently sworn obedience to His Majesty and were to bring their canoes to help our launches, we started from our camp on Sunday morning, after mass. Cortes too set out from his camp, and Sandoval led his men forward; and each company advanced in full force, capturing barricades and bridges. The Mexicans fought like brave men, but Cortes made great gains, and so did Gonzalo de Sandoval. As for us, we had already captured another barricade and bridge, which was very difficult because Guatemoc had great forces guarding them. Many of our men were wounded, one so severely that he died a little later, and more than a thousand of our Tlascalan allies were injured. Still, we followed up our victory in high spirits.

To return to Cortes and his men, they captured a deepish water-opening with a very narrow causeway across it, which the Mexicans had constructed most cunningly. For they had cleverly foreseen just what would happen; which was that after his victory Cortes and his men would press along the causeway, which would be crowded with our allies. They decided therefore that at this point they must pretend to be in flight, but continue to hurl javelins, arrows, and stones and to make little stands as though trying to put up some resistance, until they lured Cortes on to follow them.

When the Mexicans saw that Cortes was indeed following up his victory in this way, they simulated flight, as they had planned. Then, as bad fortune follows on good and great disasters succeed great prosperity, so in his headlong pursuit of the enemy, either out of carelessness or because Our Lord permitted it, Cortes and his men omitted to fill in the channel they had captured. The causeway had been deliberately built very narrow, and it was interrupted by water in some places, and full of mud and mire. When the Mexicans saw him cross that channel without filling it in they were highly delighted. They had assembled great bands of warriors under very valiant captains and posted many canoes on the lake in places where our launches could not reach them on account of great stakes. All was prepared for the moment when such a furious army of shrieking, shouting, and whistling Mexicans fell on Cortes and his men that they could not stand up to the shock of their charge. Our soldiers, captains, and standard-bearers then decided to retreat in good order. But the enemy continued to charge them furiously, and drove them back to that difficult crossing. Meanwhile our allies, of whom Cortes had brought great numbers, were so confused that they turned and fled, offering no resistance. On seeing them run away in disorder Cortes tried to hearten them with cries of: 'Stop, stop, gentlemen! Stand firm! What do you mean by turning your backs?' But he could not halt them.

Mexicans Defeat Cortes

Then, at that gap in the causeway which they had neglected to fill, on that little, narrow, broken causeway, the Mexicans, aided by their canoes, defeated Cortes, wounding him in the leg, taking sixty-six of his soldiers alive, and killing eight horses. Six or seven Mexican captains had already seized our Captain, but the Lord was pleased to help him and give him strength to defend himself, although wounded. Then, in the nick of time, that very valiant soldier Cristobal de Olea came up to him and, seeing Cortes held by so many Indians, promptly killed four of them with mighty thrusts of his sword; and another brave soldier called Lerma helped him. Such was the personal bravery of these two men that the Indian captains let Cortes go. But in defending him for the second time Olea lost his life and Lerma was almost killed. Then many other soldiers rushed up and, although badly wounded, grasped Cortes and pulled him out of his dangerous position in the mud. The quartermaster Cristobal de Olid also ran forward, and they seized Cortes by the arms to drag him out of the mud and water, and brought him a horse, on which he escaped from death. At that same moment his steward Cristobal de Guzman arrived with another horse. Meanwhile the Mexican warriors went on fighting very bravely and successfully from the rooftops, inflicting great damage on us and capturing Cristobal de Guzman, whom they carried alive to Guatemoc; and they continued to pursue Cortes and his men until they had driven them back to camp. Even after that disaster, when they reached their quarters the Mexicans continued to harry them, shouting and yelling abuse and calling them cowards.

But to turn from Cortes and his defeat to our army under Pedro de Alvarado, on the causeway from Tacuba. We were advancing most victoriously when suddenly and unexpectedly we saw a great number of Mexican bands advancing against us, with handsome standards and plumes. Uttering loud yells, they threw in front of us five heads, streaming with blood, which they had just cut off the men of Cortes' company whom they had captured.

'We will kill you too,' they cried, 'as we have killed Malinche and Sandoval, and all the men they brought with them.' With these words they closed in on us, and neither cut nor thrust, nor crossbow nor musket could keep them off. They rushed at us as if we were a target. Even so, we did not break our ranks at all as we retired. We at once commanded our Tlascalan allies to get quickly out of our way in the streets and on the causeways and at the difficult places, and this time they did so with a will. When they saw those five bloodstained heads, they said that Malinche and Sandoval and all the *Teules* with them had been killed, and that the same would happen to us, and to them, the Tlascalans. They were very much frightened, for they believed what they said.

As we were retreating, we heard the sound of trumpets from the great *cue* of Huichilobos and Tezcatlipoca, which dominates the whole city, and the beating of a drum, a very sad sound as of some devilish instrument, which could be heard six miles away; and with it came the noise of many kettle-drums, conches, horns, and whistles. At that moment, as we afterwards learnt, they were offering the hearts and blood of ten of our comrades to these two idols.

But let us return to our retreat and the great attack they made on us from the causeway, the rooftops, and the canoes on the lake. At that moment we were attacked once more by fresh bands whom Guatemoc had just sent, and he had ordered his horn to be sounded. The blowing of this horn was a signal that his captains and warriors must now fight to capture their enemies or die in the attempt, and as soon as this sound struck their ears, his bands and companies, hurling themselves on us with a terrifying and indescribable fury, endeavoured to drag us away. Even now, when I stop to think, I seem to see it all and to be present at that battle once more. It was our Lord Jesus Christ, let me repeat, who gave us strength, for we were all wounded. It was He who saved us, for otherwise we should never have reached our huts, and I praise and thank Him for it, that I escaped that time, as on other occasions, from the power of the Mexicans.

Hard Pressed and Wounded

The horsemen charged repeatedly, and with two cannon which we placed near our huts, and which were loaded and fired by turns, we managed to hold our own. The causeway was choked

Punishment of the Indians Was Necessary

I cannot omit to mention the cages of stout wooden bars that we found in the city [Cholula], full of men and boys who were being fattened for the sacrifice at which their flesh would be eaten. We destroyed these cages, and Cortes ordered the prisoners who were confined in them to return to their native districts. Then, with threats, he ordered the *Caciques* and captains and *papas* of the city to imprison no more Indians in that way and to eat no more human flesh. They promised to obey him. But since they were not kept, of what use were their promises?

Let us anticipate a little and say that these were the great cruelties about which the bishop of Chiapas, Fray Bartolome de las Casas, wrote, and was never tired of talking. He insisted that we punished the Cholulans for no reason at all, or just to amuse ourselves and because we had a fancy to. He writes so persuasively that he would convince anyone who had not witnessed the event, or had no knowledge of it, that these and the other cruelties of which he writes took place as he says, whereas the reverse is true. Let the Dominicans beware of this book of his, because they will find it contradicts the facts. . . .

If we had not inflicted that punishment, our lives would have been in great danger from the companies of Mexican warriors and Cholulans, and their barricades and breastworks. And if we had been so unfortunate as to be killed, this New Spain of ours would not have been conquered so rapidly, nor would another *armada* have dared to set out, or if it had done so it would have met with greater difficulties, because the Mexicans would have defended the ports. And they would still have remained in a state of idolatry.

Bernal Díaz del Castillo, *The Conquest of New Spain*, 1568.

with Mexicans, who pursued us as far as the houses, as if we were already conquered, and hurled javelins and stones at us. But, as I have said, we killed many of them with these cannon. The most useful man that day was a gentleman called Pedro Moreno Medrano, who now lives at Puebla. He acted as gunner, because our proper artillerymen had been either killed or wounded. He was a good soldier, and gave us great assistance. While we were defending ourselves like this, hard pressed and wounded, we did not know whether Cortes and Sandoval and their armies had been killed or routed, as the Mexicans had told us when they threw down those heads, which they had brought tied together by the hair and beards. We could get no news of them, for they were fighting about a mile and a half away, and the place where the Mexicans had defeated Cortes was even further off. We were very distressed, therefore, but by keeping together in one body, both wounded and sound, we withstood the fury of the attack, which the Mexicans believed would annihilate us. For they had already captured one of our launches, killing three soldiers and wounding the captain and the rest of the crew, though it had afterwards been rescued by another launch whose captain was Juan Jaramillo; and yet another was impaled in a place from which it could not move. Its captain was Juan de Limpias, who lost his hearing at that time, and now lives at Puebla. He himself fought so valiantly, and so encouraged the soldiers who were rowing the launch, that they broke the stakes and got away, all badly wounded, thus saving the craft, which was the first to break the stakes, a great thing for us all.

To return to Cortes, when he and nearly all his men were either killed or wounded, the Mexican bands made an attack on his camp, and cast in front of the soldiers who were defending it another four heads, dripping with blood, which were those of four men captured from Cortes' own army. But they said they were the heads of Tonatio—that is of Pedro de Alvarado—and of Sandoval, Bernal Díaz, and another *Teule*, and that they had already killed us all at Tacuba. It is said that Cortes was even more distressed than before, and that tears sprang to his eyes and the eyes of all those who were with him. Nevertheless he did not seem to weaken. He at once ordered Cristobal de Olid, the quartermaster, and his captains to be sure that the many Mexicans who were pressing in on them did not break into the camp, and to see that his men held together, the sound and the wounded alike. He then sent Andres de Tapia with three horsemen post-haste overland to Tacuba, to see if we were alive, and to tell us, if we had not been defeated, to keep watch by day and night, also in a single body. But we had already been doing this for some time. Tapia and his three horsemen came as hard as they could, though he and two of them were wounded, and when they reached our camp and found us fighting the Mexicans who were gathered against us, they rejoiced in their hearts. They told us how Cortes had been defeated and conveyed his message to us, but they did not care to tell us how many had been killed. They gave the number as about twenty-five, and said that the rest were well.

Sandoval and his men had advanced victoriously along the streets in the quarter they were invading. But after the defeat of Cortes, the Mexicans turned on them in such force that they could make no headway. Six soldiers were killed and all the rest injured, including Sandoval himself, who received three wounds, in the thigh, the head, and the left arm; and when the struggle was at its height, the enemy displayed six heads of Cortes' men whom they had killed, saying that these were the heads of Malinche, Tonatio, and other captains, and that Sandoval and his companions would meet with the same fate. They then made a fierce attack. When he saw the heads Sandoval told his men to show a bold spirit and not be dismayed. He warned them too that there must be no confusion on the narrow causeway as they retreated, and ordered his allies, who were numerous, to leave it immediately, since they would hamper him. Then, with the help of his two launches and his musketeers and crossbowmen, he very laboriously retired to his quarters, with all his men badly wounded and discouraged, and six of them dead. Once he was clear of the causeway, although still surrounded by Mexicans, he encouraged his people and their captains, charging them to be sure to keep together by day and night and thus prevent the camp from being overwhelmed. . . .

Just at that moment the two launches which Cortes kept under his command beside the causeway came in. There had been no news of them since the defeat. It appears that they had been caught on some stakes and, according to their captains' reports, surrounded by canoes which had attacked them. They all came in wounded, and said that in the first place God had aided them with a wind, and then by making every effort with their oars they had broken the stakes and escaped. Cortes was very pleased, for up to that time (although he had not said so in order not to dishearten the soldiers) he had given these launches up for lost, having heard nothing of them.

After this, Cortes strongly urged Sandoval to ride post-haste to our camp at Tacuba and see whether we were defeated, or how we stood; and if he found us alive, he was to help us to defend our camp from their assaults, and he instructed Francisco de Lugo to accompany him, for he knew very well that there were Mexican companies on the road. Indeed he told Lugo that he had already sent Andres de Tapia with three horsemen to get news of us, and feared they might have been killed on the way. Then, after taking his leave of him, he turned to embrace Sandoval, to whom he said: 'See, my son, I cannot go everywhere, because I am wounded. So I entrust you with the task of ensuring the safety of all three camps. I know that Pedro de Alvarado and all his comrades have fought valiantly, like true gentlemen. But I fear the great forces of these dogs may have overwhelmed them. As for me and my army, you can see our condition.'

Sandoval and Francisco de Lugo rode post-haste to our position, arriving a little after dusk, and found us fighting with the Mexicans who were trying to get into our camp by way of some houses we had pulled down. Others were attacking along the causeway, and many canoes were assaulting us from the lake. They had already driven one launch aground, killing two of its crew and wounding all the rest; and Sandoval saw me with six other soldiers above our waists in the lake, helping to push it off

The Siege of Tenochtitlan, 1521

At the centre of this design is Tenochtitlan, the island capital of the Aztecs. It is represented by its huge main pyramid, which stood on the site now occupied by the Cathedral of Mexico City. Around it on Lake Texcoco, Aztec warriors in canoes hold shields, clubs and spears and swords inset with obsidian; one of them (lower left) is distinguished by the Jaguar uniform of the military elite. At the corners are four towns, shown by a large House sign; in each of them mounted Spaniards, together with native allies, trample on the dismembered bodies of vanquished local inhabitants (the arrow sticking in Xochinilco, upper right, means 'conquest'). . . . After fiercely resisting Cortés when he entered their territory (roughly the modern state of Tlaxcala) on his march from the Gulf Coast, the Tlaxcalans joined him in the Spanish attack on their old enemies the Aztecs and became his stoutest allies. The siege of Tenochtitlan is one of several major campaigns depicted in their Lienzo, which the Tlaxcalans painted *c.* 1550 to celebrate their prowess and to remind the Spaniards of their indebtedness to them.

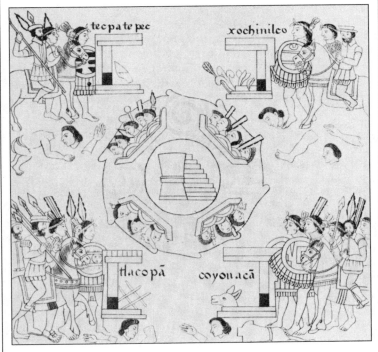

From *Image of the New World: The American Continent Portrayed in Native Texts.* Gordon Brotherston, ed. London: Thames and Hudson, 1979.

into deep water. Many Indians were attacking us, with swords captured when Cortes was defeated or with flint-edged broadswords, trying to prevent us from rescuing the launch, which, to judge by their efforts, they intended to drag off with their canoes. Indeed, they had already attached several ropes to it in order to tow it into the city. When Sandoval saw us in this condition, he cried: 'Brothers, put your backs into it and see that they do not get the launch!' And we made such an effort that we dragged it to safety, even though, as I have said, two of its crew were killed and all the rest wounded.

Just then many companies of Mexicans came down the causeway, wounding us all, including the horsemen. Sandoval too received a stone full in the face. But Pedro de Alvarado and some other horsemen went to his assistance. As so many bands were coming on, and only I and twenty soldiers were opposing them, Sandoval ordered us to retire gradually in order to save the horses; and because we did not retire as quickly as he wished he turned on us furiously and said: 'Do you want me and all my horsemen to be killed because of you? For my sake, Bernal Díaz, my friend, please fall back!' Then Sandoval received another wound, and so did his horse. By this time we had got our allies off the causeway; and facing the enemy and never turning our backs, we gradually retired, forming a kind of dam to hold up their advance. Some of our crossbowmen and musketeers shot while others were loading, the horsemen made charges, and Pedro Moreno loaded and fired his cannon. Yet despite the number of Mexicans that were swept away by his shot we could not keep them at bay. On the contrary, they continued to pursue us, in the belief that they would carry us off that night to be sacrificed.

A Terrifying Sound

When we had retired almost to our quarters, across a great opening full of water, their arrows, darts, and stones could no longer reach us. Sandoval, Francisco de Lugo, and Andres de Tapia were standing with Pedro de Alvarado, each one telling his story and discussing Cortes' orders, when the dismal drum of Huichilobos sounded again, accompanied by conches, horns, and trumpet-like instruments. It was a terrifying sound, and when we looked at the tall *cue* from which it came we saw our comrades who had been captured in Cortes' defeat being dragged up the steps to be sacrificed. When they had hauled them up to a small platform in front of the shrine where they kept their accursed idols we saw them put plumes on the heads of many of them; and then they made them dance with a sort of fan in front of Huichilobos. Then after they had danced the papas laid them down on their backs on some narrow stones of sacrifice and, cut-

78

ting open their chests, drew out their palpitating hearts which they offered to the idols before them. Then they kicked the bodies down the steps, and the Indian butchers who were waiting below cut off their arms and legs and flayed their faces, which they afterwards prepared like glove leather, with their beards on, and kept for their drunken festivals. Then they ate their flesh with a sauce of peppers and tomatoes. They sacrificed all our men in this way, eating their legs and arms, offering their hearts and blood to their idols as I have said, and throwing their trunks and entrails to lions and tigers and serpents and snakes that they kept in the wild-beast houses I have described in an earlier chapter.

On seeing these atrocities, all of us in our camp said to one another: 'Thank God they did not carry me off to be sacrificed!' My readers must remember that though we were not far off we could do nothing to help, and could only pray God to guard us from such a death. Then at the very moment of the sacrifice, great bands of Mexicans suddenly fell upon us and kept us busy on all sides. We could find no way of holding them. 'Look!' they shouted, 'that is the way you will all die, as our gods have many times promised us,' and the threats they shouted at our Tlascalan allies were so cruel and so frightening that they lost their spirit. The Mexicans threw them roasted legs of Indians and the arms of our soldiers with cries of: 'Eat the flesh of these *Teules* and of your brothers, for we are glutted with it. You can stuff yourselves on our leavings. Now see these houses you have pulled down. We shall make you build them again, much finer, with white stone and fine masonry. So go on helping the *Teules*. You will see them all sacrificed.'

Guatemoc did something more after his victory. He sent the hands and feet of our soldiers, and the skin of their faces, and the heads of the horses that had been killed, to all the towns of our allies and friends and their relations, with the message that as more than half of us were dead and he would soon finish off the rest, they had better break their alliance with us and come to Mexico, because if they did not desert us quickly he would come and destroy them.

VIEWPOINT 4

"[The Spaniards] ran everywhere . . . they invaded every room, hunting and killing."

The Conquistadors Fought Without Reason

Miguel Leon-Portilla

As with all conquests, that of Mexico may be written from two perspectives. While Bernal Díaz, author of the previous viewpoint, gave the point of view of the Spanish conquerors, the following selection gives the viewpoint of the conquered—the Aztecs.

The Aztecs believed that Cortés was Quetzalcoatl, god and culture hero who had departed to the east, promising that someday he would return from across the seas. It is thus ironic that when Cortés and his men entered Mexico, they were often welcomed not only as guests but also as gods coming home. The Aztec desire to honor the "gods" coincided with the Spanish desire for gold. Thus Motecuhzoma (Montezuma) sent out messengers with gifts. But as Cortés's forces moved toward Tenochtitlan (Mexico City), the initial "golden age" disintegrated into suspicion, manipulation, and distrust. Such distrust was often translated into brutality.

The Indians were determined to preserve their own memories of the conquest. Fray Toribio de Benevente, also known as Motolinia, arrived in June 1524 with a group of Franciscan friars. He observed the Indians' passion for history:

"Among the events of their times, the native Indians took particular note of the year in which the Spaniards entered this land, for to them it was a most remarkable happening which at first caused them great terror and amazement. They saw a strange people arrive from the sea—a feat they had never before witnessed nor had known was possible—all dressed in strange garments and so bold and warlike that, although few in number, they could invade all the provinces of this land imperiously, as if the natives were their vassals. The Indians were also filled with wonder at their horses, and the Spaniards riding on their backs. . . . They called the Spaniards 'Teteuh' meaning 'gods,' which the Spaniards corrupted into 'teules.'. . . The Indians also set down the year in which the twelve friars arrived together."

The first portion of this viewpoint was written in Nahuatl by Indian students of Fray Bernadino de Sahagun; they drew on their people's oral history, the memories of their elders who had lived through the conquest. The original version was completed about 1555. Known as the *Codex Florentino*, it was revised by Sahagun about 1585. The account of the temple massacre was gathered by Fray Diego de Duran from native sources before 1580.

As you read, consider the following questions:

1. How do Montezuma's speeches indicate he thought Cortés was the returning Quetzalcoatl?
2. What about the Aztec description of the Spaniards indicates it was written years after the events? How do the Aztecs characterize the Spaniards?
3. What impression do you have of the Aztecs? What sort of people do they seem to be?

Editor's Note: After the destruction of [the Mexican city of] Cholula, the Spaniards continued to march toward the Valley of Mexico, accompanied by their allies from Tlaxcala. The texts by Sahagun's informants, from which the passages in this chapter are taken, describe two incidents of particular interest.

When the army was among the volcanoes, in what the Indians called the Eagle Pass, it was met by new envoys from Motecuhzoma, headed by Tzihuacpopocatzin. The envoys presented many objects of gold to the strangers, and then observed their reactions to the gifts: "The Spaniards burst into smiles. . . . They hungered like pigs for that gold. . . . "

Second, the texts report the deceit of Tzihuacpopocatzin, who attempted—apparently on Motecuhzoma's orders—to pass himself off as Motecuhzoma. This effort failed, and another series of envoys was sent out—magicians again—in the hope of stopping the conquistadors. But the wizards retired before the mysterious presence of a pretended drunkard, who foretold the ruin of Mex-

ico and showed them portents. They thought the god Tezcatlipoca had appeared to them, and they hurried back to
Tenochtitlan to tell Motecuhzoma. The great Aztec *tlatoani* was
even more depressed than before and waited fatalistically for
what was to come.

The Spaniards See the Objects of Gold

Then Motecuhzoma dispatched various chiefs. Tzihuacpopocatzin was at their head, and he took with him a great many of
his representatives. They went out to meet the Spaniards in the
vicinity of Popocatepetl and Iztactepetl, there in the Eagle Pass.
They gave the "gods" ensigns of gold, and ensigns of quetzal
feathers, and golden necklaces. And when they were given these
presents, the Spaniards burst into smiles; their eyes shone with
pleasure; they were delighted by them. They picked up the gold
and fingered it like monkeys; they seemed to be transported by
joy, as if their hearts were illumined and made new.

The truth is that they longed and lusted for gold. Their bodies
swelled with greed, and their hunger was ravenous, they hungered like pigs for that gold. They snatched at the golden ensigns,
waved them from side to side and examined every inch of them.
They were like one who speaks a barbarous tongue: everything
they said was in a barbarous tongue. . . .

Speeches of Motecuhzoma and Cortes

When Motecuhzoma had given necklaces to each one, Cortes
asked him: "Are you Motecuhzoma? Are you the king? Is it true
that you are the king Motecuhzoma?"

And the king said: "Yes, I am Motecuhzoma." Then he stood up
to welcome Cortes; he came forward, bowed his head low and
addressed him in these words: "Our lord, you are weary. The
journey has tired you, but now you have arrived on the earth.
You have come to your city, Mexico. You have come here to sit on
your throne, to sit under its canopy.

"The kings who have gone before, your representatives,
guarded it and preserved it for your coming. The kings Itzcoatl,
Motecuhzoma the Elder, Axayacatl, Tizoc and Ahuitzol ruled for
you in the City of Mexico. The people were protected by their
swords and sheltered by their shields.

"Do the kings know the destiny of those they left behind, their
posterity? If only they are watching! If only they can see what I
see!

"No, it is not a dream. I am not walking in my sleep. I am not
seeing you in my dreams. . . . I have seen you at last! I have met
you face to face! I was in agony for five days, for ten days, with
my eyes fixed on the Region of the Mystery. And now you have

come out of the clouds and mists to sit on your throne again.
"This was foretold by the kings who governed your city, and
now it has taken place. You have come back to us; you have come
down from the sky. Rest now, and take possession of your royal
houses. Welcome to your land, my lords!"

Antichrist on Earth

It was only because of the mad time, the mad priests, that sadness
came among us, that Christianity came among us; for the great
Christians came here with the true God; but that was the beginning
of our distress,
the beginning of the tribute, the beginning of the alms, what made
the hidden discord appear,
the beginning of the fighting with firearms,
the beginning of the outrages,
the beginning of being stripped of everything,
the beginning of slavery for debts,
the beginning of the debts bound to the shoulders,
the beginning of the constant quarrelling,
the beginning of the suffering.
It was the beginning of the work of the Spaniards and the priests,
the beginning of the manipulation of the chiefs, schoolmasters and
officials . . .
The poor people did not protest against what they felt a slavery,
the Antichrist on earth, tiger of the peoples,
wildcat of the peoples, sucking the Indian people dry.
But the day will come when the tears of their eyes
reach God and God's justice
comes down and strikes the world.

Mayan testimony from the prophecy of the book of the Linajes, *Chilam Balam de
Chumayel*. Quoted in Miguel Leon-Portilla, *Reverso de la Conquista*.

When Motecuhzoma had finished, La Malinche translated his
address into Spanish so that the Captain could understand it.
Cortes replied in his strange and savage tongue, speaking first to
La Malinche: "Tell Motecuhzoma that we are his friends. There is
nothing to fear. We have wanted to see him for a long time, and
now we have seen his face and heard his words. Tell him that we
love him well and that our hearts are contented."
Then he said to Motecuhzoma: "We have come to your house in
Mexico as friends. There is nothing to fear."
La Malinche translated this speech and the Spaniards grasped
Motecuhzoma's hands and patted his back to show their affection
for him.
The Spaniards examined everything they saw. They dis-
mounted from their horses, and mounted them again, and dis-

mounted again, so as not to miss anything of interest.

The chiefs who accompanied Motecuhzoma were: Cacama, king of Tezcoco; Tetlepanquetzaltzin, king of Tlacopan; Itzcuauhtzin the Tlacochcalcatl, lord of Tlatelolco; and Topantemoc, Motecuhzoma's treasurer in Tlatelolco. These four chiefs were standing in a file.

The other princes were: Atlixcatzin [chief who has taken captives]; Tepeoatzin, the Tlacochcalcatl; Quetzalaztatzin, the keeper of the chalk; Totomotzin; Hecateupatilzin; and Cuappiatzin.

When Motecuhzoma was imprisoned, they all went into hiding. They ran away to hide and treacherously abandoned him!

The Spaniards Take Possession of the City

When the Spaniards entered the Royal House, they placed Motecuhzoma under guard and kept him under their vigilance. They also placed a guard over Itzcuauhtzin, but the other lords were permitted to depart.

Then the Spaniards fired one of their cannons, and this caused great confusion in the city. The people scattered in every direction; they fled without rhyme or reason; they ran off as if they were being pursued. It was as if they had eaten the mushrooms that confuse the mind, or had seen some dreadful apparition. They were all overcome by terror, as if their hearts had fainted. And when night fell, the panic spread through the city and their fears would not let them sleep.

In the morning the Spaniards told Motecuhzoma what they needed in the way of supplies: tortillas, fried chickens, hens' eggs, pure water, firewood and charcoal. Also: large, clean cooking pots, water jars, pitchers, dishes and other pottery. Motecuhzoma ordered that it be sent to them. The chiefs who received this order were angry with the king and no longer revered or respected him. But they furnished the Spaniards with all the provisions they needed—food, beverages and water, and fodder for the horses.

The Spaniards Reveal Their Greed

When the Spaniards were installed in the palace, they asked Motecuhzoma about the city's resources and reserves and about the warriors' ensigns and shields. They questioned him closely and then demanded gold.

Motecuhzoma guided them to it. They surrounded him and crowded close with their weapons. He walked in the center, while they formed a circle around him.

When they arrived at the treasure house called Teucalco, the riches of gold and feathers were brought out to them: ornaments made of quetzal feathers, richly worked shields, disks of gold, the necklaces of the idols, gold nose plugs, gold greaves and bracelets and crowns.

The Spaniards immediately stripped the feathers from the gold shields and ensigns. They gathered all the gold into a great mound and set fire to everything else, regardless of its value. Then they melted down the gold into ingots. As for the precious green stones, they took only the best of them; the rest were snatched up by the Tlaxcaltecas. The Spaniards searched through the whole treasure house, questioning and quarreling, and seized every object they thought was beautiful.

The Seizure of Motecuhzoma's Treasures

Next they went to Motecuhzoma's storehouse, in the place called Totocalco [Place of the Palace of the Birds], where his personal treasures were kept. The Spaniards grinned like little beasts and patted each other with delight.

When they entered the hall of treasures, it was as if they had arrived in Paradise. They searched everywhere and coveted everything; they were slaves to their own greed. All of Motecuhzoma's possessions were brought out: fine bracelets, necklaces with large stones, ankle rings with little gold bells, the royal crowns and all the royal finery—everything that belonged to the king and was reserved to him only. They seized these treasures as if they were their own, as if this plunder were merely a stroke of good luck. And when they had taken all the gold, they heaped up everything else in the middle of the patio.

La Malinche called the nobles together. She climbed up to the palace roof and cried: "Mexicanos, come forward! The Spaniards need your help! Bring them food and pure water. They are tired and hungry; they are almost fainting from exhaustion! Why do you not come forward? Are you angry with them?"

The Mexicans were too frightened to approach. They were crushed by terror and would not risk coming forward. They shied away as if the Spaniards were wild beasts, as if the hour were midnight on the blackest night of the year. Yet they did not abandon the Spaniards to hunger and thirst. They brought them whatever they needed, but shook with fear as they did so. They delivered the supplies to the Spaniards with trembling hands, then turned and hurried away. . . .

Editor's Note: Several indigenous texts—the Codex Ramirez, *the* XIII relación *of Alva Ixtlilxochitl and the* Codex Aubin—*describe the massacre perpetrated during the fiesta of Toxcatl, which the Aztecs celebrated in honor of the god Huitzilopochtli. "This was the most important of their fiestas," wrote Sahagun. "It was like our Easter and fell at almost the same time."*

Cortes had been absent from the city for twenty days when the massacre took place; he had gone out to fight Panfilo de Narvaez, who was coming to arrest him by order of Diego Velazques, governor of Cuba. Cortes' deputy, Pedro de Alvarado, treacherously murdered the celebrants when the festival was at its height.

Worms Swarm in the Streets

And all this happened among us. We saw it. We lived through it with an astonishment worthy of tears and of pity for the pain we suffered.

On the roads lie broken shafts and torn hair,
houses are roofless, homes are stained red,
worms swarm in the streets, walls are spattered with brains.
The water is reddish, like dyed water;
we drink it so, we even drink brine;
the water we drink is full of saltpetre.
The wells are crammed with adobe bricks.

Whatever was still alive was kept between shields, like precious treasure, between shields, until it was eaten.

We chewed on hard tzompantli wood, brackish *zacatl* fodder, chunks of adobe, lizards, vermin, dust and worms.

We eat what was on the fire, as soon as it is done we eat it together right by the fire.

We had a single price; there was a standard price for a youth, a priest, a boy and a young girl. The maximum price for a slave amounted to only two handfuls of maize, to only ten tortillas. Only twenty bundles of brackish fodder was the price of gold, jade, mantles, quetzal plumes; all valuables fetched the same low price. It went down further when the Spaniards set up their battering engine in the market place.

Now, Cuauhtemoc orders the prisoners to be brought out; the guards don't miss any. The elders and chiefs grab them by their extremities and Cuauhtemoc slits open their bellies with his own hand.

Annals of Tlatelolco, part 5, quoted in Miguel Leon-Portilla, *Image of the New World*, 1979.

The Aztecs begged permission of their king to hold the fiesta of Huitzilopochtli. The Spaniards wanted to see this fiesta to learn how it was celebrated. A delegation of the celebrants came to the palace where Motecuhzoma was a prisoner, and when their spokesman asked his permission, he granted it to them.

As soon as the delegation returned, the women began to grind seeds of the chicalote. These women had fasted for a whole year. They ground the seeds in the patio of the temple.

The Spaniards came out of the palace together, dressed in armor and carrying their weapons with them. They stalked among the women and looked at them one by one; they stared into the faces of the women who were grinding seeds. After this cold inspection, they went back into the palace. It is said that they planned to kill the celebrants if the men entered the patio.

The Statue of Huitzilopochtli, the God of War

On the evening before the fiesta of Toxcatl, the celebrants began to model a statue of Huitzilopochtli. They gave it such a human appearance that it seemed the body of a living man. Yet they made the statue with nothing but a paste made of the ground seeds of the chicalote, which they shaped over an armature of sticks.

When the statue was finished, they dressed it in rich feathers, and they painted crossbars over and under its eyes. They also clipped on its earrings of turquoise mosaic; these were in the shape of serpents, with gold rings hanging from them. Its nose plug, in the shape of an arrow, was made of gold and was inlaid with fine stones.

They placed the magic headdress of hummingbird feathers on its head. They also adorned it with an *anecuyotl*, which was a belt made of feathers, with a cone at the back. Then they hung around its neck an ornament of yellow parrot feathers, fringed like the locks of a young boy. Over this they put its nettle-leaf cape, which was painted black and decorated with five clusters of eagle feathers.

Next they wrapped it in its cloak, which was painted with skulls and bones, and over this they fastened its vest. The vest was painted with dismembered human parts: skulls, ears, hearts, intestines, torsos, breasts, hands and feet. They also put on its *maxtlatl*, or loincloth, which was decorated with images of dissevered limbs and fringed with amate paper [made from inner bark of several trees of the genus *Ficus*]. This *maxtlatl* was painted with vertical stripes of bright blue.

They fastened a red paper flag at its shoulder and placed on its head what looked like a sacrificial flint knife. This too was made of red paper; it seemed to have been steeped in blood.

The statue carried a *tehuehuelli*, a bamboo shield decorated with four clusters of fine eagle feathers. The pendant of this shield was blood-red, like the knife and the shoulder flag. The statue also carried four arrows.

Finally, they put the wristbands on its arms. These bands, made of coyote skin, were fringed with paper cut into little strips.

Early the next morning, the statue's face was uncovered by those who had been chosen for that ceremony. They gathered in front of the idol in single file and offered it gifts of food, such as round seedcakes or perhaps human flesh. But they did not carry it up to its temple on top of the pyramid.

All the young warriors were eager for the fiesta to begin. They had sworn to dance and sing with all their hearts, so that the Spaniards would marvel at the beauty of the rituals.

The procession began, and the celebrants filed into the temple patio to dance the Dance of the Serpent. When they were all together in the patio, the songs and the dance began. Those who had fasted for twenty days and those who had fasted for a year were in command of the others; they kept the dancers in file with their pine wands. (If anyone wished to urinate, he did not stop dancing, but simply opened his clothing at the hips and separated his clusters of heron feathers.)

If anyone disobeyed the leaders or was not in his proper place they struck him on the hips and shoulders. Then they drove him out of the patio, beating him and shoving him from behind. They pushed him so hard that he sprawled to the ground, and they dragged him outside by the ears. No one dared to say a word about this punishment, for those who had fasted during the year were feared and venerated; they had earned the exclusive title "Brothers of Huitzilopochtli."

The great captains, the bravest warriors, danced at the head of the files to guide the others. The youths followed at a slight distance. Some of the youths wore their hair gathered into large locks, a sign that they had never taken any captives. Others carried their headdresses on their shoulders; they had taken captives, but only with help.

Then came the recruits, who were called "the young warriors." They had each captured an enemy or two. The others called to them: "Come, comrades, show us how brave you are! Dance with all your hearts!"

The Spaniards Attack the Celebrants

At this moment in the fiesta, when the dance was loveliest and when song was linked to song, the Spaniards were seized with an urge to kill the celebrants. They all ran forward, armed as if for battle. They closed the entrances and passageways, all the gates of the patio: the Eagle Gate in the lesser palace, the Gate of the Canestalk and the Gate of the Serpent of Mirrors. They posted guards so that no one could escape, and then rushed into the Sacred Patio to slaughter the celebrants. They came on foot, carrying their swords and their wooden or metal shields.

They ran in among the dancers, forcing their way to the place where the drums were played. They attacked the man who was drumming and cut off his arms. Then they cut off his head, and it rolled across the floor.

They attacked all the celebrants, stabbing them, spearing them, striking them with their swords. They attacked some of them from behind, and these fell instantly to the ground with their entrails hanging out. Others they beheaded: they cut off their heads, or split their heads to pieces.

They struck others in the shoulders, and their arms were torn from their bodies. They wounded some in the thigh and some in the calf. They slashed others in the abdomen, and their entrails all spilled to the ground. Some attempted to run away, but their intestines dragged as they ran; they seemed to tangle their feet in their own entrails. No matter how they tried to save themselves, they could find no escape.

Some attempted to force their way out, but the Spaniards murdered them at the gates. Others climbed the walls, but they could not save themselves. Those who ran into the communal houses were safe there for a while; so were those who lay down among the victims and pretended to be dead. But if they stood up again, the Spaniards saw them and killed them.

The blood of the warriors flowed like water and gathered into pools. The pools widened, and the stench of blood and entrails filled the air. The Spaniards ran into the communal houses to kill those who were hiding. They ran everywhere and searched everywhere; they invaded every room, hunting and killing.

When the news of this massacre was heard outside the Sacred Patio, a great cry went up: "Mexicanos, come running! Bring your spears and shields! The strangers have murdered our warriors!"

This cry was answered with a roar of grief and anger: the people shouted and wailed and beat their palms against their mouths. The captains assembled at once, as if the hour had been determined in advance. They all carried their spears and shields.

Then the battle began. The Aztecs attacked with javelins and arrows, even with the light spears that are used for hunting birds. They hurled their javelins with all their strength, and the cloud of missiles spread out over the Spaniards like a yellow cloak.

The Spaniards immediately took refuge in the palace. They began to shoot at the Mexicans with their iron arrows and to fire their cannons and arquebuses. And they shackled Motecuhzoma in chains.

The Mexicans who had died in the massacre were taken out of the patio one by one and inquiries were made to discover their names. The fathers and mothers of the dead wept and lamented.

Each victim was taken first to his own home and then to the Sacred Patio, where all the dead were brought together. Some of the bodies were later burned in the place called the Eagle Urn, and others in the House of the Young Men.

CHAPTER 3

The Indians Are Dispossessed of Their Land

Chapter Preface

The selections in this chapter explore the moral and legal questions raised as Europeans moved into land previously occupied by the Indians. From the beginning of the sixteenth century to the end of the nineteenth, legal experts considered various principles to justify the taking of Indian land by white settlers. Among these principles were discovery, settlement, and efficient land use. The difficulty was that the parties involved represented radically different viewpoints. Discussions between Europeans and Indians foundered on fundamental cultural and philosophical differences. The legal, moral, and cultural problems all began with Columbus.

Certainly Columbus, on October 12, 1492, seemed punctilious in his attention to legal detail while claiming his discovery for Spain.

> At dawn we saw naked people, and I went ashore in the ship's boat, followed by Martin Alonso Pinzón, captain of the *Pinta*, and his brother Vincente Yanez Pinzón, captain of the *Niña*. I unfurled the royal banner, and the captains brought the flags which displayed a large green cross with the letters F and Y at the left and right side of the cross. Over each letter was the appropriate crown of that Sovereign. These flags were carried as a standard on all of the ships. After a prayer of thanksgiving, I ordered the captains of the *Pinta* and *Niña*, together with Rodrigo de Escobedo [secretary of the fleet], and Rodrigo Sanchez of Segovia [comptroller of the fleet] to bear faith and witness that I was taking possession of this island for the King and Queen. I made all the necessary declarations and had these testimonies carefully written down by the secretary. In addition to those named above, the entire company of the fleet bore witness to this act. To this island I gave the name *San Salvador*, in honor of our Blessed Lord.

Columbus was careful to have the secretary of the fleet and the comptroller of the fleet witness the possession. Moreover, Columbus "made all the necessary declarations," and, having adhered to legal formalities, had these witnessed, not only by the royal officials, but by the entire crew. Finally, he named the island San Salvador, conveying European nomenclature on the tiny dot on the map which the natives called Guanahaní. Was discovery—even carried out with full attention to legal propriety—enough for possession? Clearly there remained the problem that people already lived there. Equally clearly, one solution seemed to be the superimposition of one culture upon another (San Salvador for Guanahaní) and the assumption that the non-Europeans could change to conform to the newcomers: "I think they can easily be made Christians." However, it is also clear that Columbus did not *intend* in

1492 to add settlement to discovery as the basis for taking possession. Only the grounding of the *Santa Maria* necessitated building a fort and leaving some of the crew on Hispaniola. As a basis for claiming possession, this settlement could hardly count. By the time Columbus returned in 1493, La Navidad was abandoned. Its crewmen and colonists had died or disappeared.

Thus discovery alone was Columbus's basis for claiming these new territories. But additional questions emerged. Can an explorer merely sail along a new coast and claim it? If he steps ashore and lays claim, how much territory is possessed—the landing spot? the whole island? the entire continent? And what if, as would be likely in the Age of Discovery, explorers from different countries come ashore? Who, then, owned the land?

Native Rights Ignored

Initially the ethical and legal issues centered on the claims of Europeans; the native rights to the land were generally ignored. The Papal Bull of Alexander VI in 1493, dividing the new-found world between Spain and Portugal, attempted to avoid squabbling between Christian nations. Royal charters to explorers recognized that discovery was insufficient claim to possession. Elizabeth I granted Walter Raleigh the right to "discover, search, find out, and view such remote, heathen and barbarous lands, countries and territories, not actually possessed of any Christian Prince, nor inhabited by Christian peoples." This decree gave him the right, indeed the duty, to "have, hold, occupy and enjoy" these lands. Many charters contained similar language. Their additional criteria are significant. Only the lands of the heathen were fair game; while this admittedly suggests the belief in the superiority of Christianity, it also addresses a practical problem: New World discoveries should not create—nor exacerbate—Old World political tensions. In addition, the language of such grants clearly demands that something ("hold," "occupy," "enjoy") be *done* with the land. Claiming it by virtue of discovery—or even of extended exploration of the interior—was not enough. Soon this issue, *making effective use of the land*, would be turned to the Europeans' advantage in arguments favoring Indian dispossession.

While such legal documents solved some questions, they raised others. What right did the pope have to apportion the world? What right did European monarchs have to grant lands to their nationals? And, equally important, what rights did those people already living there have to the lands being claimed by Europeans? Many of these legal issues are addressed in the first two viewpoints.

Complicating the problem in North America was the fact that exploration, settlement, and dispossession occurred repeatedly. Pittsburgh, for example, was still a frontier post when Philadelphia had long been settled. Initial relations between Europeans and Indians were frequently amicable as the Europeans adapted themselves to American conditions. Fur trading, the earliest occupation, did not disrupt the man-land relationship too much. Trading posts were merely beachheads in the wilderness. But when it became clear that cash crops could be equally profitable, or when increasing numbers of immigrants sought land for themselves, the equilibrium shifted. Land itself was now in demand.

The American frontier moved progressively westward, despite government attempts to define any distant land not occupied by white settlers as "Indian territory." No mere government decree (the Proclamation of 1763 was only the first such) could keep land-hungry whites east of an imaginary barrier. Each thrust into Indian territory by small farmers caused another dislocation of Indian populations. Each dislocation resulted in two different kinds of tensions. First, Indian tribes fought against one another as eastern Indians being pushed west came into conflict with western tribes already there. Second, tension increased between whites and Indians as all Indians grew increasingly distrustful of whites who ignored treaty agreements guaranteeing the Indians possession of the land "so long as the grass shall grow and the rivers flow."

Misconceptions

Misconceptions about the Indians also created difficulties. In journals of many early settlers, they are referred to as "savages." Because the settlers saw the Indians' civilization as inferior, it was easy for them to believe the Indians had no civilization at all, and indeed perhaps lacked the rationality to achieve civilization. Many settlers saw Indians as little better than animals, and just like animals, Indians could not be said to possess land.

Even sophisticated arguments were developed along this simple idea. Henry Nash Smith's excellent and intriguing book subtitled *The American West as Symbol and Myth* (1950) has as its title *The Virgin Land*, a metaphor that clearly suggests America had known no people before the arrival of the Europeans. Historian Frederick Jackson Turner's frontier hypothesis defines the frontier as "that meeting point between civilization and savagery"—quite a contrast to an Old World concept of "frontier" as the boundary between two sovereign states. And in 1890, the Bureau of the Census declared the frontier closed, as there were no longer any areas of land with fewer than two people per square mile. *Which* people? Obviously the Bureau of the Census had long ignored the growing numbers of Indians crowded into increasingly smaller areas. Indeed, the vantage point of all these sources overlooks native populations.

Another rationalization that allowed settlers to take native lands was that all Indians were nomads. Native agricultural populations—from the Wampanoag who contributed to the success of Plymouth, to the followers of Powhatan who had cleared the fields so desired by the Virginians, to the Hohokam with their extensive agricultural irrigation projects, were ignored or conveniently forgotten. Indians, everyone knew, ranged through the woods and across the plains hunting meat and fur-bearing animals. Clearly such use of land was inefficient. Colonists argued that those who would use the land more effectively deserved to own it.

A final, probably irreconcilable land use issue between the Europeans and the Indians was their quite different understanding of the relationship between man and the land. For the Indian, the connection was intimate, organic, even religious. Many native American creation myths had Indians emerging from the earth, as from the womb. Earth, then, is the Mother, the source of life, to be respected and cherished. Certainly one could not possess her; especially emphatically, one could not sell her. And just as most Indians asked permission of the animal spirits before they killed them for meat, so too they showed concern for Mother Earth. Some Southwestern tribes, for example, removed their mounts' horseshoes in the springtime so that the pregnant and especially vulnerable earth would not be harmed. And, in the late nineteenth century, when the Bureau of Indian Affairs distributed steel plows to help the Indians become better farmers, many recipients were horrified at the thought of so brutally abusing Mother Earth's body.

From such differences arose the ultimate point of contention: whether an individual *could* own the land. The Europeans, especially those who had been dispossessed at home, saw this as a perfectly natural goal. The Indians felt that the land and all things living on it were gifts of God to be shared and conserved by all people. In such disagreements, might often makes right. Frequently in America, the force of superior numbers and more advanced technology weighed in on the side of the whites.

VIEWPOINT 1

"[N]ature ... gives no nation a right to appropriate to itself a country, except for the purpose of making use of it, and not of hindering others from deriving advantage from it."

Natural Law Justifies Dispossessing the Indians of Their Land

Emmerich von Vattel

The Swiss jurist Emmerich von Vattel (1714-1767) modernized international law, making it less theoretical and more practical. His *Law of Nations*, originally published in 1758 and reprinted in 1876 in Philadelphia, was especially popular in England and the United States, in part because of the following excerpts, which may provide legal justification for the dispossession of Indians from their lands.

As you read, consider the following questions:

1. According to Vattel, what must be avoided if the farmer is to be kept productive and happy in his most essential occupation?
2. Why does Vattel call agriculture the "most useful and necessary ... of all the arts"?
3. Which of Vattel's principles would Europeans have seized on to justify acquisition of land in the Americas? Was there any flaw in the application of these principles?
4. According to Vattel, what is the single most important step if a nation is to take possession of a country?

The Function of Society

Society is established with the view of procuring, to those who are its members, the necessaries, conveniences, and even pleasures of life, and, in general, every thing necessary to their happiness,—of enabling each individual peaceably to enjoy his own property, and to obtain justice with safety and certainty,—and, finally, of defending themselves in a body against all external violence. The nation, or its conductor, should first apply to the business of providing for all the wants of the people, and producing a happy plenty of the necessaries of life, with its conveniences and innocent and laudable enjoyments. . . .

Agriculture, the Most Necessary Art

Of all the arts, tillage, or agriculture, is doubtless the most useful and necessary, as being the source whence the nation derives its subsistence. The cultivation of the soil causes it to produce an infinite increase; it forms the surest resource and the most solid fund of riches and commerce, for a nation that enjoys a happy climate.

This object then deserves the utmost attention of the government. The sovereign ought to neglect no means of rendering the land under his jurisdiction as well cultivated as possible. He ought not to allow either communities or private persons to acquire large tracts of land, and leave them uncultivated. Those rights of common, which deprive the proprietor of the free liberty of disposing of his land—which will not allow him to enclose and cultivate it in the most advantageous manner; those rights, I say, are inimical to the welfare of the state, and ought to be suppressed, or reduced to just bounds. Notwithstanding the introduction of private property among the citizens, the nation has still a right to take the most effectual measures to cause the aggregate soil of the country to produce the greatest and most advantageous revenue possible.

The government ought carefully to avoid every thing capable of discouraging the husbandman, or of diverting him from the labours of agriculture. Those taxes—those excessive and ill-proportioned impositions, the burden of which falls almost entirely on the cultivators—and the oppressions they suffer from the officers who levy them—deprive the unhappy peasant of the means of cultivating the earth, and depopulate the country. Spain is the most fertile and the worst cultivated country in Europe. The church there possesses too much land; and the contractors for the royal magazines, being authorized to purchase, at a low price, all the corn they find in the possession of a peasant, above what is necessary for the subsistence of himself and his family, so greatly discourage the husbandman, that he sows no more corn than is barely necessary for the support of his own household. Hence the frequent scarcity in a country capable of feeding its neighbours. Another abuse injurious to agriculture is the contempt cast upon the husbandman. The tradesmen in cities—even the most servile mechanics—the idle citizens—consider him that cultivates the earth with a disdainful eye; they humble and discourage him; they dare to despise a profession that feeds the human race—the natural employment of man. A little insignificant haberdasher, a tailor, places far beneath him the beloved employment of the first consuls and dictators of Rome! China has wisely prevented this abuse: agriculture is there held in honour; and to preserve this happy mode of thinking, the emperor himself, followed by his whole court, annually, on a solemn day, sets his hand to the plough, and sows a small piece of land. Hence China is the best cultivated country in the world; it feeds an immense multitude of inhabitants who at first sight appear to the traveller too numerous for the space they occupy.

The cultivation of the soil deserves the attention of the government, not only on account of the invaluable advantages that flow from it, but from its being an obligation imposed by nature on mankind. The whole earth is destined to feed its inhabitants; but this it would be incapable of doing if it were uncultivated. Every nation is then obliged by the law of nature to cultivate the land that has fallen to its share; and it has no right to enlarge its boundaries, or have recourse to the assistance of other nations, but in proportion as the land in its possession is incapable of furnishing it with necessaries. Those nations (such as the ancient Germans, and some modern Tartars) who inhabit fertile countries, but disdain to cultivate their lands, and choose rather to live by plunder . . . are injurious to all their neighbours.

There are others, who, to avoid labour, choose to live only by hunting, and their flocks. This might, doubtless, be allowed in the first ages of the world, when the earth, without cultivation, produced more than was sufficient to feed its small number of inhabitants. But at present, when the human race is so greatly multiplied, it could not subsist if all nations were disposed to live in that manner. Those who still pursue this idle mode of life, usurp more extensive territories than, with a reasonable share of labour, they would have occasion for, and have, therefore, no reason to complain if other nations, more industrious and too closely confined, come to take possession of a part of those lands. Thus, though the conquest of the civilized empires of Peru and Mexico was a notorious usurpation, the establishment of many colonies on the continent of North America might, on their confining themselves within just bounds, be extremely lawful. The people of those extensive tracts rather ranged through than inhabited them. . . .

Indians Must Change

At the foundation of the whole social system lies individuality of property. It is, perhaps, nine times in ten, the stimulus that manhood first feels; it has produced the energy, industry, and enterprise that distinguish the civilized world, and contributes more largely to the good morals of men than those are willing to acknowledge who have not looked somewhat closely at their fellow-beings. With it come all the delights that the word *home* expresses. The comforts that follow fixed settlements are in its train; and to them belong not only an anxiety to do right, that those gratifications may not be forfeited, but industry, that they may be increased. Social intercourse and a just appreciation of its pleasures result, when you have civilized and, for the most part, moral men. This process, it strikes me, the Indians must go through, before their habits can be materially changed; and they may, after what many of them have seen and know, do it very rapidly. If, on the other hand, the large tracts of land set apart for them shall continue to be joint property, the ordinary motive to industry (and the most powerful one) will be wanting. A bare subsistence is as much as they can promise themselves. A few acres of badly cultivated corn about their cabins will be seen, instead of extensive fields, rich pastures, and valuable stock. The latter belong to him who is conscious that what he ploughs is his own, and will descend to those he loves—never to the man who does not know by what tenure he holds his miserable dwelling. . . . The history of the world proves that distinct and separate possessions make those who hold them averse to change. The risk of losing the advantages they have, men do not readily encounter. By adopting and acting on the view suggested, a large body will be created whose interests would dispose them to keep things steady. They would be the ballast of the ship.

T.A. Crawford, Commissioner of Indian Affairs, from a report dated November 25, 1838.

Hitherto we have considered the nation merely with respect to itself, without any regard to the country it possesses. Let us now see it established in a country which becomes its own property and habitation. The earth belongs to mankind in general; destined by the Creator to be their common habitation, and to supply them with food, they all possess a natural right to inhabit it, and to derive from it whatever is necessary for their subsistence, and suitable to their wants. But when the human race became extremely multiplied, the earth was no longer capable of furnishing spontaneously, and without culture, sufficient support for its inhabitants; neither could it have received proper cultivation from

98

wandering tribes of men continuing to possess it in common. It therefore became necessary that those tribes should fix themselves somewhere, and appropriate to themselves portions of land, in order that they might, without being disturbed in their labour, or disappointed of the fruits of their industry, apply themselves to render those lands fertile, and thence derive their subsistence. Such must have been the origin of the rights of property and dominion. . . . It was a sufficient ground to justify their establishment. Since their introduction, the right which was common to all mankind is individually restricted to what each lawfully possesses. The country which a nation inhabits, whether that nation has emigrated thither in a body, or the different families of which it consists were previously scattered over the country, and there uniting, formed themselves into a political society,—that country, I say, is the settlement of the nation, and it has a peculiar and exclusive right to it.

This right comprehends two things: 1. The domain, by virtue of which the nation alone may use the country for the supply of its necessities, may dispose of it as it thinks proper, and derive from it every advantage it is capable of yielding. 2. The empire, or the right of sovereign command, by which the nation directs and regulates at its pleasure every thing that passes in the country.

How May People Take Possession of the Land?

When a nation takes possession of a country to which no prior owner can lay claim, it is considered as acquiring the empire or sovereignty of it, at the same time with the domain. For, since the nation is free and independent, it can have no intention, in settling in a country, to leave to others the right of command, or any of those rights that constitute sovereignty. The whole space over which a nation extends its government becomes the seat of its jurisdiction, and is called its territory.

If a number of free families, scattered over an independent country, come to unite for the purpose of forming a nation or state, they altogether acquire the sovereignty over the whole country they inhabit: for they were previously in possession of the domain—a proportional share of it belonging to each individual family: and since they are willing to form together a political society, and establish a public authority, which every member of the society shall be bound to obey, it is evidently their intention to attribute to that public authority the right of command over the whole country.

All mankind have an equal right to things that have not yet fallen into the possession of any one; and those things belong to the person who first takes possession of them. When, therefore, a nation finds a country uninhabited, and without an owner, it may lawfully take possession of it: and, when it has sufficiently made known its will in this respect, it cannot be deprived of it by another nation. Thus navigators going on voyages of discovery, furnished with a commission from their sovereign, and meeting with islands or other lands in a desert state, have taken possession of them in the name of their nation: and this title has been usually respected, provided it was soon after followed by a real possession.

But it is questioned whether a nation can, by the bare act of taking possession, appropriate to itself countries which it does not really occupy, and thus engross a much greater extent of territory than it is able to people or cultivate. It is not difficult to determine that such a pretension would be an absolute infringement of the natural rights of men, and repugnant to the views of nature, which, having destined the whole earth to supply the wants of mankind in general, gives no nation a right to appropriate to itself a country, except for the purpose of making use of it, and not of hindering others from deriving advantage from it. The law of nations will, therefore, not acknowledge the property and sovereignty of a nation over any uninhabited countries, except those of which it has really taken actual possession, in which it has formed settlements, or of which it makes actual use. In effect, when navigators have met with desert countries in which those of other nations had, in their transient visits, erected some monument to show their having taken possession of them, they have paid as little regard to that empty ceremony as to the regulation of the popes, who divided a great part of the world between the crowns of Castile and Portugal.

But What About the New World?

There is another celebrated question, to which the discovery of the New World has principally given rise. It is asked whether a nation may lawfully take possession of some part of a vast country, in which there are none but erratic nations whose scanty population is incapable of occupying the whole. We have already observed, in establishing the obligation to cultivate the earth, that those nations cannot exclusively appropriate to themselves more land than they have occasion for, or more than they are able to settle and cultivate. Their unsettled habitation in those immense regions cannot be accounted a true and legal possession; and the people of Europe, too closely pent up at home, finding land of which the savages stood in no particular need, and of which they made no actual and constant use, were lawfully entitled to take possession of it, and settle it with colonies. The earth, as we have already observed, belongs to mankind in general, and was designed to furnish them with subsistence: if each nation had, from

The Colonial Practice

On the discovery of this immense continent, the great nations of Europe were eager to appropriate to themselves so much of it as they could respectively acquire. Its vast extent offered an ample field to the ambition and enterprise of all; and the character and religion of its inhabitants afforded an apology for considering them as a people over whom the superior genius of Europe might claim an ascendancy. The potentates of the old world found no difficulty in convincing themselves, that they made ample compensation to the inhabitants of the new, by bestowing on them civilization and Christianity, in exchange for unlimited independence. But as they were all in pursuit of nearly the same object, it was necessary, in order to avoid conflicting settlements, and consequent war with each other, to establish a principle, which all should acknowledge as the law by which the right of acquisition, which they all asserted, should be regulated, as between themselves. The principle was, that discovery gave title to the government by whose subjects, or by whose authority, it was made, against all other European governments, which title might be consummated by possession. . . .

In the establishment of these relations, the rights of the original inhabitants were, in no instance, entirely disregarded, but were necessarily, to a considerable extent, impaired. They were admitted to be the rightful occupants of the soil, with a legal as well as just claim to retain possession of it, and to use it according to their own discretion; but their rights to complete sovereignty, as independent nations, were necessarily diminished, and their power to dispose of the soil, at their own will, to whomsoever they pleased, was denied by the original fundamental principle, that discovery gave exclusive title to those who made it.

While the different nations of Europe respected the right of the natives, as occupants, they asserted the ultimate dominion to be in themselves; and claimed and exercised, as a consequence of this ultimate dominion, a power to grant the soil, while yet in possession of the natives. These grants have been understood by all, to convey a title to the grantees, subject only to the Indian right of occupancy. The history of America, from its discovery to the present day, proves, we think, the universal recognition of these principles.

Chief Justice John Marshall, from the majority opinion in *Johnson and Graham's Lessee v. M'Intosh* delivered in 1823.

the beginning, resolved to appropriate to itself a vast country, that the people might live only by hunting, fishing, and wild fruits, our globe would not be sufficient to maintain a tenth part of its present inhabitants. We do not, therefore, deviate from the views of nature in confining the Indians within narrower limits. However, we cannot help praising the moderation of the English Puritans who first settled in New England; who, notwithstanding their be-

101

ing furnished with a charter from their sovereign, purchased of the Indians the land of which they intended to take possession. This laudable example was followed by William Penn, and the colony of Quakers that he conducted to Pennsylvania. When a nation takes possession of a distant country, and settles a colony there, that country, though separated from its principal establishment, or mother-country, naturally becomes a part of the state, equally with its ancient possessions. Whenever, therefore, the political laws, or treaties, make no distinction between them, every thing said of the territory or nation, must also extend to its colonies.

Families wandering in a country, as the nations of shepherds, and ranging through it as their wants require, possess it in common: it belongs to them to the exclusion of all other nations; and we cannot, without injustice, deprive them of the tracts of country of which they make use. But, let us here recollect what we have said more than once. The savages of North America had no right to appropriate all that vast continent to themselves; and since they were unable to inhabit the whole of those regions, other nations might, without injustice, settle in some parts of them, provided they left the natives a sufficiency of land. If the pastoral Arabs would carefully cultivate the soil, a less space might be sufficient for them. Nevertheless, no other nation has a right to narrow their boundaries, unless she be under an absolute want of land. For, in short, they possess their country; they make use of it after their manner; they reap from it an advantage suitable to their manner of life, respecting which they have no laws to receive from any one. In a case of pressing necessity, I think people might, without injustice, settle in a part of that country, on teaching the Arabs the means of rendering it, by the cultivation of the earth, sufficient for their own wants, and those of the new inhabitants.

It may happen that a nation is contented with possessing only certain places, or appropriating to itself certain rights, in a country that has not an owner, without being solicitous to take possession of the whole country. In this case, another nation may take possession of what the first has neglected; but this cannot be done without allowing all the rights acquired by the first to subsist in their full and absolute independence. In such cases, it is proper that regulations should be made by treaty; and this precaution is seldom neglected among civilized nations.

VIEWPOINT 2

"Before [the] arrival of the Spaniards these barbarians possessed true dominion, both in public and private affairs."

Natural Law Does Not Justify Dispossessing the Indians of Their Land

Francisco de Vitoria

Francisco de Vitoria (probably 1486-1546), a Spanish theologian, is best remembered for his defense of the rights of the Indians in the New World. A Dominican, he was elected in 1526 to the Prime Chair of Theology at the University of Salamanca, Spain. In spite of the fact that he was a friar, he took the unusual position that it was not legitimate to wage war on people simply because they were pagans. He was critical of Spanish colonial policy, did not believe the pope had the authority to give European rulers dominion over native populations, and believed that Indians had a right to their own lands and rulers. The following viewpoint, from his "On the American Indians" ("*De Indis*"), evolved from a series of lectures. In it, he argues that although Spaniards had the right to trade in the Americas, the conquest was largely illegal or at least unjust.

As you read, consider the following questions:

1. According to de Vitoria, on what possible grounds might the Indians be seen as not true masters of their lands? Does he feel these are valid grounds for dispossession?
2. According to de Vitoria, by what unjust methods did Christians claim possessions in the New World?

The text to be re-read is 'Go ye therefore, and teach all nations, baptizing them in the name of the Father, and of the Son, and of the Holy Ghost' (Matt. 28:19). This raises the following problem: whether it is lawful to baptize the children of unbelievers against the wishes of their parents? . . .

This whole dispute and relection has arisen again because of these barbarians in the New World, commonly called Indians, who came under the power of the Spaniards some forty years ago, having been previously unknown to our world.

My present discussion of these people will be divided into three parts: first, by what right were the barbarians subjected to Spanish rule? Second, what powers has the Spanish monarchy over the Indians in temporal and civil matters? And third, what powers has either the monarchy or the Church with regard to the Indians in spiritual and religious matters? . . .

Introduction: Whether This Dispute Is Justified. . . . It may first of all be objected *that this whole dispute is unprofitable and fatuous,* not only for those like us who have no warrant to question or censure the conduct of government in the Indies irrespective of whether or not it is rightly administered, but even for those whose business it is to frame and administer that government:

1. Neither the princes of the Spains nor the ministers of their royal Councils are obliged to justify anew rights and titles which have already been deliberated and judged, especially since the territories in question are occupied in good faith and are now held in pacific possession by the Spanish Crown. . . .

2. Our princes Ferdinand and Isabella, who first occupied the Indies, are known as 'most Catholic Monarchs', and Emperor Charles V is officially entitled 'most righteous and Christian prince'. Are we to suppose that princes such as these would fail to make the most careful and meticulous inquiries into any matter to do with the security of their estate and conscience, especially one of such importance? Of course not; further cavils are unnecessary, and even insolent. . . .

Where there is some reasonable doubt as to whether an action is good or bad, just or unjust, then it is pertinent to question and deliberate, rather than acting rashly without any prior investigation of what is lawful and what is not. . . .

Returning to this business of the barbarians, . . . the matter is neither so evidently unjust of itself that one may not question whether it is just, nor so evidently just that one may not wonder whether it might be unjust. It seems rather to have arguments on both sides. At first sight, it is true, we may readily suppose that, since the affair is in the hands of men both learned and good, everything has been conducted with rectitude and justice. But when we hear subsequently of bloody massacres and of innocent individuals pillaged of their possesions and dominions, there are grounds for doubting the justice of what has been done. Hence it may be concluded that *disputation is not unprofitable.* . . .

Question 1, Article 1: On the Dominion of the Barbarians. I shall first ask:

Whether these barbarians, before the arrival of the Spaniards, had true dominion, public and private?

That is to say, whether they were true masters of their private chattels and possessions, and whether there existed among them any men who were true princes and masters of the others. It may seem in the first place that they have no right of ownership:

1. 'A slave cannot own anything as his own'. Hence everything a slave acquires belongs to his master. But these barbarians are slaves by nature. This last point is proved by Aristotle, who says with elegant precision: 'the lower sort are by nature slaves, and it is better for them as inferiors that they should be under the rule of a master'. By 'lower sort' he meant men who are insufficiently rational to govern themselves, but are rational enough to take orders; their strength resides more in their bodies than in their minds. If indeed it is true that there are such men, then none fit the bill better than these barbarians, who in fact appear to be little different from brute animals and are completely unfitted for government. It is undoubtedly better for them to be governed by others, than to govern themselves. . . . Therefore, if the barbarians were slaves, the Spaniards could appropriate them.

But on the other hand it may be argued that they were in undisputed possession of their property, both publicly and privately. Therefore, failing proofs to the contrary, they must be held to be true masters, and may not be dispossessed without due cause.

I reply that if the barbarians were not true masters before the arrival of the Spaniards, it can only have been on four possible grounds. . . . These four grounds are that they were either sinners, unbelievers, madmen, or insensate.

Question 1, Article 2: Whether Sinners Can Be True Masters. There have been some who have held that the title to any dominion is grace, and consequently that *sinners, or at least those who are in a state of mortal sin, cannot exercise dominion over anything.* . . . Anyone who accepts this conclusion may argue that the barbarians were not true masters because they were continually in a state of mortal sin.

But on the other hand, *mortal sin is no impediment to the civil right of ownership, nor to true dominion.* . . .

The initial proposition is manifestly heretical. For the Lord maketh his sun to rise on the evil and on the good, and sendeth rain on the just and on the unjust (Matt. 5:45), and so too he gives his temporal goods to the good and the bad. . . .

Question 1, Article 3: Whether Unbelievers Can Be True Masters. I reply with the following propositions:

1. *It is no impediment for a man to be a true master, that he is an unbeliever.* This can be proved first by authority, from Holy Scripture, which often calls unbelievers . . . to obey the rulers, who in their day . . . ordained that servants should obey their masters; . . .

We have also a proof based on reason. Aquinas shows that unbelief does not cancel either natural or human law, but all forms of dominion derive from natural or human law; therefore they cannot be annulled by lack of faith. . . .

The conclusion of all this is that the barbarians are not impeded from being true masters, publicly and privately, either by mortal sin in general or by the particular sin of unbelief. Nor can Christians use either of these arguments to support their title to dispossess the barbarians of their goods and lands. . . .

Question 1, Article 4: Whether Irrational Men Can Be True Masters. Let us answer with the following propositions:

1. *Irrational creatures clearly cannot have any dominion*, for dominion is a legal right, . . . Irrational creatures cannot have legal rights; therefore they cannot have any dominion. . . . This is confirmed by the absurdity of the following argument: that if brutes had dominion, then any person who fenced off grass from deer would be committing a theft, since he would be stealing food without its owner's permission.

And again: wild animals have no rights over their own bodies; still less, then, can they have rights over other things. The major premiss is proved by the fact that it is lawful to kill them with impunity, even for sport. . . .

Finally, these wild beasts and all irrational beings are subject to the power of man, even more than slaves; and therefore, if slaves cannot own anything of their own, still less can irrational beings. . . .

Question 1, Article 5: Whether Children Can Be True Masters. On the other hand what of a different question, raised in connexion with children before the age of reason: can they be legal masters? Children seem in this respect not to be any different from irrational beings. . . .

2. *Children before the age of reason can be masters.* This is self-evident, first because a child can be the victim of an injustice; therefore a child can have legal rights, therefore it can have a right of ownership, which is a legal right. Again, the possessions of an orphan minor in guardianship are not the property of the guardians; . . . they are the property of the minor. . . . Furthermore,

An Arapaho village in nineteenth-century Kansas. Buffalo meat is drying behind the seated Indians.

the foundation of dominion is the fact that we are formed in the image of God; and the child is already formed in the image of God. . . . The same does not hold of an irrational creature, since the child does not exist for another's use, like an animal, but for himself.

Question 1, Article 6: Whether Madmen Can Be True Masters. But what of madmen (I mean the incurably mad, who can neither have nor expect ever to have the use of reason)? . . .

3. *These madmen too may be true masters.* For a madman too can be the victim of an injustice; therefore he can have legal rights.

4. *The barbarians are not prevented by this, or by the argument of the previous article, from being true masters.* The proof of this is that they are not in point of fact madmen, but have judgment like other men. This is self-evident, because they have some order in their affairs: they have properly organized cities, proper marriages, magistrates and overlords, laws, industries, and commerce, all of which require the use of reason. They likewise have a form of religion, and they correctly apprehend things which are evident to other men, which indicates the use of reason. . . .

Nor could it be their fault if they were for so many thousands of years outside the state of salvation, since they were born in sin but did not have the use of reason to prompt them to seek baptism or the things necessary for salvation.

Thus if they seem to us insensate and slow-witted, I put it down mainly to their evil and barbarous education. Even amongst ourselves we see many peasants who are little different

107

from brute animals.

Question 1, Conclusion. The conclusion of all that has been said is that the barbarians undoubtedly possessed as true dominion, both public and private, as any Christians. That is to say, they could not be robbed of their property, either as private citizens or as princes, on the grounds that they were not true masters. It would be harsh to deny to them, who have never done us any wrong, the rights we concede to Saracens and Jews, who have been continual enemies of the Christian religion. Yet we do not deny the right of ownership of the latter, unless it be in the case of Christian lands which they have conquered. . . .

For the moment, the clear conclusion to the first question is therefore *that before arrival of the Spaniards these barbarians possessed true dominion, both in public and private affairs.*

Question 2: By What Unjust Titles the Barbarians of the New World Passed Under the Rule of the Spaniards. Accepting, therefore, that they were true masters, it remains to consider by what title we Christians were empowered to take possession of their territory. I shall first list the irrelevant and illegitimate titles which may be offered. . . .

Question 2, Article 1: First Unjust Title, That Our Most Serene Emperor Might Be Master of the Whole World. If this were so, then even if in the past there had been some irregularity in the Spanish title, it would be entirely wiped out in the person of our most Christian Caesar the emperor. Granting the barbarians had true dominion as explained above, they might still have superior overlords, just as lesser princes are beneath a suzerain and some kings are beneath the emperor, because it is possible for several parties to have dominion over the same thing. . . . The question, then, is whether these barbarians had some superior overlord. This doubt can refer only to the emperor and the pope; it is them I shall discuss.

It seems in the first place that the emperor is master of the whole world, and consequently of the barbarians. . . .

Things which are additional to nature ought to imitate natural things; in natural things there is always one ruler, as one heart in the body, one rational part in a soul. Therefore there should be only one ruler in the world, just as there is only one God.

But this opinion is without any foundation. . . .

1. My first proposition is that *the emperor is not master of the whole world.* The proof of this is as follows: dominion can exist only by natural law, divine law, or human law. But the emperor is not master of the world by any of these. . . .

First, as regards natural law: St Thomas rightly says that in natural law all are free other than from the dominion of fathers or husbands, who have dominion over their children and wives in natural law; therefore no one can be emperor of the world by natural law. . . .

Second, as regards divine law: we nowhere read of the emperors and masters of the world before the advent of Christ. . . .

What is certain, . . . is that dominions and empires . . . have since been handed down by inheritance or conquest or some other title until our own times, or at least down to the advent of our Saviour. So it is obvious that no one before Christ obtained an empire by divine law; and the emperor is not entitled on any such grounds to arrogate to himself the dominion of the whole world, nor, as a consequence, of these barbarians. . . .

Third, as regards human law: it is established that in this case, too, the emperor is not master of the whole world, because if he were it would be solely by authority of some enactment, and there is no such enactment. Even if there were, it would have no force, since an enactment presupposes the necessary jurisdiction; if, therefore, the emperor did not have universal jurisdiction before the enactment of the law, the enactment could not be binding on those who were not his subjects. Nor does the emperor have universal dominion by legitimate succession, gift, exchange, purchase, just war, election, or any other legal title, as is established.

Therefore the emperor has never been master of the whole world. . . .

Even if the emperor were master of the world, he could not on that account occupy the lands of the barbarians, or depose their masters and set up new ones, or impose taxes on them. . . .

From everything that has been said, therefore, it is clear that the Spaniards could not invade these lands using this first title.

Question 2, Article 2: Second Title That the Just Possession of These Countries Is on Behalf of the Supreme Pontiff.

. . .The authors of this view deduce, first, that the pope, as temporal lord, was freely empowered to make the kings of Spain princes of the barbarians; and second, that even if he was not so empowered, if the barbarians refuse to recognize the pope's temporal dominion over them he is at any rate empowered on this ground to declare war on them and impose princes upon them. In the event, both of these things happened. First the pope ceded these countries to the kings of Spain; then the barbarians were informed that the pope is the vicar and lieutenant of God on earth, that they should therefore recognize him as their superior, and that if they refused war would justly be declared upon them. . . .

I reply briefly, therefore, with a series of propositions:

1. *The pope is not the civil or temporal master of the whole world. . . .* If Our Lord Jesus Christ had no temporal dominion . . . then much less so does the pope, who is His vicar. . . .

Besides, even if Christ did have this power, it is accepted that

He did not entrust it to the pope. . . .

2. Even if the pope had such secular power over the whole world, *he could not give it to secular princes.* . . .

3. *The pope has temporal power only insofar as it concerns spiritual matters;* that is, as far as is necessary for the administration of spiritual things. . . .

4. *The pope has no temporal power over these barbarians, or any other unbelievers.* This is clear from the first and third propositions above: if the pope has no temporal power except in relation to spiritual matters, and if 1 Cor. 5:12 shows that he has no spiritual power over the barbarians, it follows that he can have no temporal power over them either.

There follows from all this the following corollary: that even if the barbarians refuse to recognize any dominion of the pope's, war cannot on that account be declared on them, nor their goods seized. This is obvious, because the pope has no such dominion. And the proof is quite clear, for, as I shall show below and as our adversaries admit, even if the barbarians refuse to receive Christ as their lord, they cannot for that reason be attacked or harmed in any way. . . . Indeed, the Saracens who live amongst Christians have never been despoiled of their goods or otherwise oppressed on this pretext; if this title was sufficient to declare war on them, it would be tantamount to saying that they can be despoiled of their goods on the grounds of their unbelief, since it is clear that no unbeliever recognizes the pope's dominion. But there is no doctor, even among our adversaries, who concedes the argument that they may be despoiled solely on the grounds of unbelief. . . .

It is clear from all that I have said that the Spaniards, when they first sailed to the land of the barbarians, carried with them no right at all to occupy their countries.

Question 2, Article 3: Third Unjust Title, That Possession of These Countries is by Right of Discovery. This title by right of discovery was the only title alleged in the beginning, and it was with this pretext alone that Columbus of Genoa first set sail. And it seems that this title is valid because:

1. All things which are unoccupied or deserted become the property of the occupier by natural law and the law of nations. . . . Hence it follows that the Spaniards, who were the first to discover and occupy these countries, must by right possess them, just as if they had discovered a hitherto uninhabited desert.

But on the other hand, against this third title, we need not argue long; as I proved above, the barbarians possessed true public and private dominion. The law of nations expressly states that goods which belong to no owner pass to the occupier. Since the goods in question here had an owner, they do not fall under this title. . . .

Question 2, Article 4: Fourth Unjust Title, That They Refuse to Ac-

110

cept the Faith of Christ. It seems that this is a legitimate title for occupying that land of the barbarians because:

1. Barbarians are obliged to accept the faith of Christ, because 'he that believeth and is baptized shall be saved, but he that believeth not shall be damned' (Mark 16:16). . . . Since the pope is the minister of Christ, at least in spiritual things, it seems that barbarians may be compelled to receive the faith of Christ at least on the authority of the pope; and that if they are asked to do so and refuse, in the law of war action may be taken against them. . . .

2. If the French refused to obey their king, the king of Spain would be empowered to compel them to obey; so if these barbarians refuse to obey God, who is the true supreme Lord, Christian princes are empowered to compel them to obey, since God's cause should clearly never be of less account than the cause of men. . . . If barbarians can be compelled to obey their own princes, much more can they be compelled to obey Christ and God.

3. If the barbarians were publicly to blaspheme against Christ, they could be compelled by war to desist from such blasphemies. We could declare war upon them if they put the Crucifix to ridicule, or in any way abused or shamed Christian things, for instance by making mockery of the sacraments of the Church or things of this kind. This is obvious, because if they were to do wrong to any Christian king, we would be empowered to avenge the wrong, even after the king were dead; so much more so, then, if they insult Christ, who is the king and Lord of Christians. . . . But unbelief is a greater sin than blasphemy, since, as St Thomas proves, unbelief is the gravest of all the sins caused by perversity of morals, being directly opposed to faith, whereas blasphemy is not directly opposed to faith, but only to the confession of faith. Unbelief also attacks the root of conversion to God, which is faith, whereas blasphemy does not. So, if Christians can punish unbelievers by war for their blasphemies against Christ, they must also be empowered to do so for their unbelief.

But on the other hand let us reply with the following conclusions:

1. First, *the barbarians, before they had heard anything about the Christian faith, were not committing the sin of unbelief merely because they did not believe in Christ.* . . . In the case of those who have never heard of Christ, unbelief is not logically a sin, but rather a punishment. . . .

Those who have never heard about a thing are invincibly ignorant, and such ignorance cannot be a sin. . . . If the faith has not been preached to them, their ignorance is invincible, since they have no means of knowing. . . .

The barbarians who have never received any news of the faith or Christian religion will be damned for their mortal sins or their

111

idolatry; but not for the sin of unbelief. If they were to do their best to live well according to the law of nature, it is a fact that the Lord would take care to enlighten them concerning the name of Christ. But it does not follow from this that, if they live evil lives, their ignorance or lack of belief in baptism and the Christian religion should be counted against them as a sin.

2. *The barbarians are not bound to believe from the first moment that the Christian faith is announced to them,* in the sense of committing a mortal sin merely by not believing a simple announcement, unaccompanied by miracles or any other kind of proof or persuasion, that the true religion is Christian, and that Christ is the Saviour and Redeemer of the universe. . . .

It is foolhardy and imprudent of anyone to believe a thing without being sure it comes from a trustworthy source, especially in matters to do with salvation. But the barbarians could not be sure of this, since they did not know who or what kind of people they were who preached the new religion to them. . . . A further confirmation is that if the Saracens were to preach their own sect in this simple way to the barbarians at the same time as the Christians, it is clear that the barbarians would not be obliged to believe the Saracens. Therefore, since they would not be able or obliged to guess which of these two was the truer religion without some more visible proof of probability on one side or the other, the barbarians are not obliged to believe the Christians either, unless the latter put forward some other motive or persuasion to convince them. . . .

From this proposition it follows that if the faith is proposed to the barbarians only in this way and they do not accept it, the Spaniards cannot use this pretext to attack them or conduct a just war against them. This is obvious, because the barbarians are innocent on this count, and have not done any wrong to the Spaniards. . . .

If the barbarians have done no wrong, there is no just cause for war. . . . Therefore this would not be a legitimate title for occupying the lands of the barbarians and despoiling their previous owners of them.

3. *If the barbarians are asked and advised to listen to peaceful persuasion about religion, but refuse to do so, they incur unpardonable mortal sin.* If their own beliefs are gravely mistaken, as we suppose they are, they can have no convincing or probable reasons for them, and are therefore obliged at least to listen and consider what anyone may advise them to hear and meditate concerning religion. . . .

4. *If the Christian faith is set before the barbarians in a probable fashion,* that is with provable and rational arguments and accompanied by manners both decent and observant of the law of nature, such as are themselves a great argument for the truth of the faith, and if this is done not once or in a perfunctory way, but diligently and observantly, *then the barbarians are obliged to accept the faith of*

Christ under pain of mortal sin. . . .
5. *It is not sufficiently clear to me that the Christian faith has up to now been announced and set before the barbarians in such a way as to oblige them to believe it under pain of fresh sin.* . . . I have not heard of any miracles or signs, nor of any exemplary saintliness of life sufficient to convert them. On the contrary, I hear only of provocations, savage crimes, and multitudes of unholy acts. From this, it does not appear that the Christian religion has been preached to them in a sufficiently pious way to oblige their acquiescence; even though it is clear that a number of friars and other churchmen have striven industriously in this cause, by the example of their lives and the diligence of their preaching, and this would have been enough, had they not been thwarted by others with different aims.
6. However probably and sufficiently the faith may have been announced to the barbarians and then rejected by them, *this is still no reason to declare war on them and despoil them of their goods.* . . . Unbelievers who have never taken up the faith such as the pagans and Jews are by no means to be compelled to believe. . . .
Besides, war is no argument for the truth of the Christian faith. Hence the barbarians cannot be moved by war to believe, but only to pretend that they believe and accept the Christian faith; and this is monstrous and sacrilegious. . . .
It is therefore clear that this title to the conquest of the lands of the barbarians, too, is neither applicable nor legitimate.
Question 2, Article 5: Fifth Unjust Title, the Sins of the Barbarians.
. . . [There are] those who say that, although the barbarians may not be invaded because of their unbelief or their refusal to accept the Christian faith, war may nevertheless be declared on them for their other mortal sins. . . .
Some sins, they say, are not against natural law, but only against positive divine law; and for these the barbarians cannot be invaded. But others, such as cannibalism, incest with mothers and sisters, or sodomy, are against nature; and for these sins they may be invaded and compelled to give them up. . . .
But on the other hand, *Christian princes, even on the authority of the pope, may not compel the barbarians to give up their sins against the law of nature, nor punish them for such sins.*
First of all, our opponent's presupposition that the pope has jurisdiction over the barbarians is false, as I have said above. . . .
Besides, the pope may not make war on Christians because they are fornicators or robbers, or even because they are sodomites; nor can he confiscate their lands and give them to other princes; if he could, since every country is full of sinners, kingdoms could be exchanged every day. And a further confirmation is that such sins are more serious in Christians, who know them to be sins,

113

than in the barbarians, who do not. . . .

Question 2, Article 6: Sixth Unjust Title, by the Voluntary Choice of the Barbarians. This is yet another title which can be and is alleged. Whenever the Spaniards first make contact with the barbarians, they notify them that the king of Spain has sent them for their benefit, and advise them to take him and accept him as their lord and king. And the barbarians have replied that they agree to do so. . . . But on the other hand . . . this title, too, is inapplicable. This is clear, first of all, because the choice ought not to have been made in fear and ignorance, factors which vitiate any freedom of election, but which played a leading part in this particular choice and acceptance. The barbarians do not realize what they are doing; perhaps, indeed, they do not even understand what it is the Spaniards are asking of them. Besides which, the request is made by armed men, who surround a fearful and defenceless crowd. . . .

Since, therefore, in these methods of choice and acceptance some of the requisite conditions for a legitimate choice were lacking, on the whole this title to occupying and conquering these countries is neither relevant nor legitimate.

Question 2, Article 7: Seventh Unjust Title, by Special Gift from God. Here is the last title that may be alleged. Some say that the Lord has by his special judgment damned all these barbarians to perdition for their abominations, and delivered them into the hands of the Spaniards just as he once delivered the Canaanites into the hands of the Jews (Num. 21:3).

But I am unwilling to enter into a protracted dispute on this argument, since it is dangerous to give credit to anyone who proclaims a prophecy of this kind contrary to common law and the rules of Scripture unless his teaching is confirmed by some miracle. The proclaimers of this prophecy offer no such miracles.

Besides, even if it were true that the Lord had decided to bring about the destruction of the barbarians, it does not follow that a man who destroyed them would thereby be guiltless. . . .

This concludes the discussion of the false and irrelevant titles for the conquest of the countries of the barbarians. . . .

It is possible that someone has elsewhere constructed a reasonable argument to establish the title and justice of this business from one of the titles mentioned above. But speaking for myself, I am unable to find any solution apart from the ones expounded here. This being so, if there were no other titles than these, it would indeed look grim for the salvation of our princes. 'For what is a man profited', says the Lord, 'if he shall gain the whole world, and lose himself, or be cast away?'

VIEWPOINT 3

"Let sentimentalists say what they will, the man who puts the soil to use must of right dispossess the man who does not, or the world will come to a standstill."

White Takeover of Indian Land: A White's View

Theodore Roosevelt

Theodore Roosevelt, the twenty-sixth president of the United States, was born in 1858. Having attended Columbia Law School after graduation from Harvard in 1880, he was well on his way toward a successful and satisfying personal and professional life. Married, by age twenty-four the author of *The Naval War of 1812*, recently elected to the New York legislature, Roosevelt seemed to have it all. Then, on February 14, 1884, two days after the birth of his first child, Roosevelt lost both his mother and his wife within a few hours. Stunned, he dropped out of politics, left his baby daughter with his sister, and went west to the North Dakota ranch which he had bought the previous year. He stayed there for two years, recovering his health and developing from a somewhat frail asthmatic to a robust outdoorsman as he actively participated in the daily life of the ranch. Roosevelt derived *Hunting Trips of a Ranchman* (1885), *Ranch Life and the Hunting Trail* (1888) and *The Wilderness Hunter* (1893) from this experience. In 1886 he returned to the east, was offered the Republican nomination for the mayor of New York City, lost the election, left for Europe and married. Returning to the United States early in 1887, he planned to write a grandiose history of European exploration and settlement of North America. The first two volumes of this work, *The*

Winning of the West, were published in 1889. The following viewpoint is excerpted from the first volume of that work.

As you read, consider the following questions:

1. Why does Roosevelt believe the Indians "have no ownership of the land"?
2. How does Roosevelt classify types of white people on the frontier? Is he sympathetic with all of them?
3. Who are some of the "sentimentalists" with whom Roosevelt takes issue? What specific points of disagreement does he have with them?
4. In addition to contrasting principles of land use and ownership, what else caused conflict between Indians and settlers?
5. Examine Roosevelt's style of writing. What argumentative techniques make his position clear? Does he ever attempt to consider an opposing viewpoint?

Border warfare . . . was a war waged by savages against armed settlers, whose families followed them into the wildnerness. Such a war is inevitably bloody and cruel; but the inhuman love of cruelty for cruelty's sake, which marks the red Indian above all other savages, rendered these wars more terrible than any others. For the hideous, unnamable, unthinkable tortures practised by the red men on their captured foes, and on their foes' tender women and helpless children, were such as we read of in no other struggle, hardly even in the revolting pages that tell the deeds of the Holy Inquisition. It was inevitable—indeed it was in many instances proper—that such deeds should awake in the breasts of the whites the grimmest, wildest spirit of revenge and hatred.

The history of the border wars, both in the ways they were begun and in the ways they were waged, makes a long tale of injuries inflicted, suffered, and mercilessly revenged. It could not be otherwise when brutal, reckless, lawless borderers, despising all men not of their own color, were thrown in contact with savages who esteemed cruelty and treachery as the highest of virtues, and rapine and murder as the worthiest of pursuits. Moreover, it was sadly inevitable that the law-abiding borderer as well as the white ruffian, the peaceful Indian as well as the painted marauder, should be plunged into the struggle to suffer the punishment that should only have fallen on their evil-minded fellows.

Looking back, it is easy to say that much of the wrong-doing could have been prevented; but if we examine the facts to find out the truth, not to establish a theory, we are bound to admit that the struggle was really one that could not possibly have been avoided. The sentimental historians speak as if the blame had been all ours, and the wrong all done to our foes, and as if it would have been possible by any exercise of wisdom to reconcile claims that were in their very essence conflicting; but their utterances are as shallow as they are untruthful. Unless we were willing that the whole continent west of the Alleghanies should remain an unpeopled waste, the hunting-ground of savages, war was inevitable; and even had we been willing, and had we refrained from encroaching on the Indians' lands, the war would have come nevertheless, for then the Indians themselves would have encroached on ours. Undoubtedly we have wronged many tribes; but equally undoubtedly our first definite knowledge of many others has been derived from their unprovoked outrages upon our people. The Chippewas, Ottawas, and Pottawatamies furnished hundreds of young warriors to the parties that devastated our frontiers generations before we in any way encroached upon or wronged them.

Land Hunger a Cause for War

Mere outrages could be atoned for or settled; the question which lay at the root of our difficulties was that of the occupation of the land itself, and to this there could be no solution save war. The Indians had no ownership of the land in the way in which we understand the term. The tribes lived far apart; each had for its hunting-grounds all the territory from which it was not barred by rivals. Each looked with jealousy upon all interlopers, but each was prompt to act as an interloper when occasion offered. Every good hunting-ground was claimed by many nations. It was rare, indeed, that any tribe had an uncontested title to a large tract of land; where such title existed, it rested, not on actual occupancy and cultivation, but on the recent butchery of weaker rivals. For instance, there were a dozen tribes, all of whom hunted in Kentucky, and fought each other there, all of whom had equally good titles to the soil, and not one of whom acknowledged the right of any other; as a matter of fact they had therein no right, save the right of the strongest. The land no more belonged to them than it belonged to Boon and the white hunters who first visited it.

On the borders there are perpetual complaints of the encroachments of whites upon Indian lands; and naturally the central government at Washington, and before it was at Washington, has usually been inclined to sympathize with the feeling that considers the whites the aggressors, for the government does not wish a war, does not itself feel any land hunger, hears of not a tenth of the Indian outrages, and knows by experience that the white borderers are not easy to rule. As a consequence, the official reports of the people who are not on the ground are apt to paint the Indian side in its most favorable light, and are often completely untrustworthy, this being particularly the case if the author of the report is an eastern man, utterly unacquainted with the actual condition of affairs on the frontier.

Indians Have No True Title to the Land

Such a man, though both honest and intelligent, when he hears that the whites have settled on Indian lands, cannot realize that the act has no resemblance whatever to the forcible occupation of land already cultivated. The white settler has merely moved into an uninhabited waste; he does not feel that he is committing a wrong, for he knows perfectly well that the land is really owned by no one. It is never even visited, except perhaps for a week or two every year, and then the visitors are likely at any moment to be driven off by a rival hunting-party of greater strength. The settler ousts no one from the land; if he did not chop down the trees, hew out the logs for a building, and clear the ground for tillage, no one else would do so. He drives out the game, however, and of course the Indians who live thereon sink their mutual animosities and turn against the intruder. The truth is, the Indians never had any real title to the soil; they had not half as good a claim to it, for instance, as the cattlemen now have to all eastern Montana, yet no one would assert that the cattlemen have a right to keep immigrants off their vast unfenced ranges. The settler and pioneer have at bottom had justice on their side; this great continent could not have been kept as nothing but a game preserve for squalid savages. Moreover, to the most oppressed Indian nations the whites often acted as a protection, or, at least, they deferred instead of hastening their fate. But for the interposition of the whites it is probable that the Iroquois would have exterminated every Algonquin tribe before the end of the eighteenth century; exactly as in recent time the Crows and Pawnees would have been destroyed by the Sioux, had it not been for the wars we have waged against the latter.

Again, the loose governmental system of the Indians made it as difficult to secure a permanent peace with them as it was to negotiate the purchase of the lands. The sachem, or hereditary peace chief, and the elective war chief, who wielded only the influence that he could secure by his personal prowess and his tact, were equally unable to control all of their tribesmen, and were powerless with their confederated nations. If peace was made with the Shawnees, the war was continued by the Miamis; if peace was made with the latter, nevertheless perhaps one small band was dissatisfied, and continued the contest on its own account; and even if all the recognized bands were dealt with, the parties of renegades or outlaws had to be considered; and in the last resort the full recognition accorded by the Indians to the right of private warfare, made it possible for any individual warrior who possessed any influence to go on raiding and murdering unchecked. Every tribe, every sub-tribe, every band of a dozen souls ruled over by a petty chief, almost every individual warrior of the least importance, had to be met and pacified. Even if peace were declared, the Indians could not exist long without breaking it. There was to them no temptation to trespass on the white man's ground for the purpose of settling; but every young brave was brought up to regard scalps taken and horses stolen, in war or peace, as the highest proofs and tokens of skill and courage, the sure means of attaining glory and honor, the admiration of men and the love of women. Where the young men thought thus, and the chiefs had so little real control, it was inevitable that there should be many unprovoked forays for scalps, slaves, and horses made upon the white borderers.

Indians lived off the land and believed that it belonged to everyone. They thought whites arrogant for claiming to own land.

As for the whites themselves, they too have many and grievous sins against their red neighbors for which to answer. They cannot be severely blamed for trespassing upon what was called the Indian's land; for let sentimentalists say what they will, the man who puts the soil to use must of right dispossess the man who does not, or the world will come to a standstill; but for many of their other deeds there can be no pardon. On the border each man was a law unto himself, and good and bad alike were left in perfect freedom to follow out to the uttermost limits their own desires; for the spirit of individualism so characteristic of American life reached its extreme of development in the backwoods. The whites who wished peace, the magistrates and leaders, had little more power over their evil and unruly fellows than the Indian sachems had over the turbulent young braves. Each man did what seemed best in his own eyes, almost without let or hindrance; unless, indeed, he trespassed upon the rights of his neighbors, who were ready enough to band together in their own defence, though slow to interfere in the affairs of others.

Misdeeds of the Borderers

Thus the men of lawless, brutal spirit who are found in every community and who flock to places where the reign of order is lax, were able to follow the bent of their inclinations unchecked. They utterly despised the red man; they held it no crime whatever to cheat him in trading, to rob him of his peltries or horses, to murder him if the fit seized them. Criminals who generally preyed on their own neighbors, found it easier, and perhaps hardly as dangerous, to pursue their calling at the expense of the redskins, for the latter, when they discovered that they had been wronged, were quite as apt to vent their wrath on some outsider as on the original offender. If they injured a white, all the whites might make common cause against them; but if they injured a red man, though there were sure to be plenty of whites who disapproved of it, there were apt to be very few indeed whose disapproval took any active shape.

Each race stood by its own members, and each held all of the other race responsible for the misdeeds of a few uncontrollable spirits; and this clannishness among those of one color, and the refusal or the inability to discriminate between the good and the bad of the other color were the two most fruitful causes of border strife. When, even if he sought to prevent them, the innocent man was sure to suffer for the misdeeds of the guilty, unless both joined together for defence, the former had no alternative save to make common cause with the latter. Moreover, in a sparse backwoods settlement, where the presence of a strong, vigorous fighter was a source of safety to the whole community, it was impossible to expect that he would be punished with severity for offences which, in their hearts, his fellow townsmen could not help regarding as in some sort a revenge for the injuries they had themselves suffered. Every quiet, peaceable settler had either himself been grievously wronged, or had been an eye-witness to wrongs done to his friends; and while these were vivid in his mind, the corresponding wrongs done the Indians were never brought home to him at all. If his son was scalped or his cattle driven off, he could not be expected to remember that perhaps the Indians who did the deed had themselves been cheated by a white trader, or had lost a relative at the hands of some border ruffian, or felt aggrieved because a hundred miles off some settler had built a cabin on lands they considered their own. When he joined with other exasperated and injured men to make a retaliatory inroad, his vengeance might or might not fall on the heads of the real offenders; and, in any case, he was often not in the frame of mind to put a stop to the outrages sure to be committed by the brutal spirits among his allies—though these brutal spirits were probably in a small minority.

A Few Naked Barbarians

What ignorance, or folly, or morbid jealousy of our national progress does it not argue, to expect that our civilized border would become stationary, and some of the fairest portions of the globe be abandoned to hopeless sterility. That a few naked wandering barbarians should stay the march of civilization and improvement, and hold in a state of perpetual unproductiveness, immense regions formed by Providence to support millions of human beings?

Lewis Cass, quoted in *North American Review*, vol. XXX, 1830.

The excesses so often committed by the whites, when, after many checks and failures, they at last grasped victory, are causes for shame and regret; yet it is only fair to keep in mind the terrible provocations they had endured. Mercy, pity, magnanimity to the fallen, could not be expected from the frontiersmen gathered together to war against an Indian tribe. Almost every man of such a band had bitter personal wrongs to avenge. He was not taking part in a war against a civilized foe; he was fighting in a contest where women and children suffered the fate of the strong men, and instead of enthusiasm for his country's flag and a general national animosity towards its enemies, he was actuated by a furious flame of hot anger, and was goaded on by memories of which merely to think was madness. His friends had been treacherously slain while on messages of peace; his house had been burned, his cattle driven off, and all he had in the world destroyed before he knew that war existed and when he felt quite guiltless of all offence; his sweetheart or wife had been carried off, ravished, and was at the moment the slave and concubine of some dirty and brutal Indian warrior; his son, the stay of his house, had been burned at the stake with torments too horrible to mention; his sister, when ransomed and returned to him, had told of the weary journey through the woods, when she carried around her neck as a horrible necklace the bloody scalps of her husband and children; seared into his eyeballs, into his very brain, he bore ever with him, waking or sleeping, the sight of the skinned, mutilated, hideous body of the baby who had just grown old enough to recognize him and to crow and laugh when taken in his arms. Such incidents as these were not exceptional; one or more, and often all of them, were the invariable attendants of every one of the countless Indian inroads that took place during the long generations of forest warfare. It was small wonder that men who had thus lost every thing should sometimes be fairly crazed by their wrongs. Again and again on the frontier we hear of some such unfortunate who has devoted all the remainder of his wretched life to the one object of taking vengeance on the whole race of the men who had darkened his days forever. Too often the squaws and pappooses fell victims of the vengeance that should have come only on the warriors; for the whites regarded their foes as beasts rather than men, and knew that the squaws were more cruel than others in torturing the prisoner, and that the very children took their full part therein, being held up by their fathers to tomahawk the dying victims at the stake.

Thus it is that there are so many dark and bloody pages in the book of border warfare, that grim and iron-bound volume, wherein we read how our forefathers won the wide lands that we inherit. It contains many a tale of fierce heroism and adventurous ambition, of the daring and resolute courage of men and the patient endurance of women; it shows us a stern race of freemen who toiled hard, endured greatly, and fronted adversity bravely, who prized strength and courage and good faith, whose wives were chaste, who were generous and loyal to their friends. But it shows us also how they spurned at restraint and fretted under it, how they would brook no wrong to themselves, and yet too often inflicted wrong on others; their feats of terrible prowess are interspersed with deeds of the foulest and most wanton aggression, the darkest treachery, the most revolting cruelty; and though we meet with plenty of the rough, strong, coarse virtues, we see but little of such qualities as mercy for the fallen, the weak, and the helpless, or pity for a gallant and vanquished foe.

VIEWPOINT 4

*"All men were made by the same Great Spirit Chief.
They are all brothers. The earth is the mother of all
people, and all people should have equal rights upon
it."*

White Takeover of
Indian Land: An Indian's
View

Chief Joseph

In June 1877, only a year after Custer's defeat, an unexpected
Indian outbreak occurred. The Nez Percé had for centuries centered their settlements on the territory where Washington, Oregon, and Idaho meet. With their horses, however, they traveled
great distances to northern Idaho and Washington, to the Pacific
and the mouth of the Columbia, and across the Bitterroots to the
Plains for hunting, war, or trade. Their relations with the whites
had always been peaceful. They welcomed Lewis and Clark in
1805; Canadian fur traders with the North West Company provided them with guns and their name, from the pieces of shell
some wore in their noses; and in the 1820s some young men were
taken to an Anglican mission school in central Canada and, returning, stirred an interest in Christianity among tribespeople.
The Reverend Spaulding, to whom Joseph refers, started a Presbyterian mission at Lapwai in 1836. Eventually, however, many
Nez Percés became disillusioned with the white man's religion.
When settlers began to pour into Oregon in the 1840s, many Indians thought the Spauldings had conspired to steal their country.
Concerned at these suspicions and frightened by the news that

the Marcus Whitmans, missionaries to the nearby Cayuse Indians, had been massacred, the Spauldings fled. The Nez Percés' suspicions that the whites were out to steal their land received confirmation when gold was found in 1860 and miners and prospectors poured in. More settlers followed. In 1863 an agreement was signed between government commissioners and some bands of the Nez Percé, ceding three quarters of their land, including the Wallowa Valley, to the whites. Chief Joseph's band was not among those present at the signing. His account of the conflict, excerpted here, was published in the April 1879 issue of *North American Review*.

As you read, consider the following questions:

1. In the excerpts used in this book, many white authors have referred to Indians as "savages," "barbarians," little better than animals. What human behavior does Chief Joseph define as "worse than a wild animal"? How does this belief influence the Indian position in the conflict over land rights?
2. How does this selection reveal the clash between two civilizations? Often settlers claimed the Indians were savages, uncivilized. According to this viewpoint, what values did the Nez Percé hold important?
3. What, according to Chief Joseph, were the historical relationships between the Nez Percé and the whites? To what or whom can these be attributed?
4. Some whites of this period began to say "the only good Indian is a dead Indian." Does Chief Joseph feel the same about whites? Does he generalize about the entire race or does he differentiate among individuals?
5. What does Chief Joseph feel to be the greatest problem with the U.S. government?

My friends, I have been asked to show you my heart. I am glad to have a chance to do so. I want the white people to understand my people. Some of you think an Indian is like a wild animal. This is a great mistake. I will tell you all about our people, and then you can judge whether an Indian is a man or not. I believe much trouble and blood would be saved if we opened our hearts more. I will tell you in my way how the Indian sees things. The white man has more words to tell you how they look to him, but it does not require many words to speak the truth. What I have to say will come from my heart, and I will speak with a straight tongue. Ah-cum-kin-i-ma-me-hut (the Great Spirit) is looking at me, and will hear me.

My name is In-mut-too-yah-lat-lat (Thunder traveling over the Mountains). I am chief of the Wal-lam-wat-kin band of Chute-pa-lu, or Nez Percés (nose-pierced Indians). I was born in eastern Oregon, thirty-eight winters ago. My father was chief before me. When a young man, he was called Joseph by Mr. Spaulding, a missionary. He died a few years ago. There was no stain on his hands of the blood of a white man. He left a good name on the earth. He advised me well for my people.

Our fathers gave us many laws, which they had learned from their fathers. These laws were good. They told us to treat all men as they treated us; that we should never be the first to break a bargain; that it was a disgrace to tell a lie; that we should speak only the truth; that it was a shame for one man to take from another his wife, or his property without paying for it. We were taught to believe that the Great Spirit sees and hears everything, and that he never forgets; that hereafter he will give every man a spirit-home according to his deserts: if he has been a good man, he will have a good home; if he has been a bad man, he will have a bad home. This I believe, and all my people believe the same.

We Met the First White Men

We did not know there were other people besides the Indian until about one hundred winters ago, when some men with white faces came to our country. They brought many things with them to trade for furs and skins. They brought tobacco, which was new to us. They brought guns with flint stones on them, which frightened our women and children. Our people could not talk with these white-faced men, but they used signs which all people understand. These men were Frenchmen, and they called our people "Nez Percés," because they wore rings in their noses for ornaments. Although very few of our people wear them now, we are still called by the same name. These French trappers said a great many things to our fathers, which have been planted in our hearts. Some were good for us, but some were bad. Our people were divided in opinion about these men. Some thought they taught more bad than good. An Indian respects a brave man, but he despises a coward. He loves a straight tongue, but he hates a forked tongue. The French trappers told us some truths and some lies.

The first white men of your people who came to our country were named Lewis and Clarke [sic]. They also brought many things that our people had never seen. They talked straight, and our people gave them a great feast, as a proof that their hearts were friendly. These men were very kind. They made presents to

125

our chiefs and our people made presents to them. We had a great many horses, of which we gave them what they needed, and they gave us guns and tobacco in return. All the Nez Percés made friends with Lewis and Clarke, and agreed to let them pass through their country, and never to make war on white men. This promise the Nez Percés have never broken. No white man can accuse them of bad faith, and speak with a straight tongue. It has always been the pride of the Nez Percés that they were the friends of the white men. When my father was a young man there came to our country a white man (Rev. Mr. Spaulding) who talked spirit law. He won the affections of our people because he spoke good things to them. At first he did not say anything about white men wanting to settle on our lands. Nothing was said about that until about twenty winters ago, when a number of white people came into our country and built houses and made farms. At first our people made no complaint. They thought there was room enough for all to live in peace, and they were learning many things from the white men that seemed to be good. But we soon found that the white men were growing rich very fast, and were greedy to possess everything the Indian had. My father was the first to see through the schemes of the white men, and he warned his tribe to be careful about trading with them. He had suspicion of men who seemed so anxious to make money. I was a boy then, but I remember well my father's caution. He had sharper eyes than the rest of our people.

My Father Wished to Be a Free Man

Next there came a white officer (Governor Stevens), who invited all the Nez Percés to a treaty council. After the council was opened he made known his heart. He said there were a great many white people in the country, and many more would come; that he wanted the land marked out so that the Indians and white men could be separated. If they were to live in peace it was necessary, he said, that the Indians should have a country set apart for them, and in that country they must stay. My father, who represented his band, refused to have anything to do with the council, because he wished to be a free man. He claimed that no man owned any part of the earth, and a man could not sell what he did not own.

Mr. Spaulding took hold of my father's arm and said, "Come and sign the treaty." My father pushed him away, and said: "Why do you ask me to sign away my country? It is your business to talk to us about spirit matters, and not to talk to us about parting with our land." Governor Stevens urged my father to sign his treaty, but he refused. "I will not sign your paper," he said; "you go where you please, so do I; you are not a child, I am no child; I

126

The author, Chief Joseph of the Nez Percé, was bewildered by the policies of the U.S. government and astonished at the whites' arrogance.

can think for myself. No man can think for me. I have no other home than this. I will not give it up to any man. My people would have no home. Take away your paper. I will not touch it with my hand."

My father left the council. Some of the chiefs of the other bands of the Nez Percés signed the treaty, and then Governor Stevens gave them presents of blankets. My father cautioned his people to take no presents, for "after a while," he said, "they will claim that you have accepted pay for your country." Since that time four bands of the Nez Percés have received annuities from the United States. My father was invited to many councils, and they tried hard to make him sign the treaty, but he was firm as the rock, and would not sign away his home. His refusal caused a difference among the Nez Percés.

Eight years later (1863) was the next treaty council. A chief called Lawyer, because he was a great talker, took the lead in this council, and sold nearly all the Nez Percés country. My father was not there. He said to me: "when you go into council with the white man, always remember your country. Do not give it away. The white man will cheat you out of your home. I have taken no pay from the United States. I have never sold our land." In this treaty Lawyer acted without authority from our band. He had no right to sell the Wallowa (winding water) country. That had always belonged to my father's own people, and the other bands had never disputed our right to it. No other Indians ever claimed Wallowa.

In order to have all people understand how much land we owned, my father planted poles around it and said:

127

"Inside is the home of my people—the white man may take the land outside. Inside this boundary all our people were born. It circles around the graves of our fathers, and we will never give up these graves to any man."

The United States claimed they had bought all the Nez Percé's country outside of Lapwai Reservation, from Lawyer and other chiefs, but we continued to live on this land in peace until eight years ago, when white men began to come inside the bounds my father had set. We warned them against this great wrong, but they would not leave our land, and some bad blood was raised. The white men represented that we were going upon the warpath. They reported many things that were false.

The United States Government again asked for a treaty council. My father had become blind and feeble. He could no longer speak for his people. It was then that I took my father's place as chief. In this council I made my first speech to white men. I said to the agent who held the council:

"I did not want to come to this council, but I came hoping that we could save blood. The white man has no right to come here and take our country. We have never accepted any presents from the Government. Neither Lawyer nor any other chief had authority to sell this land. It has always belonged to my people. It came unclouded to them from our fathers, and we will defend this land as long as a drop of Indian blood warms the hearts of our men."

The agent said he had orders, from the Great White Chief at Washington, for us to go upon the Lapwai Reservation, and that if we obeyed he would help us in many ways. "You *must* move to the agency," he said. I answered him: "I will not. I do not need your help; we have plenty, and we are contented and happy if the white man will let us alone. The reservation is too small for so many people with all their stock. You can keep your presents; we can go to your towns and pay for all we need; we have plenty of horses and cattle to sell, and we won't have any help from you; we are free now; we can go where we please. Our fathers were born here. Here they lived, here they died, here are their graves. We will never leave them." The agent went away, and we had peace for a little while.

A Man Must Love His Father's Grave

Soon after this my father sent for me. I saw he was dying. I took his hand in mine. He said: "My son, my body is returning to my mother earth, and my spirit is going very soon to see the Great Spirit Chief. When I am gone, think of your country. You are the chief of these people. They look to you to guide them. Always remember that your father never sold his country. You must stop your ears whenever you are asked to sign a treaty selling your home. A few years more, and white men will be all around you. They have their eyes on this land. My son, never forget my dying words. This country holds your father's body. Never sell the bones of your father and your mother." I pressed my father's hand and told him I would protect his grave with my life. My father smiled and passed away to the spirit-land.

I buried him in that beautiful valley of winding waters. I love that land more than all the rest of the world. A man who would not love his father's grave is worse than a wild animal.

For a short time we lived quietly. But this could not last. White men had found gold in the mountains around the land of winding water. . . . We gave up some of our country to the white men, thinking that then we could have peace. We were mistaken. The white man would not let us alone. We could have avenged our wrongs many times, but we did not. . . .

On account of the treaty made by the other bands of the Nez Percés, the white men claimed my lands. We were troubled greatly by white men crowding over the line. Some of these were good men, and we lived on peaceful terms with them, but they were not all good.

Nearly every year the agent came over from Lapwai and ordered us on to the reservation. We always replied that we were satisfied to live in Wallowa. We were careful to refuse the presents or annuities which he offered.

Through all the years since the white men came to Wallowa we have been threatened and taunted by them and the treaty Nez Percés. They have given us no rest. We have had a few good friends among white men, and they have always advised my people to bear these taunts without fighting. Our young men were quick-tempered, and I have had great trouble in keeping them from doing rash things. I have carried a heavy load on my back ever since I was a boy. I learned then that we were but few, while the white men were many, and that we could not hold our own with them. We were like deer. They were like grizzly bears. We had a small country. Their country was large. We were contented to let things remain as the Great Spirit Chief made them. They were not; and would change the rivers and mountains if they did not suit them.

Year after year we have been threatened, but no war was made upon my people until General Howard came to our country two years ago and told us that he was the white war-chief of all that country. He said: "I have a great many soldiers at my back. I am going to bring them up here, and then I will talk to you again. I will not let white men laugh at me the next time I come. The country belongs to the Government, and I intend to make you go upon the reservation.". . .

I said to General Howard: ". . . I have been in a great many councils, but I am no wiser. We are all sprung from a woman, although we are unlike in many things. We can not be made over again. You are as you were made, and as you were made you can remain. We are just as we were made by the Great Spirit, and you can not change us; then why should children of one mother and one father quarrel—why should one try to cheat the other? I do not believe that the Great Spirit Chief gave one kind of men the right to tell another kind of men what they must do."

General Howard replied: "You deny my authority, do you? You want to dictate to me, do you?"

Then one of my chiefs—Too-hool-hool-suit—rose in the council and said to General Howard: "The Great Spirit Chief made the world as it is, and as he wanted it, and he made a part of it for us to live upon. I do not see where you get authority to say that we shall not live where he placed us."

General Howard lost his temper and said: "Shut up! I don't want to hear any more of such talk. The law says you shall go upon the reservation to live, and I want you to do so, but you persist in disobeying the law" (meaning the treaty). "If you do not move, I will take the matter into my own hand, and make you suffer for your disobedience."

Too-hool-hool-suit answered: "Who are you, that you ask us to talk, and then tell me I sha'n't talk? Are you the Great Spirit? Did you make the world? Did you make the sun? Did you make the rivers to run for us to drink? Did you make the grass to grow? Did you make all these things, that you talk to us as though we were boys? If you did, then you have the right to talk as you do.". . . You can arrest me, but you can not change me or make me take back what I have said.". . .

Too-hool-hool-suit was [a] prisoner for five days before he was released.

The council broke up for that day. On the next morning General Howard came to my lodge, and invited me to go with him and White-Bird and Looking-Glass, to look for land for my people. As we rode along we came to some good land that was already occupied by Indians and white people. General Howard, pointing to this land, said: "If you will come on to the reservation, I will give you these lands and move these people off."

I replied: "No. It would be wrong to disturb these people. I have no right to take their homes. I have never taken what did not belong to me. I will not now."

We rode all day upon the reservation, and found no good land unoccupied. . . .

In the council, next day, General Howard informed me, in a haughty spirit, that he would give my people *thirty days* to go back home, collect all their stock, and move on to the reservation, saying, "If you are not here in that time, I shall consider that you want to fight, and will send my soldiers to drive you on.". . .

I knew I had never sold my country, and that I had no land in Lapwai; but I did not want bloodshed. I did not want my people killed. I did not want anybody killed. . . .

I said in my heart that, rather than have war, I would give up my country. I would give up my father's grave. I would give up everything rather than have the blood of white men upon the hands of my people. . . .

I Cannot Understand So Many Chiefs

At last I was granted permission to come to Washington and bring my friend Yellow Bull and our interpreter with me. I am glad we came. I have shaken hands with a great many friends, but there are some things I want to know which no one seems able to explain. I can not understand how the Government sends a man out to fight us . . . and then breaks his word. Such a Government has something wrong about it. I can not understand why so many chiefs are allowed to talk so many different ways, and promise so many different things. I have seen the Great Father Chief (the President), the next Great Chief (Secretary of the Interior), the Commissioner Chief (Hayt), the Law Chief (General Butler), and many other law chiefs (Congressmen), and they all say they are my friends, and that I shall have justice, but while their mouths all talk right I do not understand why nothing is done for my people. I have heard talk and talk, but nothing is done. Good words do not last long unless they amount to something. Words do not pay for my dead people. They do not pay for my country, now overrun by white men. They do not protect my father's grave. They do not pay for all my horses and cattle. Good words will not give me back my children. Good words will not make good the promise of your War Chief General Miles. Good words will not give my people good health and stop them from dying. Good words will not get my people a home where they can live in peace and take care of themselves. I am tired of talk that comes to nothing. It makes my heart sick when I remember all the good words and all the broken promises. There has been too much talking by men who had no right to talk. Too many misrepresentations have been made, too many misunderstandings have come up between the white men about the Indians. If the white man wants to live in peace with the Indian he can live in peace. There need be no trouble. Treat all men alike. Give them all the same law. Give them all an even chance to live and grow. All men were made by the same Great Spirit Chief. They are all brothers. The earth is the mother of all people, and all people should have equal rights upon it. You might as well expect the rivers to run backward as that any man who was born a free man should be contented when penned up and denied liberty to go where he pleases. If you tie a horse to a stake, do you expect he will grow fat? If you pen an Indian up on a small spot of earth, and compel him to stay there, he will not be contented, nor will he grow and prosper. I have asked some of the great white chiefs where they get their authority to say to the Indian that he shall stay in one place, while he sees white men going where they please. They can not tell me.

Treat Us Like All Other Men

I only ask of the Government to be treated as all other men are treated. If I can not go to my own home, let me have a home in some country where my people will not die so fast. I would like to go to Bitter Root Valley. There my people would be healthy; where they are now they are dying. Three have died since I left my camp to come to Washington.

When I think of our condition my heart is heavy. I see men of my race treated as outlaws and driven from country to country, or shot down like animals.

I know that my race must change. We can not hold our own with the white men as we are. We only ask an even chance to live as other men live. We ask to be recognized as men. We ask that the same law shall work alike on all men. If the Indian breaks the law, punish him by the law. If the white man breaks the law, punish him also.

Let me be a free man—free to travel, free to stop, free to work, free to trade where I choose, free to choose my own teachers, free to follow the religion of my fathers, free to think and talk and act for myself—and I will obey every law, or submit to the penalty.

Whenever the white man treats the Indian as they treat each other, then we will have no more wars. We shall all be alike—brothers of one father and one mother, with one sky above us and one country around us, and one government for all. Then the Great Spirit Chief who rules above will smile upon this land, and send rain to wash out the bloody spots made by brothers' hands from the face of the earth. For this time the Indian race are waiting and praying. I hope that no more groans of wounded men and women will ever go to the ear of the Great Spirit Chief above, and that all people may be one people.

In-mut-too-yah-lat-lat has spoken for his people.

VIEWPOINT 5

"The grass which grows out of the earth is common to all."

Indians Have an Equal Claim to the Land

John Heckewelder

John Heckewelder was a Moravian missionary to the Indians. He lived among them for nearly sixty years, learning their languages and sharing their activities. He was most familiar with the Indians of western Pennsylvania and eastern Ohio during the years 1762-1813. He crossed the Allegheny Mountains thirty times and traveled down the Ohio River from Pittsburgh many times. He observed a transitional period in this region as more whites came west. He personally knew such people as Daniel Boone and Simon Girty. The following viewpoint is excerpted from Heckewelder's book *Account of the History, Manners and Customs of the Indian Nations, Who Once Inhabited Pennsylvania and the Neighboring States,* published in Philadelphia in 1819.

As you read, consider the following questions:

1. How do the Indians' attitudes toward nature affect their behavior toward their fellows, according to Heckewelder?
2. What is the central issue relevant to Indian interpretation of "land law"?
3. Does the term "savage" seem appropriate to the people Heckewelder describes?

Not satisfied with paying this first of duties to the Lord of all, in the best manner they are able, the Indians endeavour to fulfil

133

the views which they suppose he had in creating the world. They think that he made the earth and all that it contains for the common good of mankind; when he stocked the country that he gave them with plenty of game, it was not for the benefit of a few, but of all. Every thing was given in common to the sons of men. Whatever liveth on the land, whatsoever groweth out of the earth, and all that is in the rivers and waters flowing through the same, was given jointly to all, and every one is entitled to his share. From this principle, hospitality flows as from its source. With them it is not a virtue but a strict duty. Hence they are never in search of excuses to avoid giving, but freely supply their neighbour's wants from the stock prepared for their own use. They give and are hospitable to all, without exception, and will always share with each other and often with the stranger, even to their last morsel. They rather would lie down themselves on an empty stomach, than have it laid to their charge that they had neglected their duty, by not satisfying the wants of the stranger, the sick or the needy. The stranger has a claim to their hospitality, partly on account of his being at a distance from his family and friends, and partly because he has honoured them by his visit, and ought to leave them with a good impression upon his mind; the sick and the poor because they have a right to be helped out of the common stock: for if the meat they have been served with, was taken from the woods, it was common to all before the hunter took it; if corn or vegetables, it had grown out of the common ground, yet not by the power of man, but by that of the Great Spirit. Besides, on the principle, that all are descended from one parent, they look upon themselves as but one great family, who therefore ought at all times and on all occasions, to be serviceable and kind to each other, and by that means make themselves acceptable to the head of the universal family, the great and good Mannitto. Let me be permitted to illustrate this by an example.

Who Caused the Grass to Grow?

Some travelling Indians having in the year 1777, put their horses over night to pasture in my little meadow, at Gnadenhutten on the Muskingum, I called on them in the morning to learn why they had done so. I endeavoured to make them sensible of the injury they had done me, especially as I intended to mow the meadow in a day or two. Having finished my complaint, one of them replied: "My friend, it seems you lay claim to the grass my horses have eaten, because you had enclosed it with a fence: now tell me, who caused the grass to grow? Can *you* make the grass grow? I think not, and no body can except the great Mannitto. He it is who causes it to grow both for my horses and for yours! See, friend! the grass which grows out of the earth is common to all; the game in the woods is common to all. Say, did you never eat venison and bear's meat?—"Yes, very often."—Well, and did you ever hear me or any other Indian complain about that? No; then be not disturbed at my horses having eaten only once, of what you call *your* grass, though the grass my horses did eat, in like manner as the meat you did eat, was given to the Indians by the Great Spirit. Besides, if you will but consider, you will find that my horses did not eat all your grass. For friendship's sake, however, I shall never put my horses in your meadow again."

Red Men Have Equal Rights to Unoccupied Land

It is true I am a Shawnee. My forefathers were warriors. Their son is a warrior. From them I only take my existence; from my tribe I take nothing. I am the maker of my own fortune; and oh! that I could make that of my red people, and of my country, as great as the conceptions of my mind, when I think of the Spirit that rules the universe. I would not then come to Governor Harrison, to ask him to tear the treaty, and to obliterate the landmark; but I would say to him, "Sir, you have liberty to return to your own country." The being within, communing with past ages, tells me, that once, nor until lately, there was no white man on this continent. That it then all belonged to red men, children of the same parents, placed on it by the Great Spirit that made them, to keep it, to traverse it, to enjoy its productions, and to fill it with the same race. Once a happy race. Since made miserable by the white people, who are never contented, but always encroaching. The way, and the only way to check and stop this evil, is, for all the red men to unite in claiming a common and equal right in the land, as it was at first, and should be yet; for it never was divided, but belongs to all, for the use of each. That no part has a right to sell, even to each other, much less to strangers, those who want all, and will not do with less. The white people have no right to take the land from the Indians, because they had it first; it is theirs. They may sell, but all must join. Any sale not made by all is not valid. The late sale is bad. It was made by a part only. Part do not know how to sell. It requires all to make a bargain for all. All red men have equal rights to the unoccupied land. The right of occupancy is as good in one place as in another. There cannot be two occupations in the same place. The first excludes all others. It is not so in hunting or traveling; for there the same ground will serve many, as they may follow each other all day; but the camp is stationary, and that is occupancy. It belongs to the first who sits down on his blanket or skins, which he has thrown upon the ground and till he leaves it no other has a right [to it].

Tecumseh's speech to General William H. Harrison at Vincennes, Indiana, on August 12, 1809.

135

The Indians are not only just, they are also in many respects a generous people, and cannot see the sick and the aged suffer for want of clothing. To such they will give a blanket, a shirt, a pair of leggings, mocksens, &c. Otherwise, when they make presents, it is done with a view to receive an equivalent in return, and the receiver is given to understand what that ought to be. In making presents to strangers, they are content with some trifle in token of remembrance; but when they give any thing to a trader, they at least expect double the value in return, saying that he can afford to do it, since he had cheated them so often.

They treat each other with civility, and shew much affection on meeting after an absence. When they meet in the forenoon, they will compliment one another with saying, "a good morning to you!" and in the afternoon "a good evening." In the act of shaking hands with each other, they strictly attend to the distinguishing names of relations, which they utter at the time; as for instance, "a good morning, father, grandfather, uncle, aunt, cousin," and so down to a small grandchild. They are also in the habit of saluting old people no ways related to them, by the names of grandfather and grandmother, not in a tone of condescending superiority or disguised contempt, but as a genuine mark of the respect which they feel for age. The common way of saluting where no relationship exists, is that of "friend;" when, however, the young people meet, they make use of words suitable to their years or stage in life; they will say "a good morning, comrade, favourite, beloved, &c." Even the children salute each other affectionately. "I am glad to see you," is the common way in which the Indians express themselves to one another after a short absence; but on meeting after a long absence, on the return of a messenger or a warrior from a critical or dangerous expedition, they have more to say; the former is saluted in the most cordial manner with some such expression: "I thank the Great Spirit, that he has preserved our lives to this time of our happily meeting again. I am, indeed, very glad to see you." To which the other will reply: "you speak the truth; it is through the favour of the great and good Spirit that we are permitted to meet. I am equally glad to see you." To the latter will be said: "I am glad that the Great Spirit has preserved your life and granted you a safe return to your family."

Viewpoint 6

"What use do these . . . streaked, spotted and speckled cattle [Indians] make of the soil? Do they till it? . . . This alone is human life . . . to live by tilling is more humano, by hunting is more bestiarum."

Indians Are Unworthy of Keeping Their Land

Hugh Henry Brackenridge

Hugh Henry Brackenridge (1748-1816), a resident of Pittsburgh, was an early U.S. literary figure. The following viewpoint is taken from a letter Brackenridge wrote to the editor of the *Freeman's Journal* or *North American Intelligencer*. Brackenridge sent the letter along with the testimonies of Dr. Knight and John Stover who had been captured by Indians in 1782 following Col. Crawford's punitive expedition against the Indians on the Sandusky River. First published serially in the *Freeman's Journal*, the narratives were also published in pamphlet form in Cincinnati in 1867 under the title *Indian Atrocities: Narratives of the Perils and Sufferings of Dr. Knight and John Stover, Among the Indians, During the Revolutionary War.*

As you read, consider the following questions:

1. How does Brackenridge's diction reinforce his point of view?
2. How does Brackenridge at first *seem* to agree with the author of the opposing viewpoint? How does he modify that position?
3. What principles of land law do the examples of High Priest, the man with a big belly, and Big Cat illustrate?
4. How does Brackenridge's concept of land ownership compare to Vattel's, author of viewpoint 1 in this chapter?

5. Would Heckewelder, the author of the opposing viewpoint, agree with Brackenridge's portrayal of Indians? Which author has the better claim to validity? Why?
6. Why, apparently, is Brackenridge so harsh in his portrayal?

With the narrative enclosed, I subjoin some observations with regard to the animals, vulgarly called Indians. It is not my intention to write any labored essay; for at so great a distance from the city, and so long unaccustomed to write, I have scarcely resolution to put pen to paper. Having an opportunity to know something of the character of this race of men, from the deeds they perpetrate daily round me, I think proper to say something on the subject. Indeed, several years ago, and before I left your city, I had thought different from some others with respect to the right of soil, and the propriety of forming treaties and making peace with them.

In the United States Magazine in the year 1777, I published a dissertation denying them to have a right in the soil. I perceive a writer in your very elegant and useful paper, has taken up the same subject, under the signature of "Caractacus," and unanswerably shown, that their claim to the extensive countries of America, is wild and inadmissible. I will take the liberty in this place, to pursue this subject a little.

On what is their claim founded?—Occupancy. A wild Indian with his skin painted red, and a feather through his nose, has set his foot on the broad continent of North and South America; a second wild Indian with his ears cut in ringlets, or his nose slit like a swine or a malefactor, also sets his foot on the same extensive tract of soil. Let the first Indian make a talk to his brother, and bid him take his foot off the continent, for he being first upon it, had occupied the whole, to kill buffaloes, and tall elks with long horns. This claim in the reasoning of some men would be just, and the second savage ought to depart in his canoe, and seek a continent where no prior occupant claimed the soil. Is this claim of occupancy of a very early date? When Noah's three sons, Shem, Ham, and Japhet, went out to the three quarters of the old world, Ham to Africa, Shem to Asia, Japhet to Europe, did each claim a quarter of the world for his residence? Suppose Ham to have spent his time fishing or gathering oysters in the Red Sea, never once stretching his leg in a long walk to see his vast dominions, from the mouth of the Nile, across the mountains of Ethiopia and the river Niger to the Cape of Good Hope, where the Hottentots, a cleanly people, now stay; or supposing him, like a Scots pedlar, to have traveled over many thousand leagues of that country; would this give him a right to the soil? In the opinion of some men it would establish an exclusive right. Let a man in more modern times take a journey or voyage like Patrick Kennedy and others to the heads of the Mississippi or Missouri rivers, would he gain a right ever after to exclude all persons from drinking the waters of these streams? Might not a second Adam make a talk to them and say, is the whole of this water necessary to allay your thirst, and may I also drink of it?

The whole of this earth was given to man, and all descendants of Adam have a right to share it equally. There is no right of primogeniture in the laws of nature and of nations. There is reason that a tall man, such as the chaplain in the American army we call the High Priest, should have a large spot of ground to stretch himself upon; or that a man with a big belly, like a goodly alderman of London, should have a larger garden to produce beans and cabbage for his appetite, but that an agile, nimble runner, like an Indian called the Big Cat, at Fort Pitt, should have more than his neighbors, because he has traveled a great space, I can see no reason.

Farming Is Ownership

I have conversed with some persons and found their mistakes on this subject, to arise from a view of claims by individuals in a state of society, from holding a greater proportion of the soil than others; but this is according to the laws to which they have consented; an individual holding one acre, cannot encroach on him who has a thousand, because he is bound by the law which secures property in this unequal manner. This is the municipal law of the state under which he lives. The member of a distant society is not excluded by the laws from a right to the soil. He claims under the general law of nature, which gives a right, equally to all, to so much of the soil as is necessary for subsistence. Should a German from the closely peopled country of the Rhine, come into Pennsylvania, more thinly peopled, he would be justifiable in demanding a settlement, though his personal force would not be sufficient to effect it. It may be said that the cultivation or melioration of the earth, gives a property in it. No—if an individual has engrossed more than is necessary to produce grain for him to live upon, his useless gardens, fields and pleasure walks, may be seized upon by the person who, not finding convenient ground elsewhere, choose to till them for his support.

It is a usual way of destroying an opinion by pursuing it to its consequence. In the present case we may say, that if the visiting one acre of ground could give a right to it, the visiting of a million would give a right on the same principle; and thus a few surly ill natured men, might in the earlier ages have excluded half the human race from a settlement, or should any have fixed themselves on a territory, visited before they had set a foot on it, they must be considered as invaders of the rights of others.

Obtaining the Land

The gradual extension of our Settlements will as certainly cause the Savage as the Wolf to retire; both being beasts of prey tho' they differ in shape. In a word there is nothing to be obtained by an Indian War but the Soil they live on and this can be had by purchase at less expense.

George Washington, 1783.

It is said that an individual, building a house or fabricating a machine has an exclusive right to it, and why not those who improve the earth? I would say, should man build houses on a greater part of the soil, than falls to his share, I would, in a state of nature, take away a proportion of the soil and the houses from him, but a machine or any work of art, does not lessen the means of subsistence to the human race, which an extensive occupation of the soil does.

Claims founded on the first discovery of soil are futile. When gold, jewels, manufactures, or any work of men's hands is lost, the finder is entitled to some reward, that is, he has some claims on the thing found, for a share of it.

A Claim to Profit

When by industry or the exercise of genius, something unusual is invented in medicine or in other matters, the author doubtless has a claim to an exclusive profit by it, but who will say the soil is lost, or that any one can found a claim by discovering it. The earth with its woods and rivers still exist, and the only advantage I would allow to any individual for having cast his eye first on any particular part of it, is the privilege of making the first choice of situation. I would think the man a fool and unjust, who would exclude me from drinking the waters of the Mississippi river, because he had first seen it. He would be equally so who would exclude me from settling in the country west of the Ohio, because in chasing a buffalo he had been first over it.

The idea of an exclusive right to the soil in the natives had its origin in the policy of the first discoverers, the kings of Europe. Should they deny the right of the natives from their first treading on the continent, they would take away the right of discovery in themselves, by sailing on the coast. As the vestige of the moccasin in one case gave a right, so the cruise in the other was the foundation of a claim.

Those who under these kings, derived grants were led to countenance the idea, for otherwise why should kings grant or they hold extensive tracts of country. Men become enslaved to an opinion that has been long entertained. Hence it is that many wise and good men will talk of the right of savages to immense tracts of soil.

Indians Are Like Cattle

What use do these ring, streaked, spotted and speckled cattle make of the soil? Do they till it? Revelation said to man, "Thou shalt till the ground." This alone is human life. It is favorable to population, to science, to the information of a human mind in the worship of God. Warburton has well said, that before you can make an Indian a christian you must teach him agriculture and reduce him to a civilized life. To live by tilling is *more humano*, by hunting is *more bestiarum*. I would as soon admit a right in the buffalo to grant lands, as in Killbuck, the Big Cat, the Big Dog, or any of the ragged wretches that are called chiefs and sachems. What would you think of going to a big lick or place where the beasts collect to lick saline nitrous earth and water, and addressing yourself to a great buffalo to grant you land? It is true he could not make the mark of the stone or the mountain reindeer, but he could set his cloven foot to the instrument like the great Ottomon, the father of the Turks, when he put his signature to an instrument, he put his large hand and spreading fingers in the ink and set his mark to the parchment. To see how far the folly of some would go, I had once a thought of supplicating some of the great elks or buffaloes that run through the woods, to make me a grant of a hundred thousand acres of land and prove he had brushed the weeds with his tail, and run fifty miles.

I wonder if Congress or the different States would recognize the claim? I am so far from thinking the Indians have a right to the soil, that not having made a better use of it for many hundred years, I conceive they have forfeited all pretence to claim, and ought to be driven from it.

With regard to forming treaties or making peace with this race, there are many ideas:

They have the shapes of men and may be of the human species, but certainly in their present state they approach nearer the character of Devils; take an Indian, is there any faith in him? Can you bind him by favors? Can you trust his word or confide in his promise? When he makes war upon you, when he takes you prisoner and has you in his power will he spare you? In this he de-

141

parts from the law of nature, by which, according to baron Montesquieu and every other man who thinks on the subject, it is unjustifiable to take away the life of him who submits; the conqueror in doing otherwise becomes a murderer, who ought to be put to death. On this principle are not the whole Indian nations murderers?

The author, Hugh Henry Brackenridge, considered Indians to be less than human.

Many of them may have not had an opportunity of putting prisoners to death, but the sentiment which they entertain leads them invariably to this when they have it in their power or judge it expedient; these principles constitute them murderers, and they ought to be prevented from carrying them into execution, as we would prevent a common homicide, who should be mad enough to conceive himself justifiable in killing men.

The tortures which they exercise on the bodies of their prisoners, justify extermination. Gelo of Syria made war on the Carthaginians because they oftentimes burnt human victims, and made peace with them on conditions they would cease from this unnatural and cruel practice. If we could have any faith in the promises they make we could suffer them to live, provided they would only make war amongst themselves, and abandon their hiding or lurking on the pathways of our citizens, emigrating unarmed and defenceless inhabitants; and murdering men, women and children in a defenceless situation; and on their ceasing in the meantime to raise arms no more among the American Citizens.

CHAPTER 4

Two Cultures Meet

Chapter Preface

When Columbus noted in his log for October 12, 1492, "At dawn we saw naked people," he inaugurated the process of peoples of the Old and New Worlds looking carefully, albeit sometimes warily, at each other. Columbus, a product of predominantly Catholic Europe, a renascent Spain, an Old World emerging from medieval faith to modern inquiry, described those new people from the only perspective he had.

The log entry for that very first day in America continues:

> People began to come to the beach, all as naked as their mothers bore them. . . . They are very well-built people, with handsome bodies and very fine faces, though their appearance is marred somewhat by very broad heads and foreheads, more so than I have seen in any other race. Their eyes are large and very pretty, and their skin is the color of Canary Islanders or of sunburned peasants, not at all black, as would be expected because we are on an east-west line with Hierro in the Canaries. They are tall people and their legs, with no exception, are quite straight, and none of them has a paunch. They are, in fact, well proportioned. Their hair is not kinky, but straight, and coarse like horsehair. . . . Many of the natives paint their faces; others paint their whole bodies; some only the eyes or nose. Some are painted black, some white, some red; others are of different colors. . . . The people here called this island *Guanahani* in their language, and their speech is very fluent, although I do not understand any of it. They are friendly and well-dispositioned people who bear no arms except for small spears, and they have no iron. I showed one my sword, and through ignorance he grabbed it by the blade and cut himself. . . . They took great pleasure in [receiving red caps and glass beads] and became so friendly that it was a marvel. They traded and gave everything that they had with a good will, but it seems to me that they have very little and are poor in everything.

In this passage, Columbus describes the natives' physical characteristics, their personal ornamentation, their clothing (or its absence), their speech, and their behavior. Along with this detailed description, Columbus reveals some of his conclusions about these strange islanders. What the Tainos were thinking that morning we can only guess.

Columbus was the first of a burgeoning number of writers of what is now called American contact literature, the accounts of whites and their initial meetings with native Americans in the New World. Travelers described the wonders and the horrors

144

they had seen. Explorers wrote accounts designed to encourage further financial support for their efforts. Missionaries, reporting their efforts at conversion, naturally described shocking pre-conversion practices. Land companies, wanting to lure settlers, wrote descriptions of the land and its peoples. And soldiers, writing their battle reports, analyzed the sometimes astoundingly ferocious effectiveness of their enemies. Depending on the writer's purpose, characterizations of the people of the New World tended to be polarized between the Noble Savage and the Beast.

The Noble Savage lived in a kind of new Eden, a distant place sharing the virtues of that biblical pre-fall paradise. His society was reminiscent, too, of Ovid's Golden Age:

> The age was formed of gold; in those first days
> No law or force was needed. Men did right
> Freely; without duress they kept their word. . . .
> Without law or judge all men were safe. . . .
> Earth herself
> Untouched by spade or plowshare, freely gave,
> As of her own volition, all men needed,
> And men were well content with what she gave. . . .

In this Ovidian utopia, people lived in comfort, unashamed of nakedness, uncompetitive, not thirsting for wealth or power. They were generous, hospitable, healthy in mind and body. They lived in nature and with nature, with none of the flaws of civilized society. Some philosophers concluded that man closest to nature was somehow closer to God and therefore uncorrupted. After reports of the New World reached Europe, some writers returned to this theme. Thomas More's *Utopia*, which appeared in print in 1516, introduced something of that Golden Age ideal to his readers. Perhaps because the book was based in part on More's knowledge of Vespucci's voyages, many naive sixteenth-century Europeans believed *Utopia* was a description of how things *were* in the New World rather than how they might be everywhere if society's flaws were corrected. Rousseau and Montaigne, among others, further developed the concept of the Noble Savage; probably the Pocahontas story reinforced it. The myth of the American Garden, populated by Noble Savages, lived on into twentieth-century American literature and politics.

In contrast to the Noble Savage was the Beast—threatening, unredeemed, evil, unrepentant, uncivil. The Beast or "Savage" had his roots in the mythic Wild Man of European forests, a creature somehow beyond the moral and cultural pale, whose generic, undefined evil was a folkloric bogeyman to medieval European peasants. Transposed to the Americas, the Wild Man/Beast was the negative image of the Noble Savage. Perhaps to explain the difficulties inherent in his missionary efforts, a Dominican monk, Tomas Ortíz, wrote to the Spanish Council of the Indies about such bestial beings:

> They are more given to sodomy than any other nation. There is
> no justice among them. They go naked. They have no respect either
> for love or for virginity. They are stupid and silly. They
> have no respect for truth, save when it is to their advantage.
> They are unstable. They have no knowledge of what foresight
> means. They are ungrateful and changeable. . . . They are
> brutal. . . . The older they get the worse they become. About the
> age of ten or twelve years, they seem to have some civilization,
> but later they become like real brute beasts. I may therefore affirm
> that God has never created a race more full of vice and
> composed without the least mixture of kindness or culture.

At every stage of contact, on frontiers moving constantly westward, the question was repeated: What sort of people are these? And, although there was little knowledge about what the natives of the Caribbean thought of Columbus, historians soon had evidence—as in the Aztec accounts of the conquest of Mexico or in Plains Indian oral traditions of the arrival of the first whites on strange four-footed whinneying animals—that *both* populations were assessing the other. One situation in which the mutual analysis of the other's culture was especially evident was in accounts of the Indian delegations who were brought to the U.S. Capitol to experience white culture.

Central to all of the selections in this chapter and implicit throughout the book is the question of how people look at strangers and strange ideas. Do these strangers, on the whole, demonstrate enough universal human traits—love for their children, belief in a higher power, a need to bring some sort of order to their society—that we can relate to them? (Differences in practice sometimes obscured people's similarities. For example, while most whites and Indians loved their children, New England Indians were shocked at the colonists' methods of discipline, which they considered harsh. The Indians believed children learned best by emulating positive role models, not by being punished.) Or do they practice such strange behaviors—providing the honored guest boiled puppy to feast upon, or wearing restrictive collars and inflexible shoes—that they seem incomprehensible, even alien? If we do not understand each other, we will find it difficult to live together.

VIEWPOINT 1

"Everyone gives the title of barbarism to everything that is not according to his usage."

Natives of the Americas Are Noble Savages

Michel Eyquem de Montaigne

The French essayist Michel Eyquem de Montaigne (1533-1592) was one of several European writers fascinated with the New World and its possibilities. Like Sir Thomas More, author of *Utopia*, Montaigne based his descriptions of Indian life on accounts by early explorers of Brazil. Like More's, Montaigne's writing is strongly satirical, with an underlying message that the so-called savages of the New World are in many ways more virtuous and live better lives than do the Europeans. "Of Cannibals," the essay from which the following selection is taken, was instrumental in the creation of the concept of the Noble Savage: Primitive man, living in close touch with nature and with God, is uncorrupted by the vices of society.

As you read, consider the following questions:

1. How did Montaigne learn of the inhabitants of Brazil? Why does he trust his informant? How is this relevant to the ideas he presents in the rest of the essay?
2. According to Montaigne, what is a universal reason for calling someone or something "barbarous"?
3. What is the nature of society among the barbarians, according to the author?
4. According to Montaigne, what is true courage?
5. How does Montaigne satirize European society in this selection?

When King Pyrrhus passed over into Italy, having observed the formation of the army the Romans sent out to meet him, he said, "I do not know what kind of barbarians these are" (for so the Greeks called all foreign nations), "but the disposition of this army that I see is not at all barbarous." . . . That is how we should take care not to cling to common opinions, and how we should judge by the way of reason, and not by common report.

I had with me for a long time a man that had lived ten or twelve years in that other world which has been discovered in our century, in the place where Villegaignon landed, which he called Antarctic France [Brazil]. This discovery of so vast a country seems worthy of consideration. I do not know if I can be sure that in the future there may not be another such discovery made, so many greater men than we having been deceived in this. I am afraid our eyes are bigger than our bellies and that we have more curiosity than capacity. We grasp at all, but catch nothing but wind. . . .

This man that I had was a plain ignorant fellow, which is a condition fit to bear true witness; for your sharp sort of men are much more curious in their observations and notice a great deal more, but they gloss them; and to give the greater weight to their intepretation and make it convincing, they cannot forbear to alter the story a little. They never represent things to you simply as they are, they slant them and mask them according to the aspect they saw in them; and to give authority to their judgment and to attract you to it, they are willing to contribute something there to the matter, lengthening it and amplifying it. We should have a man either of irreproachable veracity, or so simple that he has not wherewithal to contrive and to give a color of truth to false tales, and who has not espoused any cause. Mine was such a one; and, besides that, he has divers times brought me several seamen and merchants whom he had known on that voyage. I do, therefore, content myself with his information without inquiring what the cosmographers say about it.

We need topographers to make a detailed account for us of the places where they have been. But by having this advantage over us of having seen the Holy Land, they want to have the privilege of telling us stories of new things from all the rest of the world. I would have everyone write what he knows, and as much as he knows, not in this only, but in all other subjects; for such a person may have some particular knowledge and experience of the nature of a river or of a spring, who as to other things knows no more than what everybody does. Yet to make this little fragment circulate, he will undertake to write the whole body of physics. From this vice arise many great disadvantages.

What Is a Barbarian?

Now to return to my subject, I find that there is nothing barbarous and savage in this nation according to what I have been told, except that everyone gives the title of barbarism to everything that is not according to his usage; as, indeed, we have no other criterion of truth and reason than the example and pattern of the opinions and customs of the country wherein we live. There is always the perfect religion, there the perfect government, there the perfect and accomplished usage in all things. They are savages in the same way that we say fruits are wild, which nature produces of herself and by her ordinary course; whereas, in truth, we ought rather to call those wild whose natures we have changed by our artifice and diverted from the common order. In the former, the genuine, most useful, and natural virtues and properties are vigorous and active, which we have degenerated in the latter, and we have only adapted them to the pleasure of our corrupted palate. And yet, for all this, the flavor and delicacy found in various uncultivated fruits of those countries are excellent to our taste, worthy rivals of ours. It is not reasonable that art should gain the point of honor over our great and powerful mother, Nature. . . .

These nations then seem to me to be barbarous so far as having received very little fashioning from the human mind and as being still very close to their original simplicity. The laws of Nature govern them still, very little vitiated by ours; but they are in such purity that I am sometimes troubled by the fact that we were not acquainted with these people earlier when there were men who would have been better able to judge of them than we are. I am sorry that Lycurgus and Plato had no knowledge of them; for it seems to me that what we now see by experience in those nations does not only surpass all the images with which the poets have adorned the golden age and all their inventions in imagining a happy state of man, but also the conception and even the desire of philosophy. They were incapable of imagining so pure and so simple an innocence as we by experience see it; nor were they capable of believing that human society can be maintained with so little human artifice and solder. I should say to Plato that it is a nation wherein there is no manner of traffic, no knowledge of letters, no science of numbers, no name of magistrate or of political superiority; no use of servitude, riches or poverty; no contracts, no successions, no dividing of properties, no employments, except those of leisure; no respect of kindred, except for the common bond; no clothing, no agriculture, no metal, no use of wheat or wine. The very words that signify lying, treachery, dissimulation, avarice, envy, detraction, and pardon were never heard of. . . .

How Do the Barbarians Live?

For the rest, they live in a very pleasing and very temperate country, so that, according to what I have been told by my witnesses, it is rare to see a sick person there; and they assured me that they never saw any of the natives either palsied, blear-eyed, toothless, or crooked with age. They are located along the coast and are inclosed on the side towards the land with great and high mountains, having about a hundred leagues in breadth in between. They have great store of fish and flesh that have no resemblance to ours, and they eat without any other artifice than that of cooking them. The first that rode a horse there, though in several voyages he had contracted an acquaintance with them, put them into so terrible a fright in that posture that they killed him with their arrows before being able to recognize him.

Their buildings are very long and capable of holding two or three hundred people, covered with the bark of tall trees, the sections fixed to the ground at one end and leaning against and supporting one another at the peak like some of our barns, of which the covering hangs way to the ground and serves for the side walls. They have wood so hard that they cut with it and make out of it their swords and grills to cook their meat. Their beds are of cotton weave, swung from the roof like those in our vessels, each one having his own; for the women lie apart from their husbands.

They rise with the sun, and as soon as they are up, eat for the whole day, for they have no other meal than that. They do not drink then, as Suidas reports of some other people of the East who never drank at their meals; they do drink several times a day, and a great deal. Their liquor is made of a certain root and is the color of our claret. They never drink it except lukewarm. This drink will keep only two or three days, has a somewhat sharp taste, is not at all heady, is wholesome to the stomach, laxative for those who are not used to it, and a very pleasant beverage to such as are accustomed to it. Instead of bread they make use of a certain white matter like preserved coriander. I have tasted of it; the taste is sweet and somewhat insipid.

The whole day is spent in dancing. The youngest go hunting after wild beasts with bows. Some of their women are employed in heating their drink meanwhile, which is their chief duty. Some one of the old men, in the morning before they fall to eating, preaches to the whole barnful in common, walking from one end to the other and several times repeating the same sentence until he has finished the round (for these buildings are a full hundred paces long). He recommends to them only two things: valor towards their enemies and love for their wives. And they never fail to note, as their refrain, this obligation, that it is their wives who keep their drink warm and seasoned.

The Natural State of Humanity

Savage man and civilized man differ so much in the bottom of their hearts and inclinations that what constitutes the supreme happiness of one would reduce the other to despair. The former breathes only repose and freedom; he wants only to live and remain idle; and even the perfect quietude of the Stoic does not approach his profound indifference for all other objects. On the contrary, the citizen, always active, sweats, agitates himself, torments himself incessantly in order to seek still more laborious occupations; he works to death, he even rushes to it in order to get in condition to live, or renounces life in order to acquire immortality. He pays court to the great whom he hates, and to the rich whom he scorns. He spares nothing in order to obtain the honor of serving them; he proudly boasts of his baseness and their protection; and proud of his slavery, he speaks with disdain of those who do not have the honor of sharing it. What a sight the difficult and envied labors of a European minister are for a Carib! How many cruel deaths would that indolent savage not prefer to the horror of such a life. . . . Such is, in fact, the true cause of all these differences: the savage lives within himself; the sociable man, always outside of himself, knows how to live only in the opinion of others; and it is, so to speak, from their judgment alone that he draws the sentiment of his own existence. It is not part of my subject to show how, from such a disposition, so much indifference for good and evil arises along with such fine discourses on ethics; how, everything being reduced to appearances, everything becomes factitious and deceptive: honor, friendship, virtue, and often even vices themselves, about which men finally discover the secret of boasting; how, in a word, always asking others what we are and never daring to question ourselves on this subject, in the midst of so much philosophy, humanity, politeness, and sublime maxims, we have only a deceitful and frivolous exterior, honor without virtue, reason without wisdom, and pleasure without happiness. It is sufficient for me to have proved that this is not the original state of man; and that it is the spirit of society alone, and the inequality it engenders, which thus change and alter all our natural inclinations.

Jean-Jacques Rousseau, *Discourse on the Origin and Foundation of Inequality*, 1753.

The fashion of their beds, ropes, wooden swords, and the wooden bracelets with which they cover their wrists when they go to fight, and of their big canes, open at one end, by the sound of which they keep the cadence of their dances, is to be seen in several places, and among others at my house. They are close shaven all over, and much more closely than we, without any other razor than one of wood or of stone. They believe the immortality of the soul, and that those who have merited well of the gods are lodged in that part of heaven where the sun rises, and the accursed in the west.

They have some kind of priests and prophets that very rarely present themselves to the people, having their abode in the mountains. At their arrival there is a great feast and solemn assembly of many villages (each lodge, as I have described it, makes a village, and they are about a French league distant from one another). This prophet declaims to them in public, exhorting them to virtue and to their duty; but all their ethics consist in these two articles: resolution in war and affection for their wives. He also prophesies to them events to come and the results they are to expect from their enterprises; he prompts them to, or diverts them from, war. But it is on condition that, when he fails in his divination and anything happens otherwise than he has foretold, he is cut into a thousand pieces, if he is caught, and condemned for a false prophet. For that reason, the prophet who has once been mistaken is never seen again.

Divination is a gift of God, that is why it ought to be punishable to abuse it. Among the Scythians, when their diviners failed to strike it right, they were laid, bound hand and foot, upon carts laden with firewood and drawn by oxen, on which they were burned. Those who handle things subject to the conduct of human capacity are excusable in doing the best they can. But these others that come to delude us with assurances of an extraordinary faculty beyond our understanding, ought they not to be punished for the temerity of their imposture and for not making good their promise?

They have wars with the nations that live farther inland beyond their mountains, to which they go quite naked and without other arms than their bows and wooden swords pointed at one end like the points of our spears. The obstinacy of their battles is wonderful; they never end without slaughter and bloodshed; for as to running away and fear, they know not what it is. Everyone for a trophy brings home the head of an enemy he has killed and fixes it over the door of his house. After having a long time treated their prisoners well and with all the luxuries they can think of, he to whom the prisoner belongs forms a great assembly of his acquaintances. He ties a rope to one of the arms of the prisoner, by the end of which he holds him some paces away for fear of being struck, and gives to the friend he loves best the other arm to hold in the same manner; and they two, in the presence of all the assembly, dispatch him with their swords. After that they roast him and eat him among them and send some pieces to their absent friends. They do not do this, as some think, for nourishment, as the Scythians anciently did, but as a representation of an extreme revenge. . . . I am not sorry that we should take notice of the barbarous horror of such acts, but I am sorry that, seeing so clearly into their faults, we should be so blind to our own. I conceive there is more barbarity in eating a man alive than in eating him dead, in tearing by tortures and the rack a body that is still full of feeling, in roasting him by degrees, causing him to be bitten and torn by dogs and swine (as we have not only read, but lately seen, not among inveterate enemies, but among neighbors and fellow-citizens, and what is worse, under color of piety and religion), than in roasting and eating him after he is dead. . . .

We may, then, well call these people barbarians in respect to the rules of reason, but not in respect to ourselves, who, in all sorts of barbarity, exceed them. Their warfare is in every way noble and generous and has as much excuse and beauty as this human malady is capable of; it has with them no other foundation than the sole jealousy of valor. Their disputes are not for the conquests of new lands, for they still enjoy that natural abundance that supplies them without labor and trouble with all things necessary in such abundance that they have no need to enlarge their borders. And they are still in that happy stage of desiring only as much as their natural necessities demand; all beyond that is superfluous to them.

Men of the same age generally call one another brothers; those who are younger, children; and the old men are fathers to all. These leave to their heirs in common the full possession of their goods, without any manner of division, or any other title than that pure one which Nature bestows upon her creatures in bringing them into the world. If their neighbors pass over the mountains to come to attack them and obtain a victory, all the victors gain by it is only glory and the advantage of having proved themselves the better in valor and virtue. . . . They demand of their prisoners no other ransom than the confession and acknowledgment that they are overcome. But there is not one found in a whole century that will not rather choose to die than either by word or look to recede one bit from the grandeur of an invincible courage. There is not a man among them who would not rather be killed and eaten than so much as request not to be. They treat them with all liberality in order that their lives may be so much the dearer to them; and they usually entertain them with menaces of their approaching death, of the torments they are to suffer, of the preparations that are being made for that purpose, of the cutting up of their limbs, and of the feast that will be made at their expense. All this is done for the sole purpose of extorting some weak or submissive word from them, or to make them want to run away, so that they may obtain the advantage of having terrified them and shaken their constancy. For indeed, if rightly taken,

it is in this point only that a true victory consists:
No victory is complete,
But when the vanquished own their just defeat. . . .

What Is the Nature of Victory and Courage?

We get enough advantages over our enemies that are borrowed advantages, not truly our own. It is the quality of a porter, not of valor, to have sturdier arms and legs; agility is a dead and corporeal quality; it is a stroke of fortune to make our enemy stumble or to dazzle his eyes with the light of the sun; it is a trick of art and science, which may happen in any cowardly blockhead, to be a good fencer. The worth and value of a man consists in the heart and in the will; there his true honor dwells. Valor is strength, not of legs and arms, but of the heart and the soul; it does not lie in the goodness of our horse, or of our arms, but in our own. He that falls firm in his courage, *if he has fallen, he fights upon his knees.* He who, despite the danger of death near at hand, abates nothing of his assurance; who in dying still looks at his enemy firmly and disdainfully; he is beaten, not by us, but by fortune; he is killed, not conquered. The most valiant are sometimes the most unfortunate. . . .

The Nature of Freedom

As an untamed steed bristles his mane, paws the earth with his hoof, and breaks away impetuously at the very approach of the bit, whereas a trained horse patiently endures whip and spur, barbarous man does not bend his head for the yoke that civilized man wears without a murmur, and he prefers the most turbulent freedom to tranquil subjection. Therefore it is not by the degradation of enslaved peoples that man's natural dispositions for or against servitude must be judged, but by the marvels done by all free peoples to guard themselves from oppression. I know that the former do nothing but boast incessantly of the peace and repose they enjoy in their chains, and that *miserrimam servitutem pacem appellant.* But when I see the others sacrifice pleasures, repose, wealth, power, and life itself for the preservation of this sole good which is so disdained by those who have lost it; when I see animals born free and despising captivity break their heads against the bars of their prison; when I see multitudes of entirely naked savages scorn European voluptuousness and endure hunger, fire, the sword, and death to preserve only their independence, I feel that it does not behoove slaves to reason about freedom.

Jean-Jacques Rousseau, *Discourse on the Origin and Foundation of Inequality,* 1753.

True victory has as its role the struggle, not the coming off safe; and the honor of valor consists in combating, not in beating.

To return to our story. These prisoners are so far from submitting in spite of all that is done to them that, on the contrary, during the two or three months that they are kept, they bear a cheerful countenance; they urge their masters to make haste to bring them to the test; they defy them, rail at them, and reproach them with cowardice and the number of battles they have lost against those of their country. I have a song composed by a prisoner in which there is this thrust, that they come boldly, all of them, and assemble to dine upon him, for they will be eating at the same time their own fathers and grandfathers, whose flesh has served to feed and nourish his body. "These muscles," says he, "this flesh and these veins are your own, poor fools that you are. You do not recognize that the substance of your ancestors' limbs is here yet; savor them well, and you will find in them taste of your own flesh." An idea that does not smack at all of barbarity. Those that paint these people dying and reproduce the execution depict the prisoner spitting in the face of his executioners and making faces at them. In truth, to the very last gasp they never cease to brave and defy them both by word and gesture. In plain truth, here are men who are real savages in comparison with us; for either they must be absolutely so, or else we are savages; there is an amazing difference between their character and ours.

VIEWPOINT 2

"When the children of the English captives cried at anytime ... the manner of the Indians was to dash out their brains against a tree.... This was Indian captivity!"

Natives of the Americas Are Uncivilized Beasts

Cotton Mather

In 1690, the governor-general of Canada, Louis de Baude, Comte de Frontenac, sent three native American war parties to attack English forts. One of these attacked Salmon Falls, New Hampshire, before moving on to ravage settlements in Maine. During these campaigns, the bounty for scalps was lowered while that for captives was raised; thus there was an extraordinarily large number of white captives—especially women and children—taken.

The following segments are based on the first edition of Cotton Mather's *Magnalia Christi Americana* (1702), a history of New England from 1620 to 1698 through Mather's eyes. Mather (1663-1728) wrote prodigiously on topics ranging from medicine to morals, theology to education. His interest in the conversion of Indians led to his publishing a bilingual *Epistle to the Christian Indians, Giving Them a Short Account of What the English Desire Them to Know and to Do in Order to Their Happiness* (1700). Mather also served as commissioner for Indian affairs for the New England Company. Nonetheless, he could be scathing in his denunciation of the Indians, especially their atrocities.

As you read, consider the following questions:

1. Although it is impossible to deal objectively with atrocities, how does Mather intensify the reader's response to the events he describes?
2. How do the techniques Mather uses here compare to those of wartime propaganda?

On March 18 [1690] the French with Indians, being half one [and] half the other, half Indianized French and half Frenchified Indians, commanded by Monsieur Artel [Francois Hertel] and Hoop-Hood [Chief Hopehood or Wohawa], fell suddenly upon Salmon Falls [New Hampshire], destroying the best part of the town with fire and sword. Near thirty persons were slain and more than fifty were led into what the reader will by and by call the worst captivity in the world. It would be a long story to tell what a particular share in this calamity fell to the family of one Clement Short. This honest man with his pious wife and three children were killed and six or seven of their children were made prisoners, the most of which arrived safe to Canada through a thousand hardships and the most of these were with more than a thousand mercies afterwards redeemed from Canada unto their English friends again. But my readers will be so reasonable as to excuse me if I do not mention the fate of every family that hath suffered a share in the calamity of this grievous war, for 'tis impossible that I should know all that hath happened, and it would be improper for me to write all that I know. And very little is the advantage of having a name standing upon record only among unhappy sufferers.

About seven score English went out after them and came up with them. Nevertheless, through the disadvantages of their feet by the snow, they could make no hand on it. Four or five of ours were killed and as many of the enemy, but the night put an end unto the action. Ours took one prisoner, a Frenchman, who confessed that they came from Canada where both French and Indians were in pay at ten livres per month, and he particularly declared the state of Canada. This prisoner met with such kind usage from us that he became a freeman of Christ and embraced and professed the Protestant religion. But of the prisoners which the enemy took from us there were two which immediately met with a very different fate.

Three Indians hotly pursued one Thomas Toogood, and one of them overtaking him while the rest perceiving it stayed behind the hill, he yielded himself a prisoner. While the savage was getting strings to bind him, he held his gun under his arm which, Toogood observing, suddenly plucked it from his friend stark naught, threatening and protesting that he would shoot him down if he made any noise and so away he ran with it unto Quochecho [Present-day Dover, New Hampshire].

If my reader be inclined now to smile when he thinks how simple poor Isgrim looked returning to his mates behind the hill without either gun or prey or anything but strings to remember

Horatio Greenough's sculpture portrays a white settler rescuing a mother and child from an Indian. The sculpture once stood at an entrance to the nation's Capitol Building.

him of his own deserts, the smiles will all be presently turned into tears. The Indians had now made a prisoner of one Robert Rogers, and, being on their journey, they came to an hill where this man, being through his corpulency (for which he was usually nicknamed Robin Pork) and an insupportable and intolerable burden laid upon his back, not so able to travel as the rest, he absconded. The wretches, missing him, immediately went in pursuit of him, and it was not long before they found his burden cast in the way and the track of his going out of the way which they followed until they found him hidden in a hollow tree. They took him out, they stripped him, they beat him, and pricked him, and pushed him forward with their swords until they were got back to the hill. And, it being almost night, they fastened him to a tree with his hands behind him and made themselves a supper, singing, dancing, roaring, and uttering many signs of joy but with joy little enough to the poor creature who foresaw what all this tended unto. They then cut a parcel of wood, and, bringing it

158

into a plain place, they cut off the top of a small red oak tree, leaving the trunk for a stake whereto they bound their sacrifice. They first made a great fire near this tree of death, and, bringing him unto it, they bid him take his leave of his friends which he did in a doleful manner; no pen, though made of a harpy's quill, were able to describe the dolor of it! They then allowed him a little time to make his prayers unto heaven, which he did with an extreme fervency and agony. Whereupon they bound him to the stake and brought the rest of the prisoners with their arms tied each to other so setting them round the fire.

This being done, they went behind the fire and thrust it forwards upon the man with much laughter and shouting, and when the fire had burned some while upon him even till he was near stifled, they pulled it again from him. They danced about him, and at every turn they did with their knives cut collops of his flesh from his naked limbs and throw them with his blood into his face. When he was dead, they set his body down upon the glowing coals and left him tied with his back to the stake where the English army soon after found him. He was left for us to put out the fire with our tears!

Reader, who should be the father of these myrmidons? . . .

[Three Additional Relations of]
The Condition of the Captives That from
Time to Time Fell into the Hands of the Indians,
with Some Very Remarkable Accidents

RELATION OF JAMES KEY

James Key, son to John Key of Quochecho, was a child of about five years of age taken captive by the Indians at Salmon Falls, and that hellish fellow, Hope-Hood, once a servant of a Christian master in Boston, was become the master of this little Christian. This child, lamenting with tears the want of parents, his master threatened him with death if he did not refrain his tears, but these threatenings could not extinguish the natural affections of a child. Wherefore upon his next lamentations this monster stripped him stark naked and lashed both his hands round a tree and scourged him so that from the crown of the head unto the sole of his foot he was all over bloody and swollen. And when he was tired with laying on his blows on the forlorn infant, he would lay him on the ground with taunts, remembering him of his parents. In this misery the poor creature lay horribly roaring for divers days together while his master, gratified with the music, lay contriving of new torments wherewith to martyr him. It was not long before the child had a sore eye which his master said proceeded from his weeping on the forbidden accounts. Whereupon, laying hold on the head of the child with his left hand, with the thumb of his

Indian Tortures

After some miles' travel we came in sight of a large cornfield and soon after of the fort, to my great surprise, for two or three squaws met us, took off my pack, and led me to a large hut or wigwam where thirty or forty Indians were dancing and yelling round five or six poor captives who had been taken some months before from Quochecho at the same time when Major Waldein [Waldron] was most barbarously butchered by them.

I was whirled in among them, and we looked on each other with a sorrowful countenance. And presently one of them was seized by each hand and foot by four Indians who swung him up and let his back with force fall on the hard ground, till they had danced (as they call it) round the whole wigwam which was thirty or forty feet in length. But when they torture a boy, they take him up between two. This is one of their customs of torturing captives. Another is to take up a person by the middle with his head downwards and jolt him round till one would think his bowels would shake out of his mouth. Sometimes they will take a captive by the hair of the head and stoop him forward and strike him on the back and shoulder till the blood gush out of his mouth and nose. Sometimes an old shriveled squaw will take up a shovel of hot embers and throw them into a captive's bosom, and, if he cry out, the other Indians will laugh and shout and say, "What a brave action our old grandmother has done!" Sometimes they torture them with whips, etc.

John Gyles, in *Puritans Among the Indians*, 1981.

right he forced the ball of his eye quite out, therewithal telling him that when he heard him cry again he would serve the other so too and leave him never an eye to weep withal. About nine or ten days after, this wretch had occasion to remove with his family about thirty miles further, and when they had gone about six miles of the thirty, the child, being tired and faint, sat him down to rest, at which this horrid fellow, being provoked, he buried the blade of his hatchet in the brains of the child and then chopped the breathless body to pieces before the rest of the company and threw it into the river. But for the sake of these and other such truculent things done by Hope-Hood, I am resolved that in the course of our story, I will watch to see what becomes of that hideous *loup-garou* [werewolf], if he come to his end (as I am apt to think he will) before the story. . . .

RELATION OF MARY PLAISTED

Mary Plaisted, the wife of Mr. James Plaisted, was made a captive by the Indians about three weeks after her delivery of a male child. They then took her with her infant off her bed and forced her to travel in this her weakness the best part of a day without any respect of pity. At night the cold ground in the open air was her lodging, and for many a day she had no nourishment but a little water with a little bearflesh, which rendered her so feeble that she with her infant were not far from totally starved. Upon her cries to God there was at length some supply sent in by her master's taking a moose, the broth whereof recovered her. But she must now travel many days through woods and swamps and rocks, and over mountains and frost and snow, until she could stir no farther. Sitting down to rest, she was not able to rise until her diabolical master helped her up, which, when he did, he took her child from her and carried it unto a river where, stripping it of the few rags it had, he took it by the heels and against a tree dashed out its brains and then flung it into the river. So he returned unto the miserable mother, telling her she was now eased of her burden and must walk faster than she did before!

RELATION OF MARY FERGUSON

Mary Ferguson, taken captive by the Indians at Salmon Falls, declares that another maid of about fifteen or sixteen years of age taken at the same time had a great burden imposed on her. Being over-borne with her burden, she burst out into tears, telling her Indian master that she could go no further. Whereupon he immediately took off her burden and, leading her aside into the bushes, he cut off her head, and, scalping it, he ran about laughing and bragging what an act he had now done, and, showing the scalp unto the rest, he told them they should all be served so if they were not patient.

In fine, when the children of the English captives cried at anytime so that they were not presently quieted, the manner of the Indians was to dash out their brains against a tree.

And very often when the Indians were on or near the water, they took the small children and held them under water till they had near drowned them and then gave them unto their distressed mothers to quiet them.

And the Indians in their frolics would whip and beat the small children until they set them into grievous outcries and then throw them to their amazed mothers for them to quiet them again as well as they could.

This was Indian captivity!

VIEWPOINT 3

"Man, in the simplicity and loftiness of his nature, unrestrained and unfettered by the disguises of art, is surely the most beautiful model for the painter."

A White Man's View of Indian Culture

George Catlin

George Catlin (1796-1872), born in Wilkes-Barre, Pennsylvania, first became interested in Indians as a child listening to the stories told by older settlers of "Indian massacres and Indian murders." Indeed, his mother had been captured by Indians during the Wyoming Massacre of 1778. Although his father convinced him to study law, Catlin really wanted to paint. After practicing law for a few years, he moved to Philadelphia in 1823 to "commence the art of painting." He became a successful portrait painter but was still restless. When a delegation of Indians from the "Far West" passed through Philadelphia on their way to see the president, Catlin resolved to go west to paint Indians. Going beyond portrait painting, he became a recorder of native customs and cultures. In vowing to go west, he had announced, "The history and customs of such a people . . . are themes worthy of the lifetime of one man, and nothing short of the loss of my life shall prevent me visiting their country, and of becoming their historian." He spent most of the years 1832-1839 traveling widely, visiting forty-eight different tribes. He returned with 310 portraits in oil, 200 other paintings of daily life—from religious rituals to children's games—and artifacts ranging from a decorative quill to a tepee. These were exhibited in Catlin's Indian Gallery in New York, which opened September 23, 1837. The paintings from his Indian Gallery now reside in the Smithsonian. In the introduction to his book *North American Indians*, published in 1844 and excerpted here, Catlin captured trans-Mississippi Indians at that point of change before they had "fallen victims to whiskey, small-pox and the bayonet." In words and pictures, he provides "invaluable historic and ethnographic documents" of a culture soon to be changed irretrievably.

As you read, consider the following questions:

1. In what ways does Catlin reflect ideas of Rousseau and Montaigne from viewpoint 1?
2. What does Catlin say is his purpose?
3. How does the author differentiate between Indians *on* the frontier and those beyond it?
4. How would Catlin evaluate the impact of civilization on the Indian?

The early part of my life was whiled away, apparently, somewhat in vain, with books reluctantly held in one hand, and a rifle or fishing-pole firmly and affectionately grasped in the other.

At the urgent request of my father, who was a practising lawyer, I was prevailed upon to abandon these favourite themes, and also my occasional dabblings with the brush, which had secured already a corner in my affections; and I commenced reading the law for a profession, under the direction of Reeve and Gould, of Connecticut. I attended the lectures of these learned judges for two years—was admitted to the bar—and practised the law, as a sort of *Nimrodical* lawyer, in my native land, for the term of two or three years; when I very deliberately sold my law library and all (save my rifle and fishing-tackle), and converting their proceeds into brushes and paint pots; I commenced the art of painting in Philadelphia, without teacher or adviser.

I there closely applied my hand to the labours of the art for several years; during which time my mind was continually reaching for some branch or enterprise of the art, on which to devote a whole life-time of enthusiasm; when a delegation of some ten or fifteen noble and dignified-looking Indians, from the wilds of the "Far West," suddenly arrived in the city, arrayed and equipped in all their classic beauty,—with shield and helmet,—with tunic and manteau,—tinted and tasselled off, exactly for the painter's palette!

In silent and stoic dignity, these lords of the forest strutted about the city for a few days, wrapped in their pictured robes, with their brows plumed with the quills of the war-eagle, attracting the gaze and admiration of all who beheld them. After this, they took their leave for Washington City, and I was left to reflect and regret, which I did long and deeply, until I came to the following deductions and conclusions.

Black and blue cloth and civilization are destined, not only to veil, but to obliterate the grace and beauty of Nature. Man, in the simplicity and loftiness of his nature, unrestrained and unfettered by the disguises of art, is surely the most beautiful model for the painter,—and the country from which he hails is unquestionably the best study or school of the arts in the world: such I am sure, from the models I have seen, is the wilderness of North America. And the history and customs of such a people, preserved by pictorial illustrations, are themes worthy the life-time of one man, and nothing short of the loss of my life, shall prevent me from visiting their country, and of becoming their historian. . . .

To Document a Lofty Race

With these views firmly fixed—armed, equipped, and supplied, I started out in the year 1832, and penetrated the vast and pathless wilds which are familiarly denominated the great "Far West" of the North American Continent, with a light heart, inspired with an enthusiastic hope and reliance that I could meet and overcome all the hazards and privations of a life devoted to the production of a literal and graphic delineation of the living manners, customs, and character of an interesting race of people, who are rapidly passing away from the face of the earth—lending a hand to a dying nation, who have no historians or biographers of their own to pourtray with fidelity their native looks and history; thus snatching from a hasty oblivion what could be saved for the benefit of posterity, and perpetuating it, as a fair and just monument, to the memory of a truly lofty and noble race. . . .

I set out on my arduous and perilous undertaking with the determination of reaching, ultimately, every tribe of Indians on the Continent of North America, and of bringing home faithful portraits of their principal personages, both men and women, from each tribe; views of their villages, games, &c. and full notes on their character and history. I designed, also, to procure their costumes, and a complete collection of their manufactures and weapons, and to perpetuate them in a *Gallery unique*, for the use and instruction of future ages.

I claim whatever merit there may have been in the originality of such a design, as I was undoubtedly the first artist who ever set out upon such a work, designing to carry his canvass to the Rocky Mountains; and a considerable part of the following Letters were written and published in the New York Papers, as early as the years 1832 and 1833; long before the Tours of Washington

Irving, and several others, whose interesting narratives are before the world. . . .

The Indians (as I shall call them), the savages or red men of the forests and prairies of North America, are at this time a subject of great interest and some importance to the civilized world; rendered more particularly so in this age, from their relative position to, and their rapid declension from, the civilized nations of the earth. A numerous nation of human beings, whose origin is beyond the reach of human investigation,—whose early history is lost—whose term of national existence is nearly expired—three-fourths of whose country has fallen into the possession of civilized man within the short space of 250 years—twelve millions of whose bodies have fattened the soil in the mean time; who have fallen victims to whiskey, the small-pox, and the bayonet; leaving at this time but a meagre proportion to live a short time longer, in the certain apprehension of soon sharing a similar fate.

The writer who would undertake to embody the whole history of such a people, with all their misfortunes and calamities, must needs have much more space than I have allotted to this epitome; and he must needs begin also (as I am doing) with those who are *living*, or he would be very apt to dwell upon the preamble of his work, until the present living remnants of the race should have passed away; and their existence and customs, like those of ages gone bye, become subjects of doubt and incredulity to the world for whom his book was preparing. Such an historian also, to do them justice, must needs correct many theories and opinions which have, either ignorantly or maliciously, gone forth to the world in indelible characters; and gather and arrange a vast deal which has been but imperfectly recorded, or placed to the credit of a people who have not had the means of recording it themselves; but have entrusted it, from necessity, to the honesty and punctuality of their enemies. . . .

A Description

The Indians of North America are copper-coloured, with long black hair, black eyes, tall, straight, and elastic forms—are less than two millions in number—were originally the undisputed owners of the soil, and got their title to their lands from the Great Spirit who created them on it,—were once a happy and flourishing people, enjoying all the comforts and luxuries of life which they knew of, and consequently cared for:—were sixteen millions in numbers, and sent that number of daily prayers to the Almighty, and thanks for his goodness and protection. Their country was entered by white men, but a few hundred years since; and thirty millions of these are now scuffling for the goods and luxuries of life, over the bones and ashes of twelve millions

165

of red men; six millions of whom have fallen victims to the small-pox, and the remainder to the sword, the bayonet, and whiskey; all of which means of their death and destruction have been introduced and visited upon them by acquisitive white men; and by white men, also, whose forefathers were welcomed and embraced in the land where the poor Indian met and fed them with "ears of green corn and with pemican." Of the two millions remaining alive at this time, about 1,400,000, are already the miserable living victims and dupes of white man's cupidity, degraded, discouraged and lost in the bewildering maze that is produced by the use of whiskey and its concomitant vices; and the remaining number are yet unroused and unenticed from their wild haunts or their primitive modes, by the dread or love of white man and his allurements. . . .

The reader, then, to understand me rightly, and draw from these Letters the information which they are intended to give, must follow me a vast way from the civilized world; he must needs wend his way from the city of New York, over the Alleghany, and far beyond the mighty Missouri, and even to the base and summit of the Rocky Mountains, some two or three thousand miles from the Atlantic coast. He should forget many theories he has read in the books of Indian barbarities, of wanton

In this self-portrait, Catlin paints Mah-to-toh-pa's portrait while the whole tribe watches intently.

butcheries and murders; and divest himself, as far as possible of the deadly prejudices which he has carried from his childhood, against this most unfortunate and most abused part of the race of his fellow-man.

He should consider, that if he has seen the savages of North America without making such a tour, he has fixed his eyes upon and drawn his conclusions (in all probability) only from those who inhabit the frontier; whose habits have been changed—whose pride has been cut down—whose country has been ransacked—whose wives and daughters have been shamefully abused—whose lands have been wrested from them—whose limbs have become enervated and naked by the excessive use of whiskey—whose friends and relations have been prematurely thrown into their graves—whose native pride and dignity have at last given way to the unnatural vices which civilized cupidity has engrafted upon them, to be silently nurtured and magnified by a burning sense of injury and injustice, and ready for that cruel vengeance which often falls from the hand that is palsied by refined abuses, and yet unrestrained by the glorious influences of refined and moral cultivation.—That if he has laid up what he considers well-founded knowledge of these people, from books which he has read, and from newspapers only, he should pause at least, and withhold his sentence before he passes it upon the character of a people, who are dying at the hands of their enemies, without the means of recording their own annals—struggling in their nakedness with their simple weapons, against guns and gunpowder—against whiskey and steel, and disease, and mailed warriors who are continually trampling them to the earth, and at last exultingly promulgating from the very soil which they have wrested from the poor savage, the history of his cruelties and barbarities, whilst his bones are quietly resting under the very furrows which their ploughs are turning.

So great and unfortunate are the disparities between savage and civil, in numbers—in weapons and defences—in enterprise, in craft, and in education, that the former is almost universally the sufferer either in peace or in war; and not less so after his pipe and his tomahawk have retired to the grave with him, and his character is left to be entered upon the pages of history, and that justice done to his memory which from necessity, he has intrusted to his enemy.

Amongst the numerous historians, however, of these strange people, they have had some friends who have done them justice; yet as a part of all systems of justice whenever it is meted to the poor Indian, it comes invariably too late, or is administered at an ineffectual distance; and that too when his enemies are continually about him, and effectually applying the means of his destruction.

Some writers, I have been grieved to see, have written down

the character of the North American Indian, as dark, relentless, cruel and murderous in the last degree; with scarce a quality to stamp their existence of a higher order than that of the brutes:—whilst others have given them a high rank, as I feel myself authorized to do, as honourable and highly-intellectual beings; and others, both friends and foes to the red men, have spoken of them as an "anomaly in nature!"

In this place I have no time or inclination to reply to so unaccountable an assertion as this; contenting myself with the belief, that the term would be far more correctly applied to that part of the human family who have strayed farthest from nature, than it could be to those who are simply moving in, and filling the sphere for which they were designed by the Great Spirit who made them.

Uncorrupted, Indians Are Noble

From what I have seen of these people I feel authorized to say, that there is nothing very strange or unaccountable in their character; but that it is a simple one, and easy to be learned and understood, if the right means be taken to familiarize ourselves with it. Although it has its dark spots, yet there is much in it to be applauded, and much to recommend it to the admiration of the enlightened world. And I trust that the reader, who looks through these volumes with care, will be disposed to join me in the conclusion that the North American Indian in his native state, is an honest, hospitable, faithful, brave, warlike, cruel, revengeful, relentless,—yet honourable, contemplative and religious being.

If such be the case, I am sure there is enough in it to recommend it to the fair perusal of the world, and charity enough in all civilized countries, in this enlightened age, to extend a helping hand to a dying race; provided that prejudice and fear can be removed, which have heretofore constantly held the civilized portions in dread of the savage—and away from that familiar and friendly embrace, in which alone his true native character can be justly appreciated.

I am fully convinced, from a long familiarity with these people, that the Indian's misfortune has consisted chiefly in our ignorance of their true native character and disposition, which has always held us at a distrustful distance from them; inducing us to look upon them in no other light than that of a hostile foe, and worthy only of that system of continued warfare and abuse that has been for ever waged against them.

There is no difficulty in approaching the Indian and getting acquainted with him in his wild and unsophisticated state, and finding him an honest and honourable man; with feelings to meet feelings, if the above prejudice and dread can be laid aside, and

Catlin's painting of this Mandan Indian village depicts a peaceful, orderly, civilized society.

any one will take the pains, as I have done, to go and see him in the simplicity of his native state, smoking his pipe under his own humble roof, with his wife and children around him, and his faithful dogs and horses hanging about his hospitable tenement.—So the world *may* see him and smoke his friendly pipe, which will be invariably extended to them; and share, with a hearty welcome, the best that his wigwam affords for the appetite, which is always set out to a stranger the next moment after he enters.

But so the mass of the world, most assuredly, will *not* see these people, for they are too far off, and approachable to those only whose avarice or cupidity alone lead them to those remote regions, and whose shame prevents them from publishing to the world the virtues which they have thrown down and trampled under foot.

The very use of the word savage, as it is applied in its general sense, I am inclined to believe is an abuse of the word, and the people to whom it is applied. The word, in its true definition, means no more than *wild*, or *wild man*; and a wild man may have been endowed by his Maker with all the humane and noble traits that inhabit the heart of a tame man. Our ignorance and dread or fear of these people, therefore, have given a new definition to the adjective; and nearly the whole civilized world apply the word *savage*, as expressive of the most ferocious, cruel, and murderous character that can be described.

The grizzly bear is called savage, because he is blood-thirsty, ravenous and cruel; and so is the tiger, and they, like the poor red man, have been feared and dreaded (from the distance at which ignorance and prejudice have kept us from them, or from resented abuses which we have practised when we have come in close contact with them), until Van Amburgh shewed the world, that even these ferocious and unreasoning animals wanted only the friendship and close embrace of their master, to respect and to love him.

I have roamed about from time to time during seven or eight years, visiting and associating with, some three or four hundred thousand of these people, under an almost infinite variety of circumstances; and from the very many and decided voluntary acts of their hospitality and kindness, I feel bound to pronounce them, by nature, a kind and hospitable people. I have been welcomed generally in their country, and treated to the best that they could give me, without any charges made for my board; they have often escorted me through their enemies' country at some hazard to their own lives, and aided me in passing mountains and rivers with my awkward baggage; and under all of these circumstances of exposure, no Indian ever betrayed me, struck me a blow, or stole from me a shilling's worth of my property that I am aware of.

This is saying a great deal, (and proving it too, if the reader will believe me) in favour of the virtues of these people; when it is borne in mind, as it should be, that there is no law in their land to punish a man for theft—that locks and keys are not known in their country—that the commandments have never been divulged amongst them; nor can any human retribution fall upon the head of a thief, save the disgrace which attaches as a stigma to his character, in the eyes of his people about him.

And thus in these little communities, strange as it may seem, in the absense of all systems of jurisprudence, I have often beheld peace and happiness, and quiet, reigning supreme, for which even kings and emperors might envy them. I have seen rights and virtue protected, and wrongs redressed; and I have seen conjugal, filial and paternal affection in the simplicity and contentedness of nature. I have unavoidably, formed warm and enduring attachments to some of these men which I do not wish to forget—who have brought me near to their hearts, and in our final separation have embraced me in their arms, and commended me and my affairs to the keeping of the Great Spirit.

For the above reasons, the reader will be disposed to forgive me for dwelling so long and so strong on the justness of the claims of these people; and for my occasional expressions of sadness, when my heart bleeds for the fate that awaits the remainder of their unlucky race; which is long to be outlived by the rocks, by the beasts, and even birds and reptiles of the country they live in;—set upon by their fellow-man, whose cupidity, it is feared, will fix no bounds to the Indian's earthly calamity, short of the grave.

VIEWPOINT 4

"We made a show of them, and they made one of us. Which were the most civilized?"

An Indian View of Washington, D.C.

Herman J. Viola

Herman J. Viola received his B.A. from Marquette University and his Ph.D. from Indiana University. Some of Viola's major publications include *Thomas McKenney, Architect of America's Early Indian Policy* (1974), *The Indian Legacy of Charles Bird King* (1976), *After Columbus, The Smithsonian Chronicle of the North American Indians* (1990), *Exploring the West* (1987), and, with Carolyn Margolis, *Seeds of Change: A Quincentennial Commemoration* (1991). He is currently director of Quincentenary Programs at the National Museum of Natural History at the Smithsonian. In the book from which this selection is taken, *Diplomats in Buckskins*, Dr. Viola paints a sometimes poignant, sometimes comical, always readable account of Indian delegations to Washington. At times reading it is like being in a chamber of mirrors, as when, in this selection, Indians visiting Washington museums delight in identifying people and places they know in paintings produced by artists who had traveled to the West to know their subjects. The mirror effect is only increased when reporters describe the Indians' responses.

As you read, consider the following questions:

1. What, apparently, was the protocol for meeting the president? Was it always maintained?
2. Would George Catlin and his Indian Gallery have been a useful resource for government officials meeting with the Indians?
3. One of the stated purposes of bringing the Indians to Washington was to impress them with the power of the United States. Does this seem to have occurred?

In the nineteenth century, meetings between the Great Father and delegations varied little from administration to administration. Seldom was serious business transacted. Such discussions were held with officials who administered Indian affairs at the cabinet level. Audiences with the president were ceremonial interviews, courtesies of state. As a result, they would often be large gatherings, consisting of the presidential family, congressmen, Supreme Court justices, high-ranking military officers, and ambassadors from foreign countries and their families. These highly orchestrated affairs included the pomp and pageantry accorded visiting heads of state.

The meeting between President James Monroe and the O'Fallon delegation of 1821 excited considerable interest and was well-publicized in the local press. For this important occasion, the Indians were wearing new clothes, which consisted of military uniforms complete with silver epaulets, hats, and black boots. Followed by O'Fallon and the interpreters, the seventeen Indians were ushered into the president's antechamber, where they nervously awaited his arrival. They were not completely at ease in their strange clothes. "Their coats seemed to pinch them about the shoulders," one bystander noticed; "now and then they would take off their uneasy headdresses, and one sought a temporary relief by pulling off his boots." Monroe's entrance brought the assembly to attention.

Speaking from prepared notes held in one hand, the president addressed the delegates, thanking them for coming such a great distance to see him and the wonders of the white man's world. Now he hoped the Indians would want the comforts of civilized life for themselves. If so, he was prepared to send missionaries to teach their people agriculture and the lessons of Christianity. The president was also pleased that the Indians had visited forts, arsenals, and navy yards; but, he warned, they had seen only a fraction of American military strength. Few fighting men were needed at the capital; in time of war all citizens took up arms and became warriors. Thus, he urged the Indians to remain at peace with each other and not to listen to those who advised them to mistrust or fight with the United States. As Monroe spoke, the interpreters translated his speech sentence by sentence; the Indians in return nodded gravely, indicating that they understood what had been said.

When the president finished, the delegates were invited to respond. Sharitarish, spokesman for the Pawnees, stepped forward, solemnly shook hands with Monroe, and slowly delivered a long speech. "My Great Father," he said, "I have traveled a great distance to see you—I have seen you and my heart rejoices. I have heard your words . . . and I will carry them to my people as pure as they came from your mouth . . . [I] have seen your people, your homes, your vessels on the big lake, and a great many wonderful things far beyond my comprehension, which appears to have been made by the Great Spirit and placed in your hands." But, wonderful as it was, he would not trade his way of life for that of the white man. There were still plenty of buffalo to hunt and beaver to trap. "It is too soon," Sharitarish continued, "to send those good men [the missionaries] among us—we are not starving yet—we wish you to permit us to enjoy the chase until the game of our country is exhausted—until the wild animals become extinct. . . . I have grown up, and lived this long without work," he declared; "I am in hopes you will suffer me to die without it. We have everything we want—we have plenty of land, if you will keep your people off it."

The other chiefs then spoke in turn, each stressing his love for the Indian way of life. The first speakers were noticeably nervous, but each succeeding orator became less reserved until the last—claimed a witness—spoke "as loud as you ever heard a lawyer at a county court bar."

As each speaker finished, he laid a present at the president's feet. Monroe was sitting behind a mound of buffalo robes, calumets, moccasins, and feathered headdresses when the lengthy ceremony ended.

Everyone adjourned to the drawing room for cake and wine. The Indians capped the festivities by lighting their pipes and passing them to the president, Chief Justice John Marshall, and other dignitaries, who took token whiffs. By this time the visitors had endured their unfamiliar and uncomfortable clothing long enough. As a dismayed observer reported, "one of them, unable longer to bear the pressure of his boots, sat down and deliberately pulled them off. Another his coat, until the whole might have brought themselves back to a comfortable state of nature had they not been led out.". . .

Lincoln and the Indians

Ceremonies such as this were repeated countless times during the nineteenth century. Even Abraham Lincoln during the darkest moments of the Civil War had to find time to enact his role as the Great Father. Although he met with several delegations and had private audiences with prominent Indian leaders like John Ross, chief of the Cherokees, almost nothing is known of these conversations except for a few meager records. Lincoln's secretary, John Hay, jotted a few notes during a meeting with three Potawatomi Indians from Iowa. Hay's account indicates that Lincoln, like most of the Great Fathers, had little conception of In-

173

dian culture. Apparently assuming all Indians spoke the same language, he greeted his visitors with the two or three Indian words he knew. Then, despite the fact that the leader of the delegation spoke fluent English, Lincoln switched to the broken English he thought the Indians would understand—"Where live now? When go back Iowa?" Hay thought Lincoln's awkward efforts were amusing; what the Indians thought was not recorded.

One meeting between Lincoln and an Indian delegation was thoroughly documented. This was a delegation of sixteen Indians—fourteen men and two women—representing six tribes from the Southern Plains—Comanche, Kiowa, Cheyenne, Arapaho, Caddo, and Apache. A large crowd that included the families of the ministers of England, France, Prussia, and Brazil and the secretaries of state, treasury, navy, and interior, was already waiting in the East Room of the White House when the Indians arrived on the morning of March 27, 1863. Moving to one end of the long room, the Indians sat in a semicircle facing the unusually restless and noisy crowd that quickly surged around them; not everyone could get a good view, which resulted in a considerable amount of pushing and shoving. As one reporter commented, "There unfortunately seems to be an incurable habit among the good people of our country in the house of the Chief Magistrate to press forward and not give an inch to those behind." According to another observer, "Everybody seemed to find someone's bonnet or shoulder in the way, and to think himself or herself entitled to the best and most conspicuous place. . . . Still everything went off very well. These Indians are fine-looking men," he wrote. "They have all the hard and cruel lines in their faces which we might expect in savages; but they are evidently men of intelligence and force of character. They were both dignified and cordial in their manner, and listened to everything with great interest."

The Indians had been waiting about fifteen minutes when Lincoln entered the room. The interpreter introduced each of the chiefs, who came forward and gave the president a quick, vigorous handshake. Lincoln then turned to the interpreter and said: "Say to them I am very glad to see them, and if they have any thing to say, it will afford me great pleasure to hear them."

At this, Lean Bear of the Cheyennes rose and stepped forward. The chief was so nervous, however, that he asked for a chair so he could sit while speaking to the Great Father. A comfortable armchair was quickly brought forward, but the unusual request from this powerful and vigorous warrior surprised everyone. Nevertheless, despite his nervousness, Lean Bear was soon recognized as a gifted orator, with a fluent and animate style of speaking.

"The President is the Great Chief of the White People," he said; "I am the Great Chief of the Indians. Our wigwams are not so fine as this; they are small and poor. I hope the Great Chief will look upon his people with favor, and say in his wisdom what would be best for them to do. We are here to listen to his advice and carry it in our hearts. . . . I will hear all the Great Chief has to say; and when I go away I will not carry . . . [his words] in my pocket, but in my heart, where they will not be lost." Lean Bear then spoke about the many white people moving into his country. The Indians wished to live in peace, he said, but he feared the white people were not so inclined. Nevertheless, he would keep his warriors from the warpath unless the white men provoked a fight. Lean Bear also spoke of the Civil War, promising to keep his people neutral.

Spotted Wolf, another Cheyenne, was the only other delegate who chose to speak. Spotted Wolf said he was surprised to see how friendly the white people were. Everywhere he went he found only brothers. He was also amazed at all the wonderful things the delegates had seen. "When I look about me and see all these fine things, it seems like some kind of magic. I do not even know how I got here, so far away from home. It seems to me that I must have come on wings—like a bird through the air."

When no one else came forward, Lincoln addressed the delegation. "You have all spoken of the strange sights you see here, among your pale-faced brethren," he said. "But you have seen but a very small part of the pale-faced people—There are people in this wigwam, now looking at you, who have come from other countries a great deal farther off than you have come." Lincoln then launched into a geography lesson. He told the Indians that the world was a great ball, and that visitors to Washington came from all parts of that ball. As he spoke, an attendant carried a large globe into the circle. Lincoln then introduced Joseph Henry, the first secretary of the Smithsonian Institution, who gave the delegates a detailed explanation of the formation of the earth. Henry pointed out the oceans, the various countries represented by the visitors in the room, and the location of Washington in relation to the homeland of the Indians. When Henry finished speaking, Lincoln resumed his remarks. He told the Indians they would have to change their way of life if they wished to become as prosperous as the white man. In his opinion there were two primary differences in their ways of life: whites cultivated the soil and relied on bread rather than game for subsistence; whites were also a peaceful people. Despite the Civil War, Lincoln declared,"we are not, as a race, so much disposed to fight and kill one another as our red brethren."

Lincoln throughout his speech spoke slowly and paused frequently, allowing ample time for interpretation. The Indians must have liked the speech because, according to one reporter, they received it "with frequent marks of applause and approbation . . . and their countenances gave evident tokens of satisfaction." As soon as Lincoln left the room, the crowd pressed close to the Indians and, like typical tourists, gawked at their costumes and plagued them with questions, which the interpreter had to translate. The most popular of the delegates was Yellow Wolf of the Kiowas. His obvious warmth appealed to the spectators, who were overheard saying such things as: "He is a good fellow," and "There now, I like that one." Yellow Wolf was especially interesting to the crowd because he was wearing a Thomas Jefferson peace medal. The Kiowa chief explained that it had been given to one of his ancestors and was now one of his tribe's most prized possessions. . . .

Indians in the Capitol

A tour of the Capitol Building was also a requisite for the Indian visitors, but how much they benefited from the experience is open to conjecture. The Comanches who visited Washington in 1846 found the exhibits of paintings and statuary much more interesting than the speeches they heard on the house and Senate floors. They were especially delighted with the color prints by George Catlin which they saw in the library. "As they gazed upon Buffalo hunts, upon the groups of wild horses and wolves, and upon the various Indian warriors in their own costumes, and amid the scenes of their own distant homes, they could not restrain their emotions." noted one observer. "For the first time, men, women, and youths, fell into animated conversation, pointing out to each other what most interested them . . . and for the moment, seemed restored to the wild prairies or hills of Texas." The large paintings on display in the Rotunda also impressed the Comanches who recognized President James K. Polk, whom they had just met, and Sam Houston, at whose portrait they "laughed heartily.". . .

Although the Indians much preferred outdoor activities to sitting in stuffy theaters watching the ballet or the latest comedy, all delegations had to endure some exposure to these cultural events. The Indians obviously were as much of an attraction as the performances themselves, and from the amount of advance publicity given their appearances, they were sometimes used to assure a full house. Two newspapers, for instance, advertised the forthcoming appearance of the Southern Plains delegation of 1863 at Grover's Theatre on Pennsylvania Avenue near the Willard Hotel. The newspapers even printed the seating assignments for the Indians, which assured theatergoers that they would be able to see "representatives of the influential tribes in the West—all great fighting nations—[in] their peculiar paints, [and] costumes."

What the Indians thought of the entertainments is unknown, although it was unusual for a delegation to sit through an entire theatrical performance. The Winnebagos who attended a comedy in New York City did enjoy some hearty laughs, but at the wrong places. They found the love scenes especially amusing. Special effects were also lost on them. The stench of burning sulphur during a simulated earthquake caused the Indians to cover their faces with their blankets. By the end of the performance, only two of the twenty Winnebagos were still in their seats.

One of the most stirring moments in Washington's theatrical history occurred in 1837 when visiting tribesmen attended a ballet at the National Theater. Because the theater was crowded, the Indians were seated on the stage, where they almost outshone the ballerina, a Miss Nelson, in her role as the Mountain Sylph. The Indians paid no heed to the audience, for the dancer's grace and beauty held them spellbound; a crown of ostrich plumes flashed and fluttered as the Mountain Sylph darted lightly and swiftly across the stage. Suddenly, one of the Sioux warriors stood up and tossed his warbonnet of eagle feathers at Miss Nelson's feet. A second bonnet soon followed, and the ballerina stopped dancing. Tokacou, a celebrated Yankton chief, then stepped forward and handed the startled dancer his splendid robe of white wolf skins. Not to be outdone, Moukaushka arose. This gallant young warrior would die within a month from one of the white man's dread diseases, but tonight his thoughts were only of the lovely Miss Nelson. He handed her his beautifully painted buffalo robe. He was offering this treasure, the interpreter explained to the audience, "to the beauty of Washington." The quick-thinking young woman acknowledged the gifts by plucking the ostrich plumes from her crown and giving one to each delegate. "The whole scene," the Intelligencer informed its readers, was "one of extraordinary and thrilling interest." The next day the Sioux delegation was seen striding along Pennsylvania Avenue toward the Capitol. Each warrior was proudly wearing a new military uniform, silver epaulets, and hat. Tucked in each hatband was one of Miss Nelson's ostrich plumes.

When the Smithsonian Institution opened in 1850, it became a regular stop on the delegation itinerary. A gallery of Indian portraits by Charles Bird King and John Mix Stanley was especially popular, for the Indians often saw people whom they recognized. A Smithsonian clerk was present when the Pawnee delegation of 1858 visited the museum. The Indians went first to the art gallery, where they examined the portraits of Indian life with great interest. Although they seemed disappointed at not finding paintings related to their tribes, they were pleased with the gallery nonetheless. "A scene representing Indian warriors, dancing around a captive white woman and her child attracted much notice from them," the clerk recalled. "They gathered in groups in front of it and made many remarks about it in their own language.". . .

Sioux leaders in full ceremonial dress arrive by automobile at the Capitol for a 1905 meeting with U.S. leaders.

The spiritual needs of the Indians were not forgotten. As part of the christianizing effort, Indian leaders frequently attended church services and visited Sunday schools. Chief Iron Bull of the Crows delighted the students and mothers at the Bethany Sunday School by declaring he was a a believer in religious instruction. Like all Crows, he said, he prayed to the same God as the whites, but in a different way. The attitudes of most of the delegates toward these functions was probably best expressed by a cynical writer for the Washington Star when announcing that the Sioux delegation of 1891 would be at church the following Sunday. They go, he wrote, "not because they are piously inclined, but, like a great many of their white brethren, . . . to hear the music and see the people."

Whatever the Indians' response, their presence in church made good press for government officials trying to convince the public that progress was being made in the civilization of the tribes.

Although there is no known instance of a delegate harming any local residents while in the East, Washingtonians felt uneasy about the presence of Indians who, especially before the Civil War, were often armed with knives, tomahawks, and guns. More than one newspaper editorial questioned the wisdom of allowing Indians to walk the streets carrying weapons.

The most dangerous episode occurred in 1837 when two rival Sac and Fox delegations met unexpectedly on Pennsylvania Avenue. As one witness later recalled, the Indians "enlightened the terrified citizens in the art of warfare by throwing tomahawks at each other for awhile." The Indians did not frighten everyone they met. At least two delegates—a Santee Sioux in 1858 and a Chippewa in 1867—married white women they met while in Washington. The exact circumstances are unclear. Some accounts claim the women were prostitutes; others claim they were employees of the hotels where the Indians stayed. There were also many instances recorded of delegates being invited to private homes for tea or an evening by the fireside. The Oto Chief Shaumonekusse and his wife, Eagle of Delight, who visited Washington in 1822, were frequent guests of Jonathan Barber, a local physician. "She was a very good natured, mild woman," Barber wrote, whereas her husband "showed great readiness in acquiring our language, retaining anything that he was once informed, and imitating the tones of every word." The Indians also demonstrated a natural wit. On one occasion the doctor showed several members of the delegation a skeleton he kept in a closet, whereupon one of them grasped a bony hand and said, "How do you do?" In 1875 Congressman John S. Savage of Ohio held a reception at his Washington residence for a Chippewa delegation. The festivities got off to an awkward start. Everyone shook hands and stared at each other. Eventually, the Indians squatted on the floor and began to sing, keeping time by tapping their tomahawks on the floor. As one of the guests later remarked, "We made a show of them, and they made one of us. Which were the most civilized?"

VIEWPOINT 5

"A barbarous people, depending for subsistence upon the scanty and precarious supplies furnished by the chase [hunting], cannot live in contact with a civilized community."

Whites and Indians Cannot Live Side by Side

Lewis Cass

In this viewpoint written in 1829, Lewis Cass, governor of the Michigan Territory and also secretary of war under President Andrew Jackson, presents a case for Indian removal beyond the Mississippi River. Quoting every legal source he can find to support the legality of whites taking over Indian land, ignoring or rejecting real progress made by Indians such as the Cherokees, and twisting evidence to his own purposes, he argues that it would be better for the Indians to be removed from the white man and the evils he brings. His bottom line is that two peoples, one civilized and one barbarous, cannot live together.

As you read, consider the following questions:

1. Can you find any statements Cass makes that are inaccurate? How does an occasional misrepresentation of fact affect the reader's response to Cass's argument?
2. To what factors does Cass attribute the decline of the Indian population and culture?
3. Does Cass appear to have sympathy for the conditions of the Indians?

180

4. How does Cass turn what some people might consider virtues into faults?
5. Does Cass believe that assimilation is possible? Why or why not?

The destiny of the Indians, who inhabit the cultivated portions of the territory of the United States, or who occupy positions immediately upon their borders, has long been a subject of deep solicitude to the American government and people. Time, while it adds to the embarrassments and distress of this part of our population, adds also to the interest which their condition excites, and to the difficulties attending a satisfactory solution of the question of their eventual disposal, which must soon pass *sub judice*. That the Indians have diminished, and are diminishing, is known to all who have directed their attention to the subject. For any purpose we have in view, it is not necessary to go back to the remote periods of aboriginal history, and investigate the extent of the population, and their means of subsistence, and to calculate the declension of the one, and the reduction of the other, as the white man advanced in his progress from the seat covered by a buffalo robe, [The Indian tradition respecting the quantity of land first given to the white men.] first given to him on the shore of the ocean, to the dominion he now enjoys. Such an inquiry would be vain and useless. . . .

No Regrets

It would be miserable affectation to regret the progress of civilization and improvement, the triumph of industry and art, by which these regions have been reclaimed, and over which freedom, religion, and science are extending their sway. But we may indulge the wish, that these blessings had been attained at a smaller sacrifice; that the aboriginal population had accommodated themselves to the inevitable change of their condition, produced by the access and progress of the new race of men, before whom the hunter and his game were destined to disappear. But such a wish is vain. A barbarous people, depending for subsistence upon the scanty and precarious supplies furnished by the chase, cannot live in contact with a civilized community. As the cultivated border approaches the haunts of the animals, which are valuable for food or furs, they recede and seek shelter in less accessible situations. The number of these animals may be diminished, but cannot be increased, by the interference of men; and when the people, whom they supply with the means of subsistence, have become sufficiently numerous to consume the excess annually added to the stock, it is evident, that the population must become stationary, or, resorting to the principal instead of the interest, must, like other prodigals, satisfy the wants of to-day at the expense of to-morrow.

The general principles regulating the population of the human race are as applicable to wandering tribes, deriving their support from the bounties of nature, as to stationary and civilized societies, where art and industry can increase almost indefinitely those products which minister to their wants. Population and production must eventually preserve a just ratio to each other. Whether the tribes upon this continent had attained the *maximum* of their population, before the discovery, we have not now the means of ascertaining. It is certain, however, as well from a consideration of their mode of life, as from a careful examination of the earlier narratives, that, greatly as they exceeded their present numbers, they were yet thinly scattered over the country. There is no reason to believe, that vegetable productions were ever cultivated to any considerable extent by the Indians, or formed an important part of their food. Corn, and beans, and pumpkins were indigenous to the country, and were probably raised in small quantities around each Indian village. But they were left to the labor of the women, whose only instrument of agriculture was a clam-shell, or the shoulder-blade of a buffalo, tied to a stick. Their habits of life were then what they now are. They returned from their hunting grounds in the spring, and assembled in their villages. Here their few vegetables were planted. But although the seed-time came, no harvest followed; for before their corn was ripe, it was generally consumed, with that utter recklessness of the future, which forms so prominent and unaccountable a feature in their character. As the autumn approached, they separated and repaired to their *wintering* grounds, where, during eight months of the year, they were engaged alternately in the chase, and in those relaxations and amusements, peculiar to the condition of the hunter. This was the annual round of aboriginal life.

Indians' Livelihood Threatened

It is obvious, that the reduction or disappearance of the game, consequent upon the conversion of forests into fields, and the gradual advance of a civilized people, must have soon begun to press upon the means of subsistence, on which the Indians mainly depended. Other circumstances cooperated in the work of destruction. Fire-arms were introduced, and greatly facilitated the operations of the hunter. Articles of European merchandise were offered to the Indians, and they were taught the value of their furs, and encouraged to procure them. New wants arose among them. The rifle was found a more efficient instrument than the bow and arrow; blankets were more comfortable than buffalo robes; and cloth, than dressed skins. The exchange was altogether unfavorable to them. The goods they received were dear, and the peltry they furnished was cheap. A greater number of animals was necessary for the support of each family, and increased exertion was required to procure them. We need not pursue this subject further. It is easy to see the consequences, both to the Indians and their game. . . .

But a still more powerful cause has operated to produce this diminution in the number of the Indians. Ardent spirits have been the bane of their improvement; one of the principal agents in their declension and degradation. In this proposition we include only those tribes in immediate contact with our frontier settlements, or who have remained upon *reservations* guarantied to them. It has been found impracticable to prevent the sale of spirituous liquors to those who are thus situated. The most judicious laws are eluded or openly violated. The love of spirits, and the love of gain, conspire to bring together the buyer and the seller. As the penalties become heavier, and the probability of detection and punishment stronger, the prohibited article becomes dearer, and the sacrifice to obtain it greater. We shall not attempt to investigate the cause of the inordinate attachment displayed by the Indians to ardent spirits. It is probably without a parallel in all the history of man, and is certainly so, with very few exceptions, in the whole range of their own society. There is a singular uniformity in its operation, destroying the effect of individual character, and substituting a common standard of feeling and deportment. These facts are known to all, to whom the Indians themselves are known. This predisposition was the subject of observation and regret two centuries ago; and the earlier historians and travellers, while they furnish the record of its existence, furnish also the evidence of its overpowering influence and destructive consequences.

Our object is not to trace the operation of all the causes which have contributed to the diminution of the population of the Indians. We confine ourselves to those which may be fairly attributed to the coming of the Europeans among them, and which are yet exerting their influence, wherever the two races are placed in contact. As we shall attempt eventually to prove, that the only means of preserving the Indians from that utter extinction which threatens them, is to remove them from the sphere of this influence, we are desirous of showing, that no change has occurred, or probably can occur, in the principles or practice of our intercourse with them, by which the progress of their declension can be arrested, so long as they occupy their present situation. . . .

To the operation of the physical causes, which we have described, must be added the moral causes connected with their mode of life, and their peculiar opinions. Distress could not teach them providence, nor want industry. As animal food decreased, their vegetable productions were not increased. Their habits were stationary and unbending; never changing with the change of circumstances. How far the prospect around them, which to us appears so dreary, may have depressed and discouraged them, it is difficult to ascertain, as it is also to estimate the effect upon them of that superiority, which we have assumed and they have acknowledged. There is a principle of repulsion in ceaseless activity, operating through all their institutions, which prevents them from appreciating or adopting any other modes of life, or any other habits of thought or action, but those which have descended to them from their ancestors.

States Own the Land

If, as is the case, you have been permitted to abide on your lands from that period to the present, enjoying the right of the soil, and privilege to hunt, it is not thence to be inferred, that this was any thing more than a permission, growing out of compacts with your nation; nor is it a circumstance whence, now to deny to those states, the exercise of their original sovereignty. . . . No right, however, save a mere possessory one, is by the provisions of the treaty of Hopewell conceded to your nation. The soil, and the use of it, were suffered to remain with you, while the Sovereignty abided precisely where it did before, in those states within whose limits you were situated.

Secretary of War John H. Easton, addressing the Cherokees in April 1829.

That the aboriginal population should decrease under the operation of these causes, can excite no surprise. From an early period, their rapid declension and ultimate extinction were foreseen and lamented, and various plans for their preservation and improvement were projected and pursued. Many of them were carefully taught at our seminaries of education, in the hope that principles of morality and habits of industry would be acquired, and that they might stimulate their countrymen by precept and example to a better course of life. Missionary stations were established among various tribes, where zealous and pious men devoted themselves with generous ardor to the task of instruction, as well in agriculture and the mechanic arts, as in the principles of morality and religion. The Roman Catholic Church preceded the Protestant, in this labor of charity; and the *Lettres Edifiantes* are monuments of her zeal and liberality. Unfortunately, they are monuments also of unsuccessful and unproductive efforts. What tribe has been civilized by all this expenditure of treasure, and labor, and care? From the martyrdom of Le Père Brebeuf, in 1649, upon the shore of Lake Huron, to the death of the last missionary, who sacrificed himself in a cause as holy as it has proved hopeless, what permanent effect has been produced? Year after year sanguine anticipations have been formed, to be succeeded by disappointment and despondency. We are flattered with accounts of success, with explanations for the past and hopes for the future; and this, without the slightest intention to deceive. But the subject itself is calculated to excite these expectations. There are always individuals attending these establishments, who give fair promise of permanent improvement and usefulness. And as these prospects are blighted, others succeed to excite the same hopes, and to end in the same disappointment. . . .

Spanish Influences

There seems to be some insurmountable obstacle in the habits or temperament of the Indians, which has heretofore prevented, and yet prevents, the success of these labors. Whatever this may be, it appears to be confined to the tribes occupying this part of the continent. In Mexico and South America, a large portion of the aboriginal race has accommodated itself to new circumstances, and forms a constituent part of the same society with their conquerors. Under the Spanish *régime* they existed as a degraded cast; but still they were sedentary, living under the protection of the laws, and providing by labor for their comfortable subsistence.

In other parts of the continent, particularly in California and Paraguay, where the Spanish sway had but a nominal existence, the Jesuits succeeded in collecting the Indians into regular societies, in improving their morals and condition, and in controlling and directing their conduct. In the usual progress of conquest, where permanent possession is retained, the victors and vanquished become connected together, and if they do not form one people, they yet acknowledge obedience to the same laws, and look to them for protection. But from the St Lawrence to the gulph of Mexico, under the French, or British, or Spanish, or American rule, where is the tribe of Indians, who have changed their manners, who have become incorporated with their conquerors, or who have exhibited any just estimate of the improvements around them, or any wish to participate in them?. . .

The relative condition of the two races of men, who yet divide this portion of the continent between them, is a moral problem involved in much obscurity. The physical causes we have described, exasperated by the moral evils introduced by them, are sufficient to account for the diminution and deterioration of the

185

Indians. But why were not these causes counteracted by the operation of other circumstances? As civilization shed her light upon them, why were they blind to its beams? Hungry or naked, why did they disregard, or regarding, why did they neglect, those arts by which food and clothing could be procured? Existing for two centuries in contact with a civilized people, they have resisted, and successfully too, every effort to meliorate their situation, or to introduce among them the most common arts of life. Their moral and their intellectual condition have been equally stationary. And in the whole circle of their existence, it would be difficult to point to a single advantage which they have derived from their acquaintance with the Europeans. All this is without a parallel in the history of the world. That it is not to be attributed to the indifference or neglect of the whites, we have already shown. There must then be an inherent difficulty, arising from the institutions, character, and condition of the Indians themselves.

Indians Free to Govern Themselves

There [in the West] they may be secured in the enjoyment of governments of their own choice, subject to no other control from the United States than such as may be necessary to preserve peace on the frontier and between the several tribes. There the benevolent may endeavor to teach them, to raise up an interesting commonwealth, destined to perpetuate the race and to attest the humanity and justice of this Government.

Andrew Jackson, quoted in F.P. Prucha, *The Great Father*, 1984.

On this subject the world has had enough of romantic description. It is time for the soberness of truth and reality. Rousseau and the disciples of his school, with distempered imaginations and unsettled reason, may persuade themselves of the inferiority of civilized to savage life; but he who looks abroad over the forests of our country, and upon the hapless beings who roam through them, will see how much they endure, that we are spared. It is difficult to conceive that any branch of the human family can be less provident in arrangement, less frugal in enjoyment, less industrious in acquiring, more implacable in their resentments, more ungovernable in their passions, with fewer principles to guide them, with fewer obligations to restrain them, and with less knowledge to improve and instruct them. We speak of them as they are; as we have found them after a long and intimate acquaintance; fully appreciating our duties and their rights, all that they have suffered and lost, and all that we have enjoyed and acquired.

It is not our intention to undertake a delineation of the Indian character. We shall content ourselves with sketching such features as may serve to explain the difficulty which has been experienced in extending to them the benefit of our institutions, and in teaching them to appreciate their value.

Every Indian submits in youth to a process of severe mental and corporeal discipline. During its course, frequent intervals of long and rigid abstinence are enjoined, by which the system is reduced, and the imagination rendered more susceptible. Dreams are encouraged, and by these the novice is taught both his duty and his destiny, and in them his guardian *manitou*, who is to protect him in life and attend him in death, appears in the shape of some familiar animal, thenceforth to be the object of his adoration. He is taught to despise death, and during his whole life he regards it with indifference. An Indian seldom commits suicide, not because the grave does not offer him a refuge, but because patience and fortitude are the first duties of a warrior, and none but a coward can yield to pain or misfortune. This sternness of purpose is another lesson early taught.

A Stern, Unbending Fatalist

He learns also to despise labor, to become a warrior and a hunter, to associate the idea of disgrace with any other employment, and to leave to the women all the ordinary duties of life. He is a stern and unbending fatalist. Whatever of good or of evil may happen, he receives it with imperturbable calmness. If misfortunes press upon him, which he cannot resist, he can die; and he dies without a murmur. The opinions, traditions, and institutions of his own tribe, are endeared to him by habit, feeling, and authority; and from early infancy he is taught, that the Great Spirit will be offended by any change in the customs of his red children, which have all been established by him. Reckless of consequences, he is the child of impulse. Unrestrained by moral considerations, whatever his passions prompt he does. Believing all the wild and debasing superstitions which have come down to him, he has no practical views of a moral superintendence to protect or to punish him. Government is unknown among them; certainly, that government which prescribes general rules and enforces or vindicates them. The utter nakedness of their society can be known only by a personal observation. The tribes seem to be held together by a kind of family ligament; by the ties of blood, which in the infancy of society are stronger as other associations are weaker. They have no criminal code, no courts, no officers, no punishments. They have no relative duties to enforce, no debts to collect, no property to restore. They are in a state of nature, as much so as it is possible for any people to be. Injuries are redressed by revenge, and strength is the security for right. . . .

No Wish to Improve

It is easy, in contemplating the situation of such a people, to perceive the difficulties to be encountered in any effort to produce a radical change in their condition. The *fulcrum* is wanting, upon which the lever must be placed. They are contented as they are; not contented merely, but clinging with a death-grasp to their own institutions. This feeling, inculcated in youth, strengthened in manhood, and nourished in age, renders them inaccessible to argument or remonstrance. To roam the forests at will, to pursue their game, to attack their enemies, to spend the rest of their lives in listless indolence, to eat inordinately when they have food, to suffer patiently when they have none, and to be ready at all times to die; these are the principal occupations of an Indian. But little knowledge of human nature is necessary, to be sensible how unwilling a savage would be to exchange such a life for the stationary and laborious duties of civilized society. . . .

Equally fruitless and hopeless are the attempts to impart to them, in their present situation, the blessings of religion, the benefits of science and the arts, and the advantages of an efficient and stable government. The time seems to have arrived, when a change in our principles and practice is necessary; when some new effort must be made to meliorate the condition of the Indians, if we would not be left without a living monument of their misfortunes, or a living evidence of our desire to repair them. . . .

Our system of intercourse has resulted from our superiority in physical and moral power. 'The peculiar character and habits of the Indian nations, rendered them incapable of sustaining any other relation with the whites, than that of dependence and pupilage. There was no other way of dealing with them, than that of keeping them separate, subordinate, and dependent, with a guardian care thrown around them for their protection.' All this, and much more than this, is incontrovertible. They would not, or rather they could not, coalesce with the strangers who had come among them. There was no point of union between them. They were as wild, and fierce, and irreclaimable, as the animals, their co-tenants of the forests, who furnished them with food and clothing. What had they in common with the white man? Not his attachment to sedentary life; not his desire of accumulation; not his submission to law; not his moral principles, his intellectual acquirements, his religious opinions. Neither precept nor example, neither hopes nor fears, could induce them to examine, much less to adopt their improvements. The past and the future being alike disregarded, the present only employs their thoughts. They could not, therefore, become an integral part of the people who began to press upon them, as time and circumstances have elsewhere generally united the conquerors and the conquered, but still remained in juxtaposition, and in such circumstances as rendered inevitable a continued intercourse between them and their civilized neighbors. The result of all this was necessarily to compel the latter to prescribe, from time to time, the principles which should regulate the intercourse between the parties; keeping in view the great objects to be attained for their mutual benefit,— that the propensity of the Indians for war should be checked, and themselves restrained within reasonable limits; that they should be protected in all their just rights, and secured from their own improvidence, as well as from the avarice of the whites; and that the territory should be occupied for permanent improvement, whenever it was necessary for the one party, and could be spared without injury by the other. . . .

If we are asked to reconcile these apparent inconsistencies, with what may be termed the natural rights of the parties, or with the consequences which may be logically deduced from the premises, the answer is obvious. Such a reconcilement is unnecessary. The Indians themselves are an anomaly upon the face of the earth. . . .

Providence has placed them in contact with us, and with habits and feelings, which render their incorporation into our society impracticable. The sight of the war-flag, or the sound of the war-drum, operates instantly and intensely upon the warriors, and coinciding with their institutions and opinions, irresistibly impels them to war. . . .

The President offers them a country beyond the Mississippi, to be guarantied to them by the United States, where there can be no interfering claim, and which they can possess 'as long as the grass grows or the water runs.' He also promises 'to protect them, to feed them, to shield them from all encroachment.'

VIEWPOINT 6

*"[The Indian] problem resolves itself down to . . .
adopt some humane and practicable method of improving the condition of the Indians, and in the end
make them part and parcel of our great population."*

Whites and Indians Must Learn to Live Side by Side

Nelson A. Miles

When Chief Joseph of the Nez Percé and his people were fleeing for Canada, it was troops from Fort Keough under the command of Nelson A. Miles that intercepted them. After the Nez
Percé surrendered on October 5, 1877, General Miles promised
them that they could return to live peaceably on the reservation
in Idaho; this promise was overruled by General Sherman. In
some ways this disagreement reflected the dichotomy of opinion
among professional army officers. Robert Utley has noted, "Am-
bivalence . . . marked the military attitudes toward the
Indians—fear, distrust, loathing, contempt, and condescension,
on the one hand; admiration, sympathy, and even friendship on
the other." The following viewpoint, excerpted from the *North
American Review*, in 1879, reflects Miles's sympathies but also
demonstrates his pragmatism.

As you read, consider the following questions:

1. How would Miles respond to criticism of the policy of putting
   Indians, whom the army has been fighting, under control of the
   War Department? Some people felt this was a sure guarantee of
   the extermination of the Indians. How does Miles try to defuse
   this fear?

2. From what Miles says, would he agree with the statement, "The only good Indian is a dead Indian"?

3. Why, according to Miles, has Canada's treatment of its Indian population been more successful than that of the United States?

Strange as it may appear, it is nevertheless a fact that, after nearly four hundred years of conflict between the European and American races for supremacy on this continent, a conflict in which war and peace have alternated almost as frequently as the seasons, we still have presented the question, What shall be done with the Indians? If the graves of the thousands of victims who have fallen in the terrible wars of race had been placed in line, the philanthropist might travel from the Atlantic to the Pacific, and from the Lakes to the Gulf, and be constantly within sight of green mounds. And yet we marvel at the problem as if some new question of politics or morals had been presented. Indeed, wise men differ in opinion, journalists speculate, divines preach, and statesmen pronounce it still a vexed question.

The most amusing part of the quandary, however, is that it should be regarded as something new and original. After every generation has contended on deadly fields with the hope of settling the question, the home governments enacted laws, the colonies framed rules, every Administration of our Government forced to meet the difficulty, and every Congress discussed the "Indian Question," we are still brought face to face with the perplexing problem.

The real issue in the question which is now before the American people is, whether we shall continue the vacillating and expensive policy that has marred our fair name as a nation and a Christian people, or devise some practical and judicious system by which we can govern one quarter of a million of our population, securing and maintaining their loyalty, raising them from the darkness of barbarism to the light of civilization, and put an end to these interminable and expensive Indian wars.

The supposition that we are near the end of our Indian troubles is erroneous, and the fact that a condition of affairs now exists over an enormous area of our country, in which an American citizen can not travel, unguarded and unarmed, without the danger of being molested, is, to say the least, preposterous and unsatisfactory.

If, by a dispassionate and impartial discussion of the subject, some measure may be devised that will eradicate the evil, and lead to the adoption of a permanent improvement in the management of our Indian matters, one object of this paper will have been accomplished.

In considering the subject, it might be well to first examine the causes which have produced the present condition of affairs, and, in doing so, if the writer shall allude to some of the sins of his own race, it will only be in order that an unbiased judgment may be formed of both sides of the question.

Indian Wars Are Over

I now regard the Indians as substantially eliminated from the problem of the Army. There may be spasmodic and temporary alarms, but such Indian wars as have hitherto disturbed the public peace and tranquillity are not probable. The Army has been a large factor in producing this result, but it is not the only one. Immigration and the occupation by industrious farmers and miners of land vacated by the aborigines have been largely instrumental to that end, but the *railroad* which used to follow in the rear now goes forward with the picket-line in the great battle for civilization with barbarism, and has become the *greater* cause.

Gen. William T. Sherman, final report, October 27, 1883.

It will be remembered that one class or race is without representation, and has not the advantages of the press or the telegraph to bring it into communication with the intelligence of the world, and is seldom heard except in the cry of alarm and conflict along the Western frontier. If we dismiss from our minds the prejudice we have against the Indian, we shall be enabled to more clearly understand the impulses that govern both races. Sitting Bull, the great war chief of the Dakota nation, uttered one truth when he said that "there was not one white man who loved an Indian, and not a true Indian but who hated a white man."

The Indian's True Character

Could we but perceive the true character of the Indians, and learn their dispositions, not covered by the cloak of necessity, policy, and interest, we should find that they regard us as a body of false and cruel invaders of their country, while we are too apt to consider them as a treacherous and bloodthirsty race, that should be destroyed by any and all means, yet, if we consider the cause of this feeling, we might more readily understand the result.

The more we study the Indian's character, the more we appreciate the marked distinction between the civilized being and the real savage, yet we shall find that the latter is governed by the same impulses and motives that govern all other men. The want of confidence and the bitter hatred now existing between the two races have been engendered by the warfare that has lasted for centuries, and by the stories of bad faith, cruelty, and wrong, handed down by tradition from father to son until they have become second nature in both. It is unfair to suppose that one party has invariably acted rightly, and that the other is responsible for every wrong that has been committed. We might recount the treachery of the red-man, the atrocity of his crimes, the cruelties of his tortures, and the hideousness of many of his savage customs; we might undertake to estimate the number of his victims, and to picture the numberless valleys which he has illumined by the burning homes of hardy frontiersmen, yet at the same time the other side of the picture might appear equally as black with injustice.

A History of Injustice

One hundred years before the pilgrims landed at Plymouth, the Spanish Government issued a decree authorizing the enslavement of American Indians, as in accord with the law of God and man. Later they were transported to France, to San Domingo and other Spanish colonies, sold into slavery in Massachusetts, Rhode Island, Pennsylvania, Virginia, the Carolinas, Georgia, and Louisiana, and hunted with dogs in Connecticut and Florida. Practically disfranchised by our original Constitution, and deprived either by war or treaty of nearly every tract of land which to them was desirable, and to the white man valuable, they were the prey to the grasping avarice of both Jew and Gentile. Step by step a powerful and enterprising race has driven them back from the Atlantic to the far West, until now there is scarcely a spot of ground upon which the Indians have any certainty of maintaining a permanent abode.

It may be well in this connection to remember the fact that in the main the Europeans were kindly treated by the natives, when the former first landed on American shores, and when they came to make a permanent settlement were supplied with food, particularly the Plymouth and Portsmouth colonists, which enabled them to endure the severity of long and cheerless winters. For a time during the early settlement of this country, peace and good will prevailed, but only to be followed by violent and relentless warfare.

Our relations with the Indians have been governed chiefly by treaties and trade, or war and subjugation. By the first we have invariably overreached the natives, and we find the record of broken promises all the way from the Atlantic to the Pacific, while many of the fortunes of New York, Chicago, St. Louis, and San Francisco can be traced directly to Indian tradership. By war the natives have been steadily driven toward the setting sun—a subjugated, a doomed race. In council the Indians have produced men of character and intellect, and orators and diplomats of decided ability, while in war they have displayed courage and sagacity of a high order. Education, science, and the resources of the world have enabled us to overcome the savages, and they are now at the mercy of their conquerors. In our treaty relations most extravagant and sacred promises have been given by the highest authorities, and yet these have frequently been disregarded. The intrusions of the white race (occurring now more frequently than ever before), the non-compliance with treaty obligations, have been followed by atrocities that could alone satisfy a savage and revengeful spirit. We need not dwell upon the original causes that have led to the present condition of affairs. Facts that have been herein referred to make it almost impossible for the two conflicting elements to harmonize. No Administration could stop the tidal wave of immigration that is sweeping over our land; no political party could restrain or control the enterprise of our people, and no man could desire to check the march of civilization. Our progress knew no bounds. The thirst for gold and the restless desire to push beyond the horizon have carried our people over every obstacle. We have reclaimed the wilderness and made the barren desert glisten with golden harvest; settlements now cover the hunting-ground of the savages; their country has been cut and divided in every conceivable form by the innumerable railroad and telegraph lines and routes of communication and commerce; and the Indians standing in the pathway of American progress and the development of the wonderful resources of this country have become the common enemy and have been driven to the remote quarters of our territory.

During the time that this wonderful change has been wrought, it may be asked, Have the Indians as a body made any progress toward civilization? and in the light of past history we would be prompted to reply, Why should they have abandoned the modes of life which Nature had given them to adopt the customs of their enemies?

In seeking to find the evidence of enlightenment, the results are not satisfactory. It is presumed that there is not a race of wild men on the face of the globe who worship the Great Spirit more in accordance with that religion taught in the days of the patriarchs than the natives of this country, and yet after many years of contact with the civilized people we find the footprints of evil as plentiful and as common as the evidences of Christianity. Again, in early days the Indian tribes were to a considerable extent tillers of the soil, but by constant warfare, in which their fields were devastated and their crops destroyed, they have become entirely subjugated, the mere remnant of their former strength, or pushed out on the vast plains of the West where they subsist upon wild fruits and the flesh of animals. Could we obtain accurate statistics, we would undoubtedly find that there were more acres of ground cultivated by the Indians one hundred years ago than at the present time. The white race has now obtained such complete control of every quarter of the country and the means of communication with every section are now so ample that the problem resolves itself down to one of two modes of solution, viz., to entirely destroy the race by banishment and extermination, or to adopt some humane and practicable method of improving the condition of the Indians, and in the end make them part and parcel of our great population. The first proposition, though it may be found to have thousands of advocates in different sections of the country, is too abhorrent to every sense of humanity to be considered. The other method is regarded as practicable, but its adoption is considered doubtful.

Government Indian Policy

Looking at the purposes of our Government toward the Indians, we find that after subjugating them it has been our policy to collect the different tribes on reservations and support them at the expense of our people. The Indians have in the main abandoned the hope of driving back the invaders of their territory, yet there are some who still cherish the thought, and strange as it may seem it is a fact that the most noted leader among the Indians advanced such a proposition to the writer within the last two years. They now stand in the position of unruly children to indulgent parents, for whom they have very little respect, at times wrongly indulged and again unmercifully punished.

Coming down to our direct or immediate relations with them we find that our policy has been to make them wards of the nation, to be held under close military surveillance, or else to make them pensioners under no other restraint than the influence of one or two individuals. Living without any legitimate government, without any law and without any physical power to control them, what better subjects or more propitious fields could be found for vice and crime?

We have committed our Indian matters to the custody of an Indian Bureau, which for many years was a part of the military establishment of the Government; but, for political reasons and to promote party interests, this Bureau was transferred to the Department of the Interior.

Whether or not our system of Indian management has been a success during the past ten, fifty, or one hundred years, is almost answered in the asking. The Indians, the frontiersmen, the army stationed in the West, and the readers of the daily news in all

195

Guiding the Indians

Nothing is more indispensable than the protecting and guiding care of the Government during the dangerous period of transition from savage to civilized life. . . . [The Indian] is overcome by a feeling of helplessness, and he naturally looks to the "GREAT FATHER" to take him by the hand and guide him on. That guiding hand must necessarily be one of authority and power to command confidence and respect. It can be only that of the government which the Indian is accustomed to regard as a sort of omnipotence on earth. Everything depends upon the wisdom and justice of that guidance.

Secretary of the Interior Carl Schurz, *North American Review*, 1881.

parts of our country, can answer that question. Another question is frequently asked, Why is our management of Indian affairs less successful than that of our neighbors across the northern boundary? and it can be answered in a few words. Their system is permanent, decided, and just. The tide of immigration in Canada has not been as great as along our frontier; they allow the Indians to live as Indians, and do not attempt to force upon the natives the customs which to them are distasteful. In our own management it is the opinion of a very large number of our people that a change for the better would be desirable; such a measure is now under consideration, and we have the singular and remarkable phenomenon presented of the traders, the contractors, the interested officials of the West, and many of the best people of the East, advocating one scheme, while a great majority of frontier settlers, the officers of the army of long experience on the Plains, and many competent judges in the East, advocating another. The question is one of too grave importance to admit interests of a personal or partisan nature. It is one of credit or discredit to our Government, and of vital importance to our people. . . . The object is surely worthy of the effort. No body of people whose language, religion, and customs are so entirely different from ours can be expected to cheerfully and suddenly adopt our own. The change must be gradual, continuous, and in accordance with Nature's laws. The history of nearly every race that has advanced from barbarism to civilization has been through the stages of the hunter, the herdsman, the agriculturist, and finally reaching those of commerce, mechanics, and the higher arts.

It is held, first, that we as a generous people and liberal Government are bound to give to the Indians the same rights that all other men enjoy, and if we deprive them of these privileges we must then give them the best government possible. Without any legitimate government, and in a section of country where the lawless are under very little restraint, it is useless to suppose that thousands of wild savages thoroughly armed and mounted can be controlled by moral suasion. Even if they were in the midst of comfortable and agreeable surroundings, yet when dissatisfaction is increased by partial imprisonment and quickened by the pangs of hunger, a feeling that is not realized by one man in a thousand in civilized life, it requires more patience and forbearance than savage natures are likely to possess to prevent serious outbreaks.

The experiment of making a police force composed entirely of Indians is a dangerous one, unless they are under the shadow and control of a superior body of white troops, and, if carried to any great extent, will result in rearming the Indians and work disastrously to the frontier settlements. There would be a slight incongruity in a government out on the remote frontier, composed of a strictly non-combatant for chief, with a *posse comitatus* of red warriors, undertaking to control several thousand wild savages!

The available land that can be given to the Indians is being rapidly diminished; they can not be moved farther West; and some political party or administration must take the responsibility of protecting the Indians in their rights of person and property.

A New Proposal

The advantage of placing the Indians under some government strong enough to control them and just enough to command their respect is too apparent to admit of argument. The results to be obtained would be:

First. They would be beyond the possibility of doing harm, and the frontier settlements would be freed from their terrifying and devastating presence.

Second. They would be under officials having a knowledge of the Indian country and the Indian character.

Third. Their supplies and annuities would be disbursed through an efficient system of regulations.

Fourth. Besides being amenable to the civil laws, these officers would be under strict military law, subject to trial and punishment for any act that would be "unbecoming a gentleman, or prejudicial to good order."

It is therefore suggested and earnestly recommended that a system which has proved to be eminently practicable should receive at least a fair trial. As the Government has in its employ men who by long and faithful service have established reputations for integrity, character, and ability which can not be disputed—men who have commanded armies, reconstructed States, controlled hundreds of millions of public property, and who during years of experience on the frontier have opened the way for civilization and Christianity—it is believed that the services of these officials, in efforts to prevent war and elevate the Indian race, would be quite as judicious as their employment when inexperience and mismanagement have culminated in hostilities. Allowing the civilized and semi-civilized Indians to remain under the same supervision as at present, the President of the United States should have power to place the wild and nomadic tribes under the control of the War Department. Officers of known character, integrity, and experience, who would govern them and be interested in improving their condition, should be placed in charge of the different tribes. One difficulty has been, that they have been managed by officials too far away, and who knew nothing of the men they were dealing with. The Indians, as far as possible, should be localized on the public domain, in sections of country to which they are by nature adapted.

The forcing of strong, hardy, mountain Indians from the extreme North to the warmer malarial districts of the South is regarded as cruel, and should be discontinued.

Every effort should be made to locate the Indians by families, for the ties of relationship among them are much stronger than is generally supposed. By this means the Indians will become independent of their tribal relations, and will not be found congregated in large and unsightly camps, as are now usually met with about their agencies.

Much of the army transportation now used in scouting for Indians and clearing the country could be utilized in transporting their stores, breaking the ground, and preparing the way for making the Indians self-supporting.

Goals

All supplies, annuities, and disbursements of money should be made under the same system of accountability as now regulates army disbursements. The officers in charge should have sufficient force to preserve order, patrol the reservations, prevent intrusions, recover stolen property, arrest the lawless and those who take refuge in Indian camps to shield themselves from punishment for crimes or to enable them to live without labor, and to keep the Indians upon their reservations and within the limits of their treaties. The officer in charge would be enabled to control or prevent the sale of ammunition, as well as to suppress the sale of intoxicating liquors among the Indians. Many thousands of the Indian ponies, useful only for the war or the chase, should be sold and the proceeds used in the purchase of domestic stock. A large percentage of the annual appropriations should be employed in the purchase of cattle and other domestic animals; the Indians desire them, and the Plains will support hundreds of thousands of them. They will replace the buffalo, the elk, the deer, and the antelope. These cattle and other animals should be branded and given to the Indians by families; the surplus stock to be sold after three years under such restricted rules as would enable the Indians to receive full return for their property. From a pastoral people the Indians should be induced to become agriculturists; taught the seasons to plant and to harvest the variety of valuable products and the use of machinery as a means of obtaining food. The step from the first grade to the second would be easily accomplished provided the Indians were directed by a firm hand. As they accumulate property and learn industry, there would be a threefold incentive to their remaining at peace, namely, occupation, the fear of confiscation of property, and the loss of the comforts of life.

The above is no idle theory, as the writer has advocated such a policy for years, and by actual and successful experience has demonstrated that such was practicable even with the wildest tribes of the Plains, a part of whom, eighteen months before, had never shaken hands with a white man.

Courts Are Needed

Two more important measures of improvements are also needed, and should be authorized by Congress.

In all communities there will be found disturbing elements, and, to meet this difficulty, courts of justice should be instituted. Frequently outbreaks and depredations are prompted by a few mischievous characters, which could easily be checked by a proper government. This is one secret of success with the Canadian system: where disturbances occur, the guilty suffer, and not whole tribes, including innocent women and children.

As a remark from Sitting Bull has been quoted, we will now repeat the words of Joseph, who says that "the greatest want of the Indian is a system of law by which controversies between Indians, and between Indians and white men, can be settled without appealing to physical force." He says also that "the want of law is the great source of disorder among Indians. They understand the operation of laws, and, if there were any statutes, the Indians would be perfectly content to place themselves in the hands of a proper tribunal, and would not take the righting of their wrongs into their own hands, or retaliate, as they now do, without the law."

Do we need a savage to inform us of the necessity that has existed for a century? As these people become a part of our population, they should have some tribunal where they could obtain protection in their rights of person and property. . . .

The warriors may be made to care for their flocks and herds, and the industry of the Indians that is now wasted may be diverted to peaceful and useful pursuits; yet the great work of reformation must be mainly through the youth of the different tribes. The hope of every race is in the rising generation. . . . As we are under obligation to support the tribes until they become self-sustaining, it might be advisable to support as many as possible of the children of the Indians at places where they would be the least expensive to the Government, and where they would be under the best influence. As the Government has expended hundreds of thousands of dollars in building military posts that are no longer occupied or required, and as there are at these places excellent buildings and large reservations, it would be well to utilize them for educational and industrial purposes. . . . Many of the youth, . . . particularly the sons of chiefs, . . . could soon be taught the English language, habits of industry, the benefits of civilization, the power of the white race, and, after a few years, return to their people with some education, with more intelligence, and with their ideas of life entirely changed for the better. They would in turn become the educators of their own people, and their influence for good could not be estimated, while the expense of educating them would be less than at present, and thousands would be benefited thereby. The Indians, as they become civilized and educated, as they acquire property and pay taxes toward the support of the Government, should have the same rights of citizenship as all other men enjoy. . . .

A continuation of the system which has prevailed for the past twenty years will, it is believed, simply perpetuate . . . a chronic state of insecurity and hostilities. The question may as well be met and decided. A race of savages can not by any human ingenuity be civilized and Christianized within a few years of time, neither will 250,000 people with their descendants be destroyed in the next fifty years. The white man and the Indian should be taught to live side by side, each respecting the rights of the other, and both living under wholesome laws, enforced with ample authority and exact justice. Such a government would be most gratifying and beneficial to the Indians, while those men who have invested their capital, and with wonderful enterprise are developing the unparalleled and inexhaustible wealth that for ages has lain dormant in the Western mountains, those people who have left the overcrowded centers of the East, and whose humble homes are now dotting the plains and valleys of the far West, as well as those men who are annually called upon to endure greater exposure and suffering than is required by the troops of any other nation on the globe, would hail with great satisfaction any system that would secure a substantial and lasting peace.

CHAPTER 5

Learning from Each Other

Chapter Preface

Frederick Jackson Turner presented his essay "The Significance of the Frontier in American History" at the Chicago World's Fair in 1893. In it he explored the influence of the frontier on the formation of the American character:

> The frontier is the line of most rapid and effective Americanization. The wilderness masters the colonist. It finds him a European in dress, industries, tools, modes of travel, and thought. It takes him from the railroad car and puts him in the birch canoe. It strips off the garments of civilization and arrays him in the hunting shirt and the moccasin. It puts him in the log cabin of the Cherokee and Iroquois and runs an Indian palisade around him. Before long he has gone to planting Indian corn and plowing with a sharp stick; he shouts the war cry and takes the scalp in orthodox Indian fashion. In short, at the frontier the environment is at first too strong for the man. He must accept the conditions which it furnishes, or perish, and so he fits himself into the Indian clearings and follows the Indian trails. Little by little he transforms the wilderness, but the outcome is not the old Europe. . . . The fact is that here is a new product that is American. At first the frontier was the Atlantic coast. It was the frontier of Europe in a very real sense. Moving westward, the frontier became more and more American. As successive terminal moraines result from successive glaciations, so each frontier leaves its traces behind it, and when it becomes a settled area the region still partakes of the frontier characteristics. Thus the advance of the frontier has meant a steady movement away from the influence of Europe, a steady growth of independence on American lines.

In short, at successive stages of the frontier, the settler became acculturated to his new environment by adopting native ways. In his contact with the American land and the American Indians, he adopted new patterns of thought and behavior.

Whenever two cultures meet, almost always *both* are changed. This is indeed what happened, especially in North America, as Europeans and Indians lived in proximity. In many instances, acculturation occurred quite informally as one people observed and imitated the other. Such changes generally occurred when neither felt superior to the other or when there were pragmatic benefits to be gained by the change. In other instances, acculturation was the result of specific plans of one people to change the other. Such a pattern was early established by the English in New England.

As James Axtell, author of *The European and the Indian*, observes:

To many early settlers, primitive New England was a living hell ignited by its barbarous inhabitants. The Indians threatened to push them into the sea, and nearly succeeded on several occasions, but the threat of physical annihilation was never so alarming to English sensibilities—perhaps because they were blinded to the possibility by their supreme righteousness—as the Indian himself. To the English he stood proudly and defiantly against all that they stood for, all that was good and Christian and civilized. The Indian, in their lights, was immoral, pagan, and barbarous. So, characteristically, they tried to remake him in their own image through the time-honored but formal institutions of English education—the church, the school, and the college. Needless to say, they failed miserably.

But try it they did. In this chapter alone we see acculturation efforts by the Moravian church, the United States government, and an off-reservation boarding school. All of these illustrate a century and a half of formal efforts by whites to change Indian behavior.

Exchanges Along the Frontier

Along the frontier, *both* cultures learned from the other by choice or by necessity. Indians taught the English rudimentary survival skills: how to plant corn and nurture it, where to catch fish, and how, generally, to survive in what at first had seemed a harsh and alien environment. In the process, much basic vocabulary was exchanged. The settlers introduced chicks, cows, and pigs, while the Indians brought succotash, wampum, pemmican, and moccasin.

Some, like the missionaries, realized that they had to acquire a far more abstract vocabulary if they were to effectively preach to the Indians. Thus, to make the Indians more English, more civilized, the most effective missionaries learned the language and customs of their future converts. While Cotton Mather might on occasion revile the Indians as "Lazy Drones," "most impudent Lyars," and "Ravenous howling Wolves," John Heckewelder went among them believing that

> the sure way to obtain correct ideas, and a true knowledge of the characters, customs, manners &c. of the Indians, and to learn their history, is to dwell among them for some time, and having acquired their language, the information wished for will be obtained in the common way; that is, by paying attention to their discourses with each other on different subjects, and occasionally asking them questions; always watching for the proper opportunity, when they do not suspect your motives, and are disposed to be free and open with you.

Heckewelder understood that the best way to change another's behavior was to meet him where he was. To do so, one must understand, rather than revile, the other's culture.

Military Exchanges

Even when relations were less than amicable between the settlers and the Indians, each learned from the other. The Indians quickly recognized the advantage of European technology; the gun soon supplemented the bow and arrow. While Europeans were superior in technology, they had much to learn about tactics. James Axtell described the inferior methods of seventeenth-century English troops: "completely armed, with corselets, muskets, bandoleers, rests and swords . . . beat up the drum, flew their colors and marched in serried ranks into the nearest campaign field to 'bid them battle.'" While the martial display may have been impressive as ceremony, the Indians generally were the more effective fighters.

This is recognized by Col. Henry Bouquet, a Swiss professional soldier for the English. In 1763 he was ordered to bring supplies and reinforcements to the garrison at Fort Pitt in Pennsylvania. Remembering General Braddock's disastrous defeat, Bouquet elected to fight the Indians on their own terms and defeated them at Bushy Run. In so doing, he forced the Indians to lift the siege of Fort Pitt. Bouquet wrote of his Indian opponents:

> Like beasts of prey, they are patient, deceitful, and rendered by habit almost insensible to the common feelings of humanity. Their barbarous custom of scalping their enemies, in the heat of action; the exquisite tortures often inflicted by them on those reserved for a more deliberate fate; their general ferocity of manners, and the success wherewith they have often been flush'd, have conspired to render their name terrible, and some times to strike a panic even into our bravest and best disciplined troops. . . . They fight only when they think to have the advantage, but cannot be forced to it, being sure by their speed to elude the most eager pursuit. Their dress consists of the skins of some wild beast, or a blanket, a shirt either of linen, or of dressed skins, a breech clout, leggings, reaching half way up the thigh, and fastened with a belt, with mokawsons on their feet. They use no ligatures that might obstruct the circulation of their blood, or agility of their limbs. They shave their head, reserving only a small tuft of hair on the top; and slit the outer part of their ears. . . . When they prepare for an engagement they paint themselves black, and fight naked. Their arms are a fusil, or rifle, a powder horn, a shot pouch, a tomahawk, and a scalping knife hanging to their neck. . . . Thus lightly equipped do the savages lie in wait to attack, at some difficult pass, the European soldier, heavily accoutred, harassed by a tedious march, and encumbered with an unwieldy convoy. Experience has convinced us that it is not our interest to be at war with them; but if after having tried all means to avoid it, they force us to it . . . we should endeavor to fight them upon more equal terms, and regulate our Maneuvers upon those of the enemy we are to engage, and the nature of the country we are to act in. . . . They

seldom expose their persons to danger, and depend entirely upon their dexterity in concealing themselves during an engagement, never appearing openly, unless they have struck their enemies with terror, and have thereby rendered them incapable of defense. From whence it might be inferred that, if they were beat two or three times, they would lose that confidence inspired by success, and be less inclined to engage in wars which might end fatally for them. But this cannot reasonably be expected, till we have troops trained to fight them in their own way, with the additional advantage of European courage and discipline.

The Indians acquired European technology; the Europeans began to adopt Indian tactics. Militarily, a reciprocal acculturation took place.

Attitudes of Cultural Superiority

However, when it was not advantageous to adopt Indian practices, the settlers, generally seeing themselves superior to the "savages," sought to make the Indians over in the image of the whites. For the better part of five centuries, white educators and religious figures have tried to impart their values to the Indians. However, on the frontier, the Indian was culturally secure. There, *he* was the teacher. Some whites who wanted to escape the restraints of government and church chose to adopt the Indian lifestyle. They were often more receptive to the Indians' teaching than the Indians would ever be to the missionaries'. In fact, after recovering from their initial shock and fear, a surprising number of whites captured by the Indians chose to remain with their captors. In 1782 J. Hector St. John de Crèvecoeur wrote in *Letters from an American Farmer*:

> By what power does it come to pass, that children who have been adopted when young among these people, can never be prevailed upon to readopt European manners; for *thousands* of Europeans are Indians and we have no examples of even *one* of those Aborigines having from choice become Europeans!

Embarrassing as such "white Indians" must have been to those who wanted to proselytize, educate, and civilize the Indians, they do raise questions about the wisdom of assuming one's own culture to be superior. For, repeatedly on American frontiers, the process of acculturation was reciprocal. When Western civilization became dominant, the Indian, perceiving the strengths of his own culture, resisted.

VIEWPOINT 1

"Education is to be the medium through which the rising generation of Indians are to be brought into fraternal and harmonious relationship with their white fellow-citizens."

Indians Must Be Educated to Adopt Civilized Ways

T. J. Morgan

After serving as an officer during the Civil War and being ordained a Baptist minister, T.J. Morgan devoted his life to public education. He served as Commissioner of Indian Affairs from 1889-1893. He wanted to integrate all Indian schools—the common schools on the reservations, agency boarding schools, and national industrial schools like Carlisle—into one system comparable to the public school system of the states. "The Indian youth," he said, "should be instructed in their rights, privileges and duties as American citizens; should be taught to love the American flag; should be imbued with genuine patriotism and made to feel that the United States, and not some paltry reservation, is their home. . . . Education should seek the disintegration of the tribes, and not their segregation. They should be educated, not as Indians, but as Americans. In short, public schools should do for them what they are so successfully doing for all the other races in this country—assimilate them." The following viewpoint is taken from Morgan's report to the secretary of the interior on December 1, 1889.

As you read, consider the following questions:

1. What are the major goals of Indian education, according to Morgan?
2. What parts of the program seem geared specifically to cultural assimilation?
3. The proposal reflects the late nineteenth-century reform movements. What are the attitudes toward the Indians expressed here?

Editor's Note: The first part of this viewpoint was written by the commissioner of education, W.T. Harris, as an introduction to Morgan's report.

In presenting to the correspondents of this Bureau this reprint of a report of the Commissioner of Indian Affairs, I hope to furnish matter of a high degree of interest. It is my belief that the well-wishers for the Indian have reasons to rejoice at the prospect before them of a humane settlement of the long pending question. A century of ineffective effort to civilize the Indian, instead of discouraging the missionary spirit of our nation, has had the effect of continually increasing its fervor. It has become clear that earlier endeavors failed because they were not radical enough. In the early history of the colonies, it was believed that the ethnical difference between the white man and the Indian is a superficial one, one easily eradicated by a little book education, or by religious conversion unaided by other agencies. Modern studies in ethnology have made us acquainted with the depth to which the distinctions of civilization penetrate. We do not now expect to work the regeneration of a people except by changing the industrial habits, the manners and customs, the food and clothing, the social and family behavior, the view of the world, and the religious conviction systematically and co-ordinately.

The adoption of changes in industry and the fashion of clothing and drink does not signify very much without the adoption of enlightened views and religious convictions corresponding. On the other hand, the attempt to grasp new religious convictions, those of Christianity, without the simultaneous adoption of the minor habits is not likely to produce a full and permanent regeneration. It is understood that the habits of life, the social and industrial organization of society, offer a symbol of the deeper ideas formulated in the religion of the people. Even Christianity becomes quite a different religion when professed by lower races clinging to a social form of life not founded on productive industry. In a country whose social system is founded on caste it varies from the form of religion existing in a community with a democratic form of government and with a system of free productive industry.

On this account the new education for our American Indians as it has been founded in recent years by devoted men and women, undertakes to solve the problem of civilizing them by a radical system of education not merely in books, nor merely in religious ceremonies, but in matters of clothing, personal cleanliness, matters of dietary, and especially in habits of industry.

To work out this thorough system in all its details, it is found necessary, or at least desirable, to obtain control of the Indian at an early age, and to seclude him as much as possible from the tribal influence. The boarding-school has thus far been quite effectual in forming new habits and new wants and desires in the pupil. It has kindled in him aspirations which would permanently transform him if he lived in an environment of civilization. But it has been found that when the pupils return from their boarding schools to their native tribes on the borders that they often succumbed to the influences of the old environment. They are not strong enough to withstand the aggregate influence of old and young men and women who have retained the old forms and who look upon innovation as idle and useless, not to say sacrilegious.

It is evident that the only remedy for this defect is to be found in the course recommended by General Morgan in the report herewith presented. The Indian youth must be educated *en masse*. They must be educated in the thorough manner of the boarding-school, and they must all be educated, so that the environment of each individual shall be favorable to his persistence in the habits formed at school.

It is evident, moreover, that the protraction of the period of school education is a very important item, especially at the beginning of this experiment. One year or two years, or even three years of school education, is not so economical as five years or ten years of school training. Because the short period of school training will make little impression on the form of tribal life—it will not tend to change the patriarchal life to a form of a society founded on productive industry. And while the patriarchal or tribal form exists our own civilization must protect itself from the dangers which menace it from that lower form of civilization by supporting military forces or an armed police on the tribal frontiers. This looks towards a continual heavy expense, or, on the other hand, towards the cruel policy of extermination.

Again, as to the matter of economy, the recommendations of General Morgan to establish high school and college instruction are, in my opinion, quite wise. At first glance they seem to recommend an extravagant outlay of money, but I am persuaded that this extravagance is only seeming and not real. It will be found that very few Indian children will show a sufficient capacity to complete the primary course of instruction before the age of 16 or 17 years, and there will not remain sufficient time before mature life to take up secondary and higher instruction. This is the case, indeed, even with our children of European descent. Only four in one hundred take up secondary instruction, and only one in one hundred take up higher instruction.

It will be safe to use all influences to encourage Indian youth to enter high school and college courses. All who undertake this will fit themselves for directive power among their people at home, and will powerfully aid in civilizing their fellows. From the higher educated persons will naturally come the chieftains, and in general the men who make combinations and manage work that requires systematic co-ordination. Even if the chieftains are selected from men naturally gifted with directive power over their fellow-men, they will necessarily employ as counselors, as personal aids, as clerks, and business agents the educated among their followers. And these educated agents will create the forms of doing and acting, and thereby effectually furnish the directive power.

Brought before the bar of the awakened conscience of the great mass of the American people, there can be but one verdict possible regarding the system proposed by the Commissioner of Indian Affairs. We owe it to ourselves and to the enlightened public opinion of the world to save the Indian, and not destroy him. We can not save him and his patriarchal or tribal institution both together. To save him we must take him up into our form of civilization. We must approach him in the missionary spirit and we must supplement missionary action by the aid of the civil arm of the State. We must establish compulsory education for the good of the lower race. . . .

W.T. Harris, Commissioner of Education

Morgan's Report

When we speak of the education of the Indians, we mean that comprehensive system of training and instruction which will convert them into American citizens, put within their reach the blessings which the rest of us enjoy, and enable them to compete successfully with the white man on his own ground and with his own methods. Education is to be the medium through which the rising generation of Indians are to be brought into fraternal and harmonious relationship with their white fellow-citizens, and with them enjoy the sweets of refined homes, the delight of social intercourse, the emoluments of commerce and trade, the advantages of travel, together with the pleasures that come from literature, science, and philosophy, and the solace and stimulus afforded by a true religion.

That such a great revolution for these people is possible is becoming more and more evident to those who have watched with an intelligent interest the work which, notwithstanding all its hindrances and discouragements, has been accomplished for them during the last few years. It is no longer doubtful that, under a wise system of education, carefully administered, the condition of this whole people can be radically improved in a single generation.

Promotion of Indian Schools

The Indian must have a knowledge of the English language, that he may associate with his white neighbors and transact business as they do. He must have practical industrial training to fit him to compete with others in the struggle for life. He must have a Christian education to enable him to perform the duties of the family, the State, and the Church.

Lake Mohonk Conference, 1884.

Under the peculiar relations which the Indians sustain to the Government of the United States, the responsibility for their education rests primarily and almost wholly upon the nation. This grave responsibility, which has now been practically assumed by the Government, must be borne by it alone. It can not safely or honorably either shirk it or delegate it to any other party. The task is not by any means an herculean one. The entire Indian school population is less than that of Rhode Island. The Government of the United States, now one of the richest on the face of the earth, with an overflowing Treasury, has at its command unlimited means, and can undertake and complete this work without feeling it to be in any degree a burden. Although very imperfect in its details, and needing to be modified and improved in many particulars, the present system of schools is capable, under wise direction, of accomplishing all that can be desired.

In order that the Government shall be able to secure the best results in the education of the Indians, certain things are desirable, indeed, I might say necessary, viz:

First. Ample provision should be made at an early day for the accommodation of the entire mass of Indian school children and youth. To resist successfully and overcome the tremendous downward pressure of inherited prejudice and the stubborn conservatism of centuries, nothing less than universal education should be attempted.

Second. Whatever steps are necessary should be taken to place these children under proper educational influences. If, under any circumstances, compulsory education is justifiable, it certainly is in this case. Education, in the broad sense in which it is here used, is the Indian's only salvation. With it they will become honorable, useful, happy citizens of a great republic, sharing on equal terms in all its blessings. Without it they are doomed either to destruction or to hopeless degradation.

Third. The work of Indian education should be completely systematized. The camp schools, agency boarding-schools, and the great industrial schools should be related to each other so as to form a connected and complete whole. So far as possible there should be a uniform course of study, similar methods of instruction, the same textbooks, and a carefully organized and well-understood system of industrial training.

Fourth. The system should be conformed, so far as practicable, to the commonschool system now universally adopted in all the States. It should be non-partisan, non-sectarian. The teachers and employés should be appointed only after the most rigid scrutiny into their qualifications for their work. They should have a stable tenure of office, being removed only for cause. They should receive for their service wages corresponding to those paid for similar service in the public schools. They should be carefully inspected and supervised by a sufficient number of properly qualified superintendents.

Fifth. While, for the present, special stress should be laid upon that kind of industrial training which will fit the Indians to earn an honest living in the various occupations which may be open to them, ample provision should also be made for that general literary culture which the experience of the white race has shown to be the very essence of education. Especial attention should be directed toward giving them a ready command of the English language. To this end, only English should be allowed to be spoken, and only English-speaking teachers should be employed in schools supported wholly or in part by the Government.

Sixth. The scheme should make ample provision for the higher education of the few who are endowed with special capacity or ambition, and are destined to leadership. There is an imperative necessity for this, if the Indians are to be assimilated into the national life.

Seventh. That which is fundamental in all this is the recognition of the complete manhood of the Indians, their individuality, their right to be recognized as citizens of the United States, with the same rights and privileges which we accord to any other class of people. They should be free to make for themselves homes wherever they will. The reservation system is an anachronism which has no place in our modern civilization. The Indian youth should be instructed in their rights, privileges, and duties as American citizens; should be taught to love the American flag; should be imbued with a genuine patriotism, and made to feel that the United States, and not some paltry reservation, is their home. Those charged with their education should constantly strive to awaken in them a sense of independence, self-reliance, and self-respect.

Eighth. Those educated in the large industrial boarding-schools should not be returned to the camps against their will, but should be not only allowed, but encouraged to choose their own vocations, and contend for the prizes of life wherever the opportunities are most favorable. Education should seek the disintegration of the tribes, and not their segregation. They should be educated, not as Indians, but as Americans. In short, the public school should do for them what it is so successfully doing for all the other races in this country, assimilate them.

Training the Young

Any plan for civilization which does not provide for training the young, even though at a largely increased expenditure, is short-sighted and expensive.

Edward P. Smith, Commissioner of Indian Affairs, 1873.

Ninth. The work of education should begin with them while they are young and susceptible, and should continue until habits of industry and love of learning have taken the place of indolence and indifference. One of the chief defects which have heretofore characterized the efforts made for their education has been the failure to carry them far enough, so that they might compete successfully with the white youth, who have enjoyed the far greater advantages of our own system of education. Higher education is even more essential to them than it is for white children.

Tenth. Special pains should be taken to bring together in the large boarding-schools members of as many different tribes as possible, in order to destroy the tribal antagonism and to generate in them a feeling of common brotherhood and mutual respect. Wherever practicable, they should be admitted on terms of equality into the public schools, where, by daily contact with white children, they may learn to respect them and become respected in turn. Indeed, it is reasonable to expect that at no distant day, when the Indians shall have all taken up their lands in severalty and have become American citizens, there will cease to be any necessity for Indian schools maintained by the Government. The Indians, where it is impracticable for them to unite with their white neighbors, will maintain their own schools.

Eleventh. Co-education of the sexes is the surest and perhaps only way in which the Indian women can be lifted out of that position of servility and degradation which most of them now occupy, on to a plane where their husbands and the men generally will treat them with the same gallantry and respect which is accorded to their more favored white sisters.

Twelfth. The happy results already achieved at Carlisle, Hampton, and elsewhere, by the so-called "outing system," which consists in placing Indian pupils in white families where they are taught the ordinary routine of housekeeping, farming, etc., and are brought into intimate relationship with the highest type of American rural life, suggests the wisdom of a large extension of the system. By this means they acquire habits of industry, a practical acquaintance with civilized life, a sense of independence, enthusiasm for home, and the practical ability to earn their own living. This system has in it the "promise and the potency" of their complete emancipation.

Thirteenth. Of course, it is to be understood that, in addition to all of the work here outlined as belonging to the Government for the education and civilization of the Indians, there will be requisite the influence of the home, the Sabbath-school, the church, and religious institutions of learning. There will be urgent need of consecrated missionary work and liberal expenditure of money on the part of individuals and religious organizations in behalf of these people. Christian schools and colleges have already been established for them by missionary zeal, and others will doubtless follow. But just as the work of the public schools is supplemented in the States by Christian agencies, so will the work of Indian education by the Government be supplemented by the same agencies. There need be no conflict and no unseemly rivalry. The Indians, like any other class of citizens, will be free to patronize those schools which they believe to be best adapted to their purpose.

VIEWPOINT 2

"No people [are] so rude, as to be without any rules of politeness."

Indians Already Have Civilized Cultures

Benjamin Franklin

Benjamin Franklin was long interested in and generally sympathetic to the Indians. He chided the delegates at the Albany Conference in 1754 by reminding them of the Iroquois Confederacy and pointing out that it was hard to believe that thirteen colonies couldn't agree to a political union when "Six Nations of ignorant savages" could. During his term in the Pennsylvania legislature he defended Indians' rights. The following viewpoint reflects some of his thinking on the civilizations of the Indians versus the whites.

As you read, consider the following questions:

1. According to Franklin, should Indians be called "savages"? Who should in his opinion?
2. What is Franklin's advice about how to treat people of other cultures?
3. Does Franklin seem to prefer one culture to another?

Savages we call them, because their manners differ from ours, which we think the perfection of civility; they think the same of theirs.

Perhaps, if we could examine the manners of different nations with impartiality, we should find no people so rude, as to be without any rules of politeness; nor any so polite, as not to have some remains of rudeness.

"Good For Nothing"

The Indian men, when young, are hunters and warriors; when old, counselors; for all their government is by counsel of the sages; there is no force, there are no prisons, no officers to compel obedience, or inflict punishment. Hence they generally study oratory, the best speaker having the most influence. The Indian women till the ground, dress the food, nurse and bring up the children, and preserve and hand down to posterity the memory of public transactions. These employments of men and women are accounted natural and honorable. Having few artificial wants, they have abundance of leisure for improvement by conversation. Our laborious manner of life, compared with theirs, they esteem slavish and base; and the learning, on which we value ourselves, they regard as frivolous and useless. An instance of this occurred at the Treaty of Lancaster, in Pennsylvania, *anno* 1744, between the government of Virginia and the Six Nations. After the principal business was settled, the commissioners from Virginia acquainted the Indians by a speech, that there was at Williamsburg a college, with a fund for educating Indian youth; and that, if the chiefs of the Six Nations would send down half a dozen of their sons to that college, the government would take care that they should be well provided for, and instructed in all the learning of the white people. It is one of the Indian rules of politeness not to answer a public proposition the same day that it is made; they think it would be treating it as a light matter, and that they show it respect by taking time to consider it, as of a matter important. They therefore deferred their answer till the day following; when their speaker began, by expressing their deep sense of the kindness of the Virginia government, in making them that offer

"for we know," says he, "that you highly esteem the kind of learning taught in those Colleges, and that the maintenance of our young men, while with you, would be very expensive to you. We are convinced, therefore, that you mean to do us good by your proposal, and we thank you heartily. But you, who are wise, must know that different nations have different conceptions of things; and you will therefore not take it amiss, if our ideas of this kind of education happen not to be the same with yours. We have had some experience of it. Several of our young people were formerly brought up at the colleges of the northern provinces; they were instructed in all your sciences; but, when they came back to us, they were bad runners, ignorant of every means of living in the woods, unable to bear either cold or hunger, knew neither how to build a cabin, take a deer, or kill an enemy, spoke our language imperfectly, were therefore nei-

215

The author, Benjamin Franklin. Franklin's dealings with the Indians led him to respect their cultures.

ther fit for hunters, warriors, nor counselors; they were totally good for nothing. We are however not the less obliged by your kind offer, though we decline accepting it; and, to show our grateful sense of it, if the gentlemen of Virginia will send us a dozen of their sons, we will take great care of their education, instruct them in all we know, and make *men* of them."

Having frequent occasions to hold public councils, they have acquired great order and decency in conducting them. The old men sit in the foremost ranks, the warriors in the next, and the women and children in the hindmost. The business of the women is to take exact notice of what passes, imprint it in their memories, for they have no writing, and communicate it to their children. They are the records of the council, and they preserve tradition of the stipulations in treaties a hundred years back; which, when we compare with our writings, we always find exact. He that would speak, rises. The rest observe a profound silence. When he has finished and sits down, they leave him 5 or 6 minutes to recollect, that, if he has omitted anything he intended to say, or has anything to add, he may rise again and deliver it. To interrupt another, even in common conversation, is reckoned highly indecent. How different this is from the conduct of a polite British House of Commons, where scarce a day passes without some confusion that makes the speaker hoarse in calling *to order*; and how different from the mode of conversation in many polite companies of Europe, where, if you do not deliver your sentence with great rapidity, you are cut off in the middle of it by the impatient loquacity of those you converse with, and never suffered to finish it.

The politeness of these savages in conversation is indeed carried to excess, since it does not permit them to contradict or deny the truth of what is asserted in their presence. By this means they indeed avoid disputes, but then it becomes difficult to know their minds, or what impression you make upon them. The missionaries who have attempted to convert them to Christianity, all complain of this as one of the great difficulties of their mission. The Indians hear with patience the truths of the Gospel explained to them, and give their usual tokens of assent and approbation; you would think they were convinced. No such matter. It is mere civility.

Encounter with a Missionary

A Swedish minister, having assembled the chiefs of the Susquehanah Indians, made a sermon to them, acquainting them with the principal historical facts on which our religion is founded; such as the fall of our first parents by eating an apple, the coming of Christ to repair the mischief, His miracles and suffering, &c. When he had finished, an Indian orator stood up to thank him.

"What you have told us," says he, "is all very good. It is indeed bad to eat apples. It is better to make them all into cider. We are much obliged by your kindness in coming so far to tell us those things which you have heard from your mothers. In return, I will tell you some of those we have heard from ours":

> In the beginning, our fathers had only the flesh of animals to subsist on; and if their hunting was unsuccessful, they were starving. Two of our young hunters, having killed a deer, made a fire in the woods to broil some parts of it. When they were about to satisfy their hunger, they beheld a beautiful young woman descend from the clouds, and seat herself on that hill, which you see yonder among the blue mountains. They said to each other, it is a spirit that has smelled our broiling venison, and wishes to eat of it; let us offer some to her. They presented her with the tongue. She was pleased with the taste of it, and said, "Your kindness shall be rewarded. Come to this place after thirteen moons, and you shall find something that will be of great benefit in nourishing you and your children to the latest generations." They did so, and, to their surprise, found plants they had never seen before, but which, from that ancient time, have been constantly cultivated among us, to our great advantage. Where her right hand had touched the ground, they found maize; where her left hand had touched it, they found kidney beans; and where her backside had sat on it, they found tobacco."

The good missionary, disgusted with this idle tale, said, "What I delivered to you were sacred truths; but what you tell me is mere fable, fiction, and falsehood." The Indian, offended, replied, "My brother, it seems your friends have not done you justice in your education; they have not well instructed you in the rules of common civility. You saw that we, who understand and practice those rules, believed all your stories; why do you refuse to believe ours?"

Manners and Hypocrisy

When any of them come into our towns, our people are apt to crowd round them, gaze upon them, and incommode them, where they desire to be private; this they esteem great rudeness, and the effect of the want of instruction in the rules of civility and good manners. "We have," say they, "as much curiosity as you, and when you come into our towns, we wish for opportunities of looking at you; but for this purpose we hide ourselves behind bushes, where you are to pass, and never intrude ourselves into your company."

Their manner of entering one another's village has likewise its rules. It is reckoned uncivil in traveling strangers to enter a village abruptly, without giving notice of their approach. Therefore, as soon as they arrive within hearing, they stop and hollow, remaining there till invited to enter. Two old men usually come out to them, and lead them in. There is in every village a vacant dwelling, called the strangers' house. Here they are placed, while the old men go round from hut to hut acquainting the inhabitants that strangers are arrived, who are probably hungry and weary; and every one sends them what he can spare of victuals, and skins to repose on. When the strangers are refreshed, pipes and tobacco are brought; and then, but not before, conversation begins, with inquiries who they are, whither bound, what news, &c.; and it usually ends with offers of service, if the strangers have occasion of guides, or any necessaries for continuing their journey; and nothing is exacted for the entertainment.

The same hospitality, esteemed among them as a principal virtue, is practiced by private persons; of which Conrad Weiser, our interpreter, gave me the following instances. He had been naturalized among the Six Nations, and spoke well the Mohawk language. In going through the Indian country, to carry a message from our Governor to the Council at Onondaga, he called at the habitation of Canassatego, an old acquaintance, who embraced him, spread furs for him to sit on, placed before him some boiled beans and venison, and mixed some rum and water for his drink. When he was well refreshed, and had lit his pipe, Canassatego began to converse with him, asked how he had fared the many years since they had seen each other, whence he then came, what occasioned the journey, &c. Conrad answered all his questions; and when the discourse began to flag, the Indian, to continue it, said, "Conrad, you have lived long among the white people, and know something of their customs; I have been sometimes at Albany, and have observed that once in seven days they shut up their shops and assemble all in the great house; tell me what it is for? What do they do there?" "They meet there," says Conrad, "to hear and learn *good things.*" "I do not doubt," says the Indian, "that they tell you so; they have told me the same; but I doubt the truth of what they say, and I will tell you my reasons. I went lately to Albany to sell my skins and buy blankets, knives, powder, rum, &c. You know I used generally to deal with Hans Hanson; but I was a little inclined this time to try some other merchant. However, I called first upon Hans, and asked him what he would give for beaver. He said he could not give any more than four shillings a pound; 'but,' says he, 'I cannot talk on business now; this is the day when we meet together to learn *good things,* and I am going to the meeting.' So I thought to myself, 'Since we cannot do any business today, I may as well go to the meeting too,' and I went with him. There stood up a man in black, and began to talk to the people very angrily. I did not understand what he said; but, perceiving that he looked much at me and at Hanson, I imagined he was angry at seeing me there; so I went out, sat down near the house, struck fire, and lit my pipe, waiting till the meeting should break up. I thought too, that the man had mentioned something of beaver, and I suspected it might be the subject of their meeting. So, when they came out, I accosted my merchant. 'Well, Hans,' says I, 'I hope you have agreed to give more than four shillings a pound.' 'No,' says he, 'I cannot give so much; I cannot give more than three shillings and sixpence.' I then spoke to several other dealers, but they all sung the same song, three and sixpence, three and sixpence. This made it clear to me, that my suspicion was right; and, that whatever they pretended of meeting to learn *good things,* the real purpose was to consult how to cheat Indians in the price of beaver. Consider but a little, Conrad, and you must be of my opinion. If they met so often to learn *good things,* they would certainly have learned some before this time. But they are still ignorant. You know our practice. If a white man, in traveling through our country, enters one of our cabins, we all treat him as I treat you; we dry him if he is wet, we warm him if he is cold, and give him meat and drink that he may allay his thirst and hunger; and we spread soft furs for him to rest and sleep on. We demand nothing in return. But, if I go into a white man's house at Albany, and ask for victuals and drink, they say, 'Where is your money?' and if I have none, they say, 'Get out, you Indian dog.' You see they have not yet learned those little *good things,* that we need no meetings to be instructed in, because our mothers taught them to us when we were children. And therefore it is impossible their meetings should be, as they say, for any such purpose, or have any such effect; they are only to contrive the *cheating of Indians in the price of beaver.*"

VIEWPOINT 3

"An Indian is an independent person who is not inclined to seek advice nor to change his mind to please anyone. It is a tremendous thing when such a one decides to surrender himself to Jesus."

Indians Should Be Christianized

Abraham Steiner

Abraham Steiner was a member of the *Unitas Fratrum*, or Unity of the Brethren, the oldest international Protestant denomination. Founded in Bohemia and Moravia in 1457, it "quickly spread across Europe, established missions in every continent, and now, under the name of the Moravian Church, finds its chief home in the United States. . . . It is missionary work that constitutes their most glorious achievement; and, among their many noble undertakings in this field, none surpassed the mission to the Delaware and Mohican Indians of the United States and Canada," according to Paul Wallace, editor of Steiner's journal.

In 1740 the first group of Pennsylvania Moravians founded Nazareth, Pennsylvania; the following year, on Christmas eve, 1741, Bethlehem, Pennsylvania, was established. Once established, the Moravian colony set about establishing missions and schools among the Indians. Schooling was to be stressed along with religion.

In the spring of 1789 Abraham Steiner accompanied Johann Heckewelder, an elder of the Moravian church, while he made one of his many trips west from Bethlehem. The following viewpoint is taken from Steiner's journal account of these travels. The two men went to see about surveying the lands Congress had set aside for the Moravian convert Indians on the Muskingum River in Ohio. In the journal we see what life was like on the unsettled Indian frontier in the years following the American Revolution. Also apparent is the arduous life of the missionary and the real joy of making converts.

As you read, consider the following questions:

1. What sorts of hazards and difficulties do the missionaries face on this trip?
2. What evidence is there of an unsettled frontier? What remains of the primitive? What changes have been made by settlers?
3. What evidence is there that missionaries have had an impact on the Indians?

---

*A*braham *Steiner's Account of his Journey with Johann Heckewelder from Bethlehem to Pettquotting on the Huron River near Lake Erie, and Return. 1789.*

[April] 21st. Half a mile beyond the ferry we came to Yellow Breeches Creek which, though sometimes a wild and dangerous stream, we were able to ride across without difficulty. 5 miles from Carlisle we saw a Presbyterian pulpit in the woods. These pulpits are built on a tree in the woods where people camp. A flight of three or four steps lead up to the pulpit, over which a small roof is built. At 1 o'clock in the afternoon we came to Carlisle, 16 miles from the ferry. We had a fine view of the place as we approached. This beautiful little town lies on an open plain. East of the town there are 5 long two-story buildings, each about 100 feet in length, built of brick, besides several smaller buildings, and an arsenal built of rough stone. During the war these buildings were put up by the States for workingmen attached to the army; they are, however, no longer maintained, and are now occupied only by Dr. Nesbitt, President of the local college, and a few young theological students. The town has about 350 handsome and for the most part two-story houses, most of which are built of handsome blue limestone, with which this vicinity abounds. The Courthouse is not large, but handsome, the prison small, and the market good. There are 3 churches, and the inhabitants, half of whom are German and half English, are mostly Presbyterians, Roman Catholics, German Lutherans and Reformed. The Methodists, too, have a meeting place here. There is a college here [Dickinson] but not in very good condition, and also two English schools; business is good, and there are many stores. There is a good printing press, and almost all trades are carried on here, in particular the making of nails and good beer. . . .

On the 22nd we rode 14 miles through dry land where there are no springs, to Shippensburg, where we had breakfast. . . . We saw several acquaintances here. We saw also our first packhorses. They put packs on them which they have to carry over the mountains. The drivers do not set off before 8 or 9 o'clock in the morning, but they drive all day till late in the evening. There are often 40 or 50 horses together. From here it is 10 miles to the foot of the Blue Mountain, where a German innkeeper lives named Kiefer. From this point on we had mountains to climb. There are 3 high ones here, one right after the other, which they call the Blue Mountains. A few years ago there was only a path over them, but now there is as good a road as can be expected on such mountains. . . .

The 23rd. We passed the place where Fort Littleton formerly stood. . . . Formerly Sideling Hill was much dreaded by travellers because of the rough steep road and the huge rocks on it. But here you can see what an efficient government can do in such a case. . . . There used to be very good hunting in these mountains and there are still many deer. . . . We ferried over the Juniata because the river was too high for fording. The road then follows a ridge; one has the Juniata on both sides. . . . On the north side of the road the bank is very high and steep, & the road runs close to the edge. Once, it is said, a man went over here with a wagon & 4 horses, & nothing has been heard of him since. . . . At night we came to Snakespring, 11 miles from the Crossing, and stopped at Diefenbach's, a German Innkeeper's. While we were on the road it rained fairly hard, but once we were inside the house there came a downpour with thunder & lightning. Snakespring is said to have received its name from the Indian traders, who used to have a trading post here. Once a lot of them got together here and had a celebration, during which they killed a snake, fried it in the fire & ate it, & afterwards called the place Snakespring.

On the 24th . . . we reached our friend Bonnet's, 4 miles beyond Bedford, where we stayed till next morning & were well looked after. . . . Here & on the adjoining plantation there are more than 200 acres of cleared pasture-land, and more can be cleared. Mr. Bonnet makes several 100 pounds a year from passing travelers for hay and pasturage, and some of his neighbors do almost as well. Here the great road to Pittsburg divides into two main roads, the one called the Pennsylvania Road [by way of Ligonier], the other the Glades Road [by way of Berlin]. . . .

On the 25th we had a good road for 5 miles farther till we came to Anderson's at the foot of the famous Allegheny Mountain. . . . A strong wind was blowing as we climbed, and it was still blowing hard while we were on top. The road up the mountain is rather stony, & all along the lower half small springs come out of the mountain on the left and run down the road. It is not particularly steep, and you can get up if you climb slowly and don't mind tired legs. Left of the road, all down the side of the mountain, the soil is very rich & this is called the "Garden Spot." It produces tall weeds, & all kinds of timber and shrubs are found here growing together. There are cherry, walnut, locust, sassafras, mulberry, ash, chestnut, hickory, elm, maple, beech, oak, aspen, etc. On the right hand side a beautiful little brook goes tumbling down. On the far side of the brook the mountain rises rather higher and the soil is poorer. Here are Spruce, white & pitch pine, cedar & boxwood. It is flat on top of the mountain, and it continues like that with some little variations to Laurel Hill, so that it may be said that Laurel Hill stands on Allegheny Mountain. The soil on the mountain top is mostly a black, rich loam, but it is cold; the grain often freezes, but grass grows in abundance. It is fairly well settled, and although there are not many plantations to be seen along the way, the people are already complaining that their neighbors are too close to them. . . .

On the 26th we could not get warm all day. We crossed Laurel Hill today. . . . It began to snow, & it kept on snowing until evening when the snow was 2 inches deep. Thunder & lightning accompanied the snow & it was intensely cold. . . . We spent the night with a German named Ried, who keeps a good inn. . . . Mr. Hufnagel & 2 other gentlemen from Greensburg also spent the night here. The former said a great many nice things about our Indian mission, condemned in the strongest terms the murder of the Indians on the Muskingum, & was angry because the ringleaders had not been punished.

On the 27th we went on to Greensburg. . . . Many Germans live in this neighborhood. . . . A man named Steinmez told us that his neighbors, who have driven cattle to Detroit, praise the Moravian Indians & say there are no better Christians than they. In this vicinity, which is called the German Settlement, the Indians committed many murders during the last war. We went on another 8 miles through beautiful country to a German by the name of Waldhauer, who would not let us go on. So we spent the night with him & rested well. . . . A lot of people from this area are moving to the Missury. They are having particular trouble with rascals who owe them money, slip quietly off to the Youghiogany, where boats are always ready to pull out, and go down from there by way of the Monnonghahela & Ohio to the Mississippi. . . .

On the 28th we . . . reached Pittsburg by 3 o'clock. . . . General Gibson told us that his boat would leave in the morning for Kentucky & would stop at Marietta. We wanted to go along. But then one person advised us for it and another against it, until Br. Heckewelder found Mr. Isaac Williams, who lives in Sandusky and only recently has come from there. He said he had been sent with a "speech" from all the nations to Gov. St. Clair, which, however, as the Governor was not at home, he would take back again. This was the gist of the message: that the Indians will not allow the land which had been ceded at the last Treaty to be surveyed, and no forts are to be built on it, and, more particularly, they have made up their minds to kill all surveyors who go out. He added that the Indians say they were forced to the last Treaty. They neglected their fall hunting because of it; it lasted until winter, & they became poor, naked, & hungry. This drove them to accept certain terms in hopes of getting some food and clothing, but as they found themselves for the most part cheated, they merely laughed at the Treaty when they returned from it, and did not honor it at all. The Indians have decided to make an attack on the New England settlement on the Muskingum. They were resolved to fight for their land, and then if they lost it they would lose it like men. At this time there were many Indians on the Muskingum who were there only to keep watch. If we now surveyed the tract for the Moravian Indians on the Muskingum, it might cause trouble, & if soldiers were present it would be all the worse, & what would 20 or 30 soldiers be for the Indians lying in wait for them in the woods. Mr. Connelly from Detroit was present & confirmed this. They entreated us under no circumstances to survey the land, it would certainly cause trouble. They advised us, instead, to go to our Brethren at Pettquotting, where we could best inform ourselves about the matter. Not knowing what to do, we decided to stay here for a few days. All honest people here are sorry for the poor Indians, who lose their land without getting anything for it. They say the Treaty cost a lot, and most of the Indians got nothing. Some who were to have got something thought it was not even worth while to put out their hands for it, it was so small. . . .

On the 30th we were invited to breakfast with Mr. Nicholson, an "Interpreter of Indian languages," who advised us to survey our land, & would not hear of any danger. . . .

May 1st. Mr. Wilson, who had come from Washington [Pennsylvania] yesterday, brought us the certain news that the Indians on Dunker Creek had killed several white people and stolen some horses. He advised against surveying the land at this time, and so did almost everyone. So we prepared to go to Pettquotting. . . .

On the 10th it rained. We met a number of Indians who were going with skins to Beaver Creek, where General Gibson had directed them to come for trading because many of them were afraid to go to Pittsburg. After them came Anton (Wellochalent), formerly one of the Brethren, but he had reverted. He had just now shot a bear. He gave us a ham from it. We let our party go on ahead. Br. Heckewelder reminded him of the grace he had once experienced. He replied that he had never intended to leave the Moravians, but, when his whole family was murdered, that not only grieved him but also so infuriated him that he resolved to go to war, & he had been weak enough to do so. Now he had avenged himself & had no longer any hatred of the white people. He often thought of going back to the Moravians, but believed he was too wicked. Br. Heckewelder said: "The thought of returning to the congregation comes from the Saviour, he has taken hold of you & will not easily let you go. He will forgive you everything if you turn to him." Anton said: "You speak words of comfort to me. I will soon return." And so we parted. Anton was once a very good man. He did much for the white people, saved their lives, & during the war brought them himself to safety, often at risk of his life. He had a good wife & lovely, promising children. These were all killed in the great massacre on the Muskingum. . . .

The 12th. In the morning 2 young Delaware Indians came to our camp. The father of one of them was a brother-in-law of the woman who was travelling with us. They were friendly & confirmed the report of the horse-stealing at Wheeling. The Delawares are said to have delivered a Speech to these Mingoes, to get them to mend their ways, but to no effect, & the Delawares are said to have gone quietly off because they saw it was no use. These same Mingoes are said to have stolen 11 horses from Mr. Ludlow, a surveyor, & then returned. On the way we saw the grave of an Indian who, at sugar-making in the spring, ate so much sugar that his stomach swelled and he died. . . .

On the 20th we came to the road that turns off to Pettquotting. . . . We met 2 Indians, who gave us directions about our road. The plains were becoming wetter and more extensive, broken only by an occasional long narrow strip of oak trees, the hollow ones being full of bees. Now and again we saw single large sandstones, and small round, stony hills, where innumerable crawfish live & make holes in the ground. Everywhere little round hillocks had been thrown up. Otherwise the whole region was as flat as a board. The horses walked on hard ground for miles, up to their knees in water, & under the water white violets grew. . . . 5 miles from Pettquotting we came into woods again and broken country. Better than a mile from the town was a peeled tree, on which, was written with charcoal in Delaware the whole verse, "The Saviour's blood & righteousness." This made us a good road sign. At last we saw the town before us. On a hill, at the fence of the nearest plantation, we called to the Indians working in the field. As soon as they recognized us, they dropped their hoes & ran to meet us. Several who were on the other side of the stream hurried across, & everybody welcomed us, accompanied us across the field to the river, & then over into the town, which we reached about 3 o'clock. Here we were welcomed by the Zeisbergers & the Edwards & Jung, & the Indian Brethren & Sisters swarmed about us until evening. It was an amazing sight to see a crowd of people who had once been heathen & are now true Christians & lovers of Jesus & his flock. The place is named Pettquotting after a high round hill, 5 miles from here. The town [New Salem, two miles from Milan] is set on a hill which is washed by the Huron River on the west, & has a deep, narrow valley on the east. The hill is fairly dry, but so narrow that not more than two rows of houses can stand on it, and these have only very small gardens or none at all. Towards the south the hill becomes a large, wet plain. Every cellar on this high, wet place has to have a drain. The schoolhouse is beautiful, with fireplaces on both sides, & a nice fence across the front. Not far from it, on the other side of the street, is the church. It is roomy, bark-covered, without board flooring & without windows, with 2 doors, good benches including some for the children, & candlesticks & candles. The bell hangs outside on a forked tree with a tiny roof built over it. The buildings in town are rather irregular & small, but most of them are well-built & all give protection against rain & cold. There are, however, no glass windows here, only a few paper ones. Those who have any glass save it. The graveyard is near the town, to the southeast. When a grave is dug in the wet season, it stands full of water. But there is no better place. It is 3 1/2 miles by land to Lake Erie northeast of here, and 5 1/2 miles by water down the river. Huron River is here about 12 rods wide, 30 feet deep. It is also called Bald Eagle Creek from a large eagle's nest found at the rivermouth. This is the only drinking water. In summer, when it is quiet, the water is stagnant & bad. When the winds blow in from the lake, the lake water comes up the river to above the town, & this is the best drinking water. The bottoms down river are for the most part wet; up river they are dry & rich, with not many swamps. They produce everything in abundance when not too wet. All the high land is too wet. Trees of all the usual kinds grow here. Sugar trees, ginseng, & deer are scarce in this vicinity. They trap many raccoons and also beaver & otter here. There are bears, too, and many bees in the woods. There are plenty of fish in the river, especially very large catfish, and at times there are many geese & ducks. The Indians have horses, cattle, chickens, & many pigs. They can live well if they plant enough.

On Ascension Day, the 21st, we had only 2 services as it was rainy. We consulted the Brethren about our problem. They were against our surveying the land on the Muskingum at this time, but they wanted the opinion and advice of some of the Assistants. During the spring there had been a great uproar among some of the bad Indians at the thought of the Christians now moving to the Muskingum. They had settled down, but if the land were now surveyed they would be in an uproar again and might ruin the whole congregation. If someone were connected with the business whom they knew to be a former teacher, it would be so much the worse. We should not tell the Indians why we were here, for fear it might get to the ears of the bad Indians. West of here live wicked bands among whom are utterly godless whites & Indians. They are always in a stir, and are said to live in a pitiful condition. Br. David was very busy this week preparing his address for Holy Communion. . . .

Regarding Treatment of the Indians

There is another point which seems to me to deserve notice, that is the censure that is thrown upon our forefathers for their treatment of the natives of the country they came to inhabit. It seems wholly out of place for the present generation to judge their conduct. After the knowledge I have of Indian character & knowing the constant teasing & the perplexity there is in getting along with them & taking into consideration the sentiments of the civilized world, I am rather surprised that the Indians received so kind treatment & their conduct was so long borne. None but those who have intercourse with the Indians can tell the great demand it makes upon one's patience to deal with them. I often think of what the Ps. said, "O that I had some hiding place in the wilderness, then would I flee away & be at rest."

If they [the natives] should remain constantly about us the whole year, it would to all human view soon kill us. It is their leaving for a part of the year that affords us time & opportunity to renew our strength & prepare for our labors anew. I fully coincide [concur] with the views expressed by a lady of this Mission, probably the most devoted of any one in the Mission, that they could not endure their labors if it were not for the respite they have in the summer season when the natives are absent after roots & fish.

Elkanah Walker, diary, 1844.

The 23rd. We had Communion in the evening. All communicants came afterwards to Br. David's room. The Brethren all kissed one another, the Sisters did the same among themselves, & Brethren & Sisters shook hands with one another in mutual fellowship. It is a great thing to see a congregation drawn from raw heathendom fully enjoying the reward & bounties of Jesus, & loving one another like true Christians.

On the 25th a conference was held with Samuel & Wilhelm. Much as they wished to see our affair succeed & to help us themselves, they were nevertheless of opinion we should drop the matter for the time being. Their reasons were exactly the same as those the white Brethren had advanced. They thought that, since the Indians did not want the Christians to go to the Muskingum and supposed they would have to as soon as the land was surveyed, all who had relatives at this place would take them away and very likely some wicked band would come and take the rest away. They said: "You cannot conceive how closely they watch us, and they are worse than you imagine. They are determined that no surveyor shall set foot on that land. Perhaps the matter will be cleared up after the Council meets at Deep River near Detroit, where Brant is expected." We discussed the matter further during the week, and came to the conclusion: "God forbid! It were better the land were never surveyed than that the least harm should befall the mission. The land should rather be sacrificed for the mission than the mission for the land.". . .

The 31st was Pentecost, which the Indians observe as an important day. There was a baptism of 3 Brethren and 1 Sister. Two of those baptized were sons of William Henry, who formerly was known as Killbuck or Gelelemind. One of them had lived 4 years at Princeton, & had attended the college there. The persons baptized were dressed in white & wore blue gowns over their garments because it was cool. Reed mats were spread before them. After an address by Br. David, the sacristans hauled water in 4 buckets with a tin basin in each. The men & women Assistants removed their gowns, & after they had worshipped they were led into Br. David's house & had dry clothes put on them. When it was all over, all the Brethren kissed the newly baptized Brethren, & the Sisters kissed the newly baptized Sister. The Brethren shook hands with the Sister, & the Sisters shook hands with the Brethren. Everyone was happy to see new partakers in the blessedness they themselves enjoyed. Things go very well, on the whole, among the young people here. A great longing fires them to surrender themselves to Him who gave His life for them. An Indian is an independent person who is not inclined to seek advice nor to change his mind to please anyone. It is a tremendous thing when such a one decides to surrender himself to Jesus, and still more so when it is a young Indian who is just as independent & who in addition has to fight the temptations of the world. Towards evening there was a lovefeast for the whole congregation. The church was crowded. There were some Chippewas present, who had come because they had heard that today was Sunday. At the lovefeast everything went off very well. Br. David told the Indians about the congregations at Bethlehem & other places, & assured them they were remembered by them. It was a happy day for the Indian congregation. I should mention with what eagerness the Indians go to school to learn reading, writing, & hymns. Br. David conducts school here by himself, in various classes, from morning till night. School stops only during the busiest planting & harvesting seasons. Men, women, & children attend it. At other times you see, here & there, a little group in a corner, learning reading and hymns from one another. You may hear them in the evening singing hymns in their houses until late at night.

On the 1st of June, from morning till noon, there were Indians with us saying good-bye. When we left at 2 o'clock, they assembled once more and went through it all over again. The whole hill, from the houses on down, was covered with people following us with their eyes as long as they could. . . .

On the 9th we forded Muddy Run, crossed some plains, & then came to the best high land we had seen on our whole journey. At 5 o'clock we reached the Allegheny, & before dark were again in Pittsburg,—

Where we stayed the 10th & 11th. We could do little business here. The people in whom we were chiefly interested were busy listening to the inquiry then being conducted in the church by 6 pastors from the neighbourhood into the dispute between the Presbyterian congregation and their pastor. Messrs. Morrison & Connelly told us they thanked God they had returned safely. They had gone in the spring to the mouth of the Cayahaga with flour, & thought themselves fortunate not to have known at the time the danger they were in. Had the war parties that were lying in wait not missed them, they would have been at their mercy. Everybody, by the way, advised us to take the advice of our Brethren & not survey the land at this time. We said good-bye to the Indian Brethren & our hosts, &—

On the 12th left Pittsburg. . . .

On the 24th, [June] arrived in Bethlehem.

VIEWPOINT 4

"The red man prefers to believe that the Spirit of God is not breathed into man alone, but that the whole created universe is a sharer in the immortal perfection of its Maker."

Indians Wish to Keep Their Own Religion

Charles Alexander Eastman

When the Santee Sioux of Minnesota rose up against white settlers in 1862, government retaliation was swift. Many of the Sioux fled into exile in Canada; among them was four-year-old Charles Alexander Eastman, born "Pitiful Last" but later called "Ohiyesa—The Winner." He did not see a white person until he was sixteen. Later, he attended Dartmouth College and, in 1890, earned his medical degree from Boston University. He thus lived in and observed both worlds—the Indians' and the whites'. This is evident in the following viewpoint explaining native American religious beliefs, excerpted from Eastman's book *The Soul of the Indian*, published in 1911.

As you read, consider the following questions:

1. How did the native American respond to missionary teaching? What in their own religion might explain this?
2. What is the "Great Mystery"? How was it worshipped by the Sioux?
3. What evidence is there in the viewpoint that Eastman knows of Christianity and its practices?
4. What elements of Indian religion might be misunderstood by Europeans? What elements are similar to those of other religions?

The original attitude of the American Indian toward the Eternal, the "Great Mystery" that surrounds and embraces us, was as simple as it was exalted. To him it was the supreme conception, bringing with it the fullest measure of joy and satisfaction possible in this life.

The worship of the "Great Mystery" was silent, solitary, free from all self-seeking. It was silent, because all speech is of necessity feeble and imperfect; therefore the souls of my ancestors ascended to God in wordless adoration. It was solitary, because they believed that He is nearer to us in solitude, and there were no priests authorized to come between a man and his Maker. None might exhort or confess or in any way meddle with the religious experience of another. Among us all men were created sons of God and stood erect, as conscious of their divinity. Our faith might not be formulated in creeds, nor forced upon any who were unwilling to receive it; hence there was no preaching, proselyting, nor persecution, neither were there any scoffers or atheists.

There were no temples or shrines among us save those of nature. Being a natural man, the Indian was intensely poetical. He would deem it sacrilege to build a house for Him who may be met face to face in the mysterious, shadowy aisles of the primeval forest, or on the sunlit bosom of virgin prairies, upon dizzy spires and pinnacles of naked rock, and yonder in the jeweled vault of the night sky! He who enrobes Himself in filmy veils of cloud, there on the rim of the visible world where our Great-Grandfather Sun kindles his evening camp-fire, He who rides upon the rigorous wind of the north, or breathes forth His spirit upon aromatic southern airs, whose war-canoe is launched upon majestic rivers and inland seas—He needs no lesser cathedral!

Hambeday

That solitary communion with the Unseen which was the highest expression of our religious life is partly described in the word *hambeday*, literally "mysterious feeling," which has been variously translated "fasting" and "dreaming." It may better be interpreted as "consciousness of the divine."

The first *hambeday*, or religious retreat, marked an epoch in the life of the youth, which may be compared to that of confirmation or conversion in Christian experience. Having first prepared himself by means of the purifying vapor-bath, and cast off as far as possible all human or fleshly influences, the young man sought out the noblest height, the most commanding summit in all the surrounding region. Knowing that God sets no value upon material things, he took with him no offerings or sacrifices other than symbolic objects, such as paints and tobacco. Wishing to appear before Him in all humility, he wore no clothing save his moccasins and breech-clout. At the solemn hour of sunrise or sunset he took up his position, overlooking the glories of earth and facing the "Great Mystery," and there he remained, naked, erect, silent, and motionless, exposed to the elements and forces of His arming, for a night and a day to two days and nights, but rarely longer. Sometimes he would chant a hymn without words, or offer the ceremonial "filled pipe." In this holy trance or ecstasy the Indian mystic found his highest happiness and the motive power of his existence.

A Response to Missionaries

They do us no good. If they are not useful to the white people and do them no good, why do they send them among the Indians? If they are useful to the white people and do them good, why do they not keep them at home? They [the white men] are surely bad enough to need the labor of everyone who can make them better. These men [the missionaries] know we do not understand their religion. We cannot read their book—they tell us different stories about what it contains, and we believe they make the book talk to suit themselves. If we had no money, no land and no country to be cheated out of these black coats would not trouble themselves about our good hereafter. The Great Spirit will not punish us for what we do not know. He will do justice to his red children. These black coats talk to the Great Spirit, and ask for light that we may see as they do, when they are blind themselves and quarrel about the light that guides them. These things we do not understand, and the light which they give us makes the straight and plain path trod by our fathers, dark and dreary. The black coats tell us to work and raise corn; they do nothing themselves and would starve to death if someone did not feed them. All they do is to pray to the Great Spirit; but that will not make corn and potatoes grow; if it will why do they beg from us and from the white people. The red men knew nothing of trouble until it came from the white men; as soon as they crossed the great waters they wanted our country, and in return have always been ready to teach us to quarrel about their religion. . . . We are few and weak, but may for a long time be happy if we hold fast to our country, and the religion of our fathers.

Red Jacket, response to a man who asked why he was opposed to missionaries, 1824.

When he returned to the camp, he must remain at a distance until he had again entered the vapor-bath and prepared himself for intercourse with his fellows. Of the vision or sign vouchsafed to him he did not speak, unless it had included some commission which must be publicly fulfilled. Sometimes an old man, standing upon the brink of eternity, might reveal to a chosen few the oracle of his long-past youth.

What Is the Nature of Virtue?

The native American has been generally despised by his white conquerors for his poverty and simplicity. They forget, perhaps, that his religion forbade the accumulation of wealth and the enjoyment of luxury. To him, as to other single-minded men in every age and race, from Diogenes to the brothers of Saint Francis, from the Montanists to the Shakers, the love of possessions has appeared a snare, and the burdens of a complex society a source of needless peril and temptation. Furthermore, it was the rule of his life to share the fruits of his skill and success with his less fortunate brothers. Thus he kept his spirit free from the clog of pride, cupidity, or envy, and carried out, as he believed, the divine decree—a matter profoundly important to him.

It was not, then, wholly from ignorance or improvidence that he failed to establish permanent towns and to develop a material civilization. To the untutored sage, the concentration of population was the prolific mother of all evils, moral no less than physical. He argued that food is good, while surfeit kills; that love is good, but lust destroys; and not less dreaded than the pestilence following upon crowded and unsanitary dwellings was the loss of spiritual power inseparable from too close contact with one's fellow-men. All who have lived much out of doors know that there is a magnetic and nervous force that accumulates in solitude and that is quickly dissipated by life in a crowd; and even his enemies have recognized the fact that for a certain innate power and self-poise, wholly independent of circumstances, the American Indian is unsurpassed among men.

The red man divided mind into two parts,—the spiritual mind and the physical mind. The first is pure spirit, concerned only with the essence of things, and it was this he sought to strengthen by spiritual prayer, during which the body is subdued by fasting and hardship. In this type of prayer there was no beseeching of favor or help. All matters of personal or selfish concern, as success in hunting or warfare, relief from sickness, or the sparing of a beloved life, were definitely relegated to the plane of the lower or material mind, and all ceremonies, charms, or incantations designed to secure a benefit or to avert a danger, were recognized as emanating from the physical self.

Religious Symbolism

The rites of this physical worship, again, were wholly symbolic, and the Indian no more worshiped the Sun than the Christian adores the Cross. The Sun and the Earth, by an obvious parable, holding scarcely more of poetic metaphor than of scientific truth, were in his view the parents of all organic life. From the Sun, as the universal father, proceeds the quickening principle in nature, and in the patient and fruitful womb of our mother, the Earth, are hidden embryos of plants and men. Therefore our reverence and love for them was really an imaginative extension of our love for our immediate parents, and with this sentiment of filial piety was joined a willingness to appeal to them, as to a father, for such good gifts as we may desire. This is the material or physical prayer.

A Good Indian's Dilemma

Even when an Indian was baptized as the missionaries insisted, racial bigotry kept him from gaining fuller acceptance by whites. The Fox, or Mesquakie, Indians of the southern Great Lakes region provide this ironic anecdote about a convert's can't-win plight.

Once there was an Indian who became a Christian. He became a very good Christian; he went to church, and he didn't smoke or drink, and he was good to everyone. He was a very good man. Then he died. First he went to the Indian hereafter, but they wouldn't take him because he was a Christian. Then he went to Heaven, but they wouldn't let him in—because he was an Indian. Then he went to Hell, but they wouldn't admit him there either, because he was so good. So he came alive again, and he went to the Buffalo Dance and the other dances and taught his children to do the same thing.

Anonymous, from *Native American Testimony,* 1991.

The elements and majestic forces in nature, Lightning, Wind, Water, Fire, and Frost, were regarded with awe as spiritual powers, but always secondary and intermediate in character. We believed that the spirit pervades all creation and that every creature possesses a soul in some degree, though not necessarily a soul conscious of itself. The tree, the waterfall, the grizzly bear, each is an embodied Force, and as such an object of reverence.

The Indian loved to come into sympathy and spiritual communion with his brothers of the animal kingdom, whose inarticulate souls had for him something of the sinless purity that we attribute to the innocent and irresponsible child. He had faith in their instincts, as in a mysterious wisdom given from above; and while he humbly accepted the supposedly voluntary sacrifice of their bodies to preserve his own, he paid homage to their spirits in prescribed prayers and offerings.

The Importance of the Supernatural

In every religion there is an element of the supernatural, varying with the influence of pure reason over its devotees. The Indian was a logical and clear thinker upon matters within the
scope of his understanding, but he had not yet charted the vast
field of nature or expressed her wonders in terms of science. With
his limited knowledge of cause and effect, he saw miracles on every hand,—the miracle of life in seed and egg, the miracle of
death in lightning flash and in the swelling deep! Nothing of the
marvelous could astonish him; as that a beast should speak, or
the sun stand still. The virgin birth would appear scarcely more
miraculous than is the birth of every child that comes into the
world, or the miracle of the loaves and fishes excite more wonder
than the harvest that springs from a single ear of corn.

Who may condemn his superstition? Surely not the devout
Catholic, or even Protestant missionary, who teaches Bible miracles as literal fact! The logical man must either deny all miracles
or none, and our American Indian myths and hero stories are
perhaps, in themselves, quite as credible as those of the Hebrews
of old. If we are of the modern type of mind, that sees in natural
law a majesty and grandeur far more impressive than any solitary infraction of it could possibly be, let us not forget that, after
all, science has not explained everything. We have still to face the
ultimate miracle,—the origin and principle of life! Here is the
supreme mystery that is the essence of worship, without which
there can be no religion, and in the presence of this mystery our
attitude cannot be very unlike that of the natural philosopher,
who beholds with awe the Divine in all creation.

It is simple truth that the Indian did not, so long as his native
philosophy held sway over his mind, either envy or desire to imitate the splendid achievements of the white man. In his own
thought he rose superior to them! He scorned them, even as a
lofty spirit absorbed in its stern task rejects the soft beds, the lux-
urious food, the pleasure-worshiping dalliance of a rich neighbor.
It was clear to him that virtue and happiness are independent of
these things, if not incompatible with them.

An Evaluation of Christianity

There was undoubtedly much in primitive Christianity to appeal to this man, and Jesus' hard sayings to the rich and about the
rich would have been entirely comprehensible to him. Yet the religion that is preached in our churches and practiced by our congregations, with its element of display and self-aggrandizement,
its active proselytism, and its open contempt of all religions but
its own, was for a long time extremely repellent. To his simple

mind, the professionalism of the pulpit, the paid exhorter, the moneyed church, was an unspiritual and unedifying thing, and it was not until his spirit was broken and his moral and physical constitution undermined by trade, conquest, and strong drink, that Christian missionaries obtained any real hold upon him. Strange as it may seem, it is true that the proud pagan in his secret soul despised the good men who came to convert and to enlighten him!

Nor were its publicity and its Phariseeism the only elements in the alien religion that offended the red man. To him, it appeared shocking and almost incredible that there were among this people who claimed superiority many irreligious, who did not even pretend to profess the national faith. Not only did they not profess it, but they stooped so low as to insult their God with profane and sacrilegious speech! In our own tongue His name was not spoken aloud, even with utmost reverence, much less lightly or irreverently.

We Never Quarrel About Religion

Brother! We do not understand these things. We are told that your religion was given to your forefathers, and has been handed down from father to son. We also have a religion which was given to our forefathers, and has been handed down to us their children. We worship that way. It teacheth us to be thankful for all the favors we receive, to love each other, and to be united. We never quarrel about religion. . . .

Red Jacket, from *Native American Testimony*, 1991.

More than this, even in those white men who professed religion we found much inconsistency of conduct. They spoke much of spiritual things, while seeking only the material. They bought and sold everything: time, labor, personal independence, the love of woman, and even the ministrations of their holy faith! The lust for money, power, and conquest so characteristic of the Anglo-Saxon race did not escape moral condemnation at the hands of his untutored judge, nor did he fail to contrast this conspicuous trait of the dominant race with the spirit of the meek and lowly Jesus.

He might in time come to recognize that the drunkards and licentious among white men, with whom he too frequently came in contact, were condemned by the white man's religion as well, and must not be held to discredit it. But it was not so easy to overlook or to excuse national bad faith. When distinguished emissaries from the Father at Washington, some of them ministers of the gospel and even bishops, came to the Indian nations, and pledged to them in solemn treaty the national honor, with prayer and mention of their God; and when such treaties, so made, were promptly and shamelessly broken, is it strange that the action should arouse not only anger, but contempt? The historians of the white race admit that the Indian was never the first to repudiate his oath. . . .

The Unwritten Scriptures

A missionary once undertook to instruct a group of Indians in the truths of his holy religion. He told them of the creation of the earth in six days, and of the fall of our first parents by eating an apple.

The courteous savages listened attentively, and, after thanking him, one related in his turn a very ancient tradition concerning the origin of the maize. But the missionary plainly showed his disgust and disbelief, indignantly saying: "What I delivered to you were sacred truths, but this that you tell me is mere fable and falsehood!"

"My brother," gravely replied the offended Indian, "it seems that you have not been well grounded in the rules of civility. You saw that we, who practice these rules, believed your stories; why, then, do you refuse to credit ours?"

Every religion has its Holy Book, and ours was a mingling of history, poetry, and prophecy, of precept and folk-lore, even such as the modern reader finds within the covers of his Bible. This Bible of ours was our whole literature, a living Book, sowed as precious seed by our wisest sages, and springing anew in the wondering eyes and upon the innocent lips of little children. Upon its hoary wisdom of proverb and fable, its mystic and legendary lore thus sacredly preserved and transmitted from father to son, was based in large part our customs and philosophy.

Naturally magnanimous and open-minded, the red man prefers to believe that the Spirit of God is not breathed into man alone, but that the whole created universe is a sharer in the immortal perfection of its Maker. His imaginative and poetic mind, like that of the Greek, assigns to every mountain, tree, and spring its spirit, nymph, or divinity, either beneficent or mischievous. The heroes and demigods of Indian tradition reflect the characteristic trend of his thought, and his attribution of personality and will to the elements, the sun and stars, and all animate or inanimate nature.

VIEWPOINT 5

"You are to consider yourself as one of our people."

A White Man Learns About Indian Culture

James Smith

In 1755 Maj. Gen. Edward Braddock amassed two thousand English and American troops for an assault on Fort Duquesne (later Fort Pitt and now Pittsburgh), held by the French. To bring supplies to this force, colonists began to build a road through the wilderness. Among the road builders was eighteen-year-old James Smith, who was captured by the Caughnawagas, a branch of the Mohawks who were friendly to the French. He was a prisoner at the French-held Fort Duquesne when the celebrating Indians returned from annihilating Braddock's forces. He saw victorious warriors with scalps and other battle trophies and a dozen naked prisoners brought in to be burned to death. For the next five years he lived among the Caughnawagas. He was adopted by them and promptly treated as an equal, with all the benefits and responsibilities of other tribesmen. At times he fell short of their expectations. Most of the following viewpoint describes how Smith learned how to behave in his new extended family.

In 1759 he escaped and returned to his Pennsylvania home. When the frontier came under Indian attack in 1763, Smith, now with a reputation as an Indian expert, organized a company of Rangers, who wore Indian clothes, and often painted themselves to look like Indians, for defense of the colonies. (The Rangers were yet another evidence of acculturation—in a military sense. Unlike the English regular soldiers under Braddock who as Redcoats had marched in traditional rank and file to their decimation, the Rangers were an irregular force.) Smith later advanced to the rank of colonel during the Revolutionary War. He then moved to Kentucky, serving for a time in its state legislature. He also spent much of his time as a missionary to the Indians.

As you read, consider the following questions:

1. What did Smith need to learn in order to fit into his adoptive tribe? How did the Indians teach him?
2. Some sources in this book refer to the Indians as "savages." Would Smith agree?

In May 1755, the province of Pennsylvania agreed to send out three hundred men to cut a wagon road from Fort Loudon to join Braddock's road near the Turkey Foot or three forks of Yohogania. My brother-in-law, William Smith, Esquire, of Conococheague, was appointed commissioner in charge of these road cutters. . . .

We went on with the road without interuption until near the Allegheny Mountain. Then I was sent back to hurry up some provision wagons that were on the way after us. Finding the wagons were coming on as fast as possible, I returned up the road towards the Allegheny Mountain in company with one Arnold Vigoras.

About four or five miles above Bedford, three Indians had made a blind of bushes, stuck in the ground as though they grew naturally. Here they concealed themselves about fifteen yards from the road. When we came opposite them, they fired upon us and killed my fellow traveler. Their bullets did not touch me, but my horse made a violent start and threw me. The Indians immediately ran up and took me prisoner. . . .

Two of these Indians stood by me whilst the other scalped my comrade. We then set off and ran at a smart rate through the woods for about fifteen miles. That night we slept on the Allegheny Mountain, without fire.

The next morning the Indians divided the last of their provision, which they had brought from Fort Duquesne, and gave me an equal share—about two or three ounces of mouldy biscuit. This and a young ground hog about as large as a rabbit, roasted and also equally divided, was all the provision we had until we came to Loyal-Hanna Creek, which was about fifty miles. A great part of the way we came through exceedingly rocky laurel thickets, without any path.

When we came to the west side of Laurel Hill, they gave the scalp halloo, which is a long yell or halloo for every scalp or prisoner they have. The last of these scalp halloos was followed with quick and sudden shrill shouts of joy and triumph. We were answered by the firing of a number of guns on Loyal-Hanna Creek, one after another, quicker than one could count, by another party of Indians. As we advanced near this party they increased their repeated shouts of joy and triumph, but I did not share their excessive mirth.

When we came to this camp, we found they had plenty of turkeys and other meat there. I had never before eaten venison without bread or salt, yet, as I was hungry, it relished very well. There we stayed that night, and the next morning the whole of us marched on our way for Fort Duquesne. The following night we joined another camp of Indians, with nearly the same ceremony, attended with great noise and joy among all except one.

As I was unacquainted with this mode of firing and yelling of the savages, I concluded that there were thousands of Indians there, ready to receive General Braddock. But, what added to my surprise, I saw numbers running toward me, stripped naked, excepting breechclouts, and painted in the most hideous manner with various colors—red, black, brown, blue, etc.

As they approached, they formed themselves into two long ranks, about two or three yards apart. I was told by an Indian that could speak English that I must run betwixt these ranks and they would flog me all the way. If I ran quickly, it would be so much the better, as they would quit when I got to the end of the ranks.

There appeared to be a general rejoicing around me. I could find nothing like joy in my breast, but I started the race with all the resolution and vigor I was capable of. I was flogged the whole way. When I got near the end of the lines, I was struck with something that appeared to me to be a stick, which caused me to fall to the ground.

Recovering my senses, I endeavored to renew my race. As I arose, someone cast sand in my eyes, which blinded me, so that I could not see where to run. They continued beating me most intolerably, until I was at length insensible. Before I lost my senses, I remember my wishing them to strike the fatal blow. I thought they intended killing me, but were too long about it. . . .

The first thing I remember was my being in the fort, amidst the French and Indians, and a French doctor standing by me. . . .

I was then sent to the hospital and carefully attended by the doctors, and recovered quicker than I expected.

Some time after, I was visited by the Delaware Indian already mentioned, who was at the taking of me. Though he spoke bad English, I found him to be a man of considerable understanding. I asked him if I had done anything that had offended the Indians, which caused them to treat me so unmercifully. He said no, it was only an old custom, like saying how do you do. After that, he said, I would be well used.

I asked him if I should be permitted to remain with the French. He said no—and told me that as soon as I recovered I must not only go with the Indians, but must be made an Indian myself. . . .

Becoming an Indian

The day after my arrival a number of Indians collected about me, and one of them began to pull the hair out of my head. He had some ashes on a piece of bark, in which he frequently dipped his fingers in order to take the firmer hold. And so he went on, as if he had been plucking a turkey, until he had all the hair clean out of my head, except a small spot about three or four inches square on my crown. They cut this off with a pair of scissors, excepting three locks, which they dressed up in their own mode. Two of these they wrapped round with a narrow beaded garter made for that purpose, and the other they plaited at full length and then stuck full of silver brooches.

After this they bored my nose and ears, and fixed me up with earrings and nose jewels. They ordered me to strip off my clothes and put on a breechclout, which I did. Then they painted my head, face and body in various colors. They put a large belt of wampum on my neck, and silver bands on my hands and right arm.

Next, an old chief led me out in the street and gave the alarm halloo, "*Coo-wigh!*" several times, repeated quickly. At this, all that were in the town came running and stood round the old chief, who held me by the hand in their midst.

At that time I knew nothing of their mode of adoption, and had seen them put to death all they had taken. As I never could find that they saved a man alive at Braddock's defeat, I did not doubt they were about to put me to death in some cruel manner.

The old chief, holding me by the hand, made a long speech very loud, and handed me to three young squaws. They led me by the hand down the bank into the river until the water was up to our middle.

The squaws made signs to me to plunge myself into the water. I did not understand them. I thought the result of the council was I should be drowned, and these young ladies were the executioners. All three took violent hold of me. For some time I opposed them with all my might, which occasioned loud laughter among the multitude on the bank of the river.

At length one of the squaws resorted to speaking a little English (for I believe they began to be afraid of me) and said, "No hurt you!" At this I gave myself up to their ladyships, who were as good as their word. Though they plunged me under water and washed and rubbed me severely, I could not say they hurt me much.

These young women then led me up to the council house, where some of the tribe were ready with new clothes for me. They gave me a new ruffled shirt, which I put on, a pair of leggings done off with ribbons and beads, a pair of moccasins, and garters dressed with beads, porcupine quills, and red hair—also a tinsel-laced cloak.

They again painted my head and face with various colors, and tied a bunch of red feathers to one of the locks they had left on the crown of my head, which stood up five or six inches. They seated me on a bearskin and gave me a pipe, tomahawk, and polecat-skin pouch which contained tobacco and dry sumach leaves, which they mix with their tobacco—also flint, steel, and spunk, a kind of dry wood they use as tinder.

When I was seated, the Indians came in dressed and painted in their grandest manner. They took their seats and for a considerable time there was a profound silence. Everyone was smoking, but not a word was spoken among them. Finally one of the chiefs made a speech which was delivered to me by an interpreter.

An Insight

We had always regarded the capture of whites by Indians as dreadful; yet I saw nothing dreadful in taking Billy home with me. In fact, I had even thought of Billy as fortunate to be thus captured; and certainly he seemed to be enjoying himself. It came to me that the Indians who stole my people may not have felt they were doing anything particularly terrible; indeed, may have thought, as I did of Billy, that their captives were fortunate. Could it, I wondered, have been possible that my ancestors even took a certain amount of pleasure in the experience? Was there a possibility, even, that the behavior of those savages from St. Francis was no worse than that of white men?

These ideas, I suspected, were unorthodox and not to be publicly mentioned unless I wished to get into more trouble in Portsmouth.

Kenneth Roberts, *Northwest Passage*, 1937.

"My son, you are now flesh of our flesh and bone of our bone. By the ceremony which was performed this day, every drop of white blood was washed out of your veins. You are taken into the Caughnawaga nation and initiated into a warlike tribe. You are adopted into a great family, and now received with great solemnity in the place of a great man. You are one of us by an old strong law and custom.

"My son, you have nothing to fear. We are under the same obligation to love, support and defend you that we are to love and defend one another. You are to consider yourself as one of our people."

I did not believe this fine speech, but since that time I have found there was much sincerity in it. From that day I never knew them to make any distinction between me and themselves in any respect whatever. If they had plenty of clothing, I had plenty; if we were scarce of provisions, we all shared one fate.

After this ceremony was over, I was introduced to my new kin, and told that I was to attend a feast that evening, which I did. And as the custom was, they gave me a bowl and wooden spoon, which I carried with me to the place, where there was a number of large brass kettles full of boiled venison and green corn. Everyone advanced with his bowl and spoon and had his share given him. After this, one of the chiefs made a short speech, and then we began to eat. . . .

Shortly after this I was given a gun and went out on a long hunting trip with Mohawk Solomon and some of the Caughnawagas. After some time we came upon some fresh buffalo tracks.

I had observed that the Indians were upon their guard, and afraid of an enemy, for until now they and the southern nations had been at war. As we were following the buffalo tracks, Solomon seemed to be upon his guard. He went very slowly, and would frequently stand and listen.

We came to where the tracks were very plain in the sand.

"They are surely buffalo tracks," I said.

"Hush, you know nothing. May be buffalo tracks, may be Catawba," Solomon answered.

He went very cautiously until we found some fresh buffalo dung.

He smiled. "Catawba cannot make so."

He then stopped and told me an odd story about the Catawbas. He said that once the Catawbas came near one of the Caughnawaga hunting camps, and at some distance from the camp lay in ambush. In order to decoy the Caughnawagas out, the Catawbas sent two or three warriors in the night, past the camp, with buffalo hoofs fixed on their feet, so as to make artificial tracks.

In the morning those in the camp followed these tracks, thinking they were buffalo, until they were fired on by the Catawbas, and several of them killed. The others fled, collected a party and pursued the Catawbas.

But the wily Catawbas had brought with them rattlesnake poison, collected from the bladder at the root of the snakes' teeth. They had also brought small reeds, which they made sharp at the end and dipped in this poison. They stuck these in the ground among the grass, along their own tracks, in such a position that they might stick into the legs of the pursuers. When the Catawbas found that a number of the enemy were lame, being artificially snake bit, and they were all going back, the Catawbas turned upon the Caughnawagas and killed and scalped all that were lame.

When Solomon had finished this story and found I understood him, he concluded: "You don't know Catawba. Velly bad Indian, Catawba. All one devil Catawba."

Our hunting party encamped on a creek. One day I was told to take the dogs with me and go down the creek—perhaps I might kill a turkey. Since it was in the afternoon, I was also told not to go far from the creek, and to take care not to get lost.

When I had gone some distance down the creek I came upon fresh buffalo tracks. I had a number of dogs with me to stop the buffalo and decided I would follow them and kill one.

A little before sundown, I despaired of catching up with the buffalo. I was then thinking how I might get to camp before night. The buffalo had made several turns, and if I took the track back to the creek, it would be dark before I could get to camp. Therefore I thought I would take a near way through the hills, and strike the creek a little below the camp.

But it was cloudy weather and I was a very young woodsman: I could find neither creek or camp. When night came on, I fired my gun several times and hallooed, but received no answer.

Early the next morning the Indians were out after me. As I had with me ten or a dozen dogs, and the grass and weeds were rank, they could readily follow my track. When they came up with me they appeared to be in a very good humor.

I asked Solomon if he thought I was running away.

"No, no," he said, "you go too much clooked."

On my return to camp they took my gun from me. For this rash step I was reduced to a bow and arrows for nearly two years. . . .

Life Among the Squaws

While the hunters were all out, exerting themselves to the utmost of their ability, the squaws and boys (in which class I was) were scattered out, hunting red haws, black haws, and hickory nuts. As it was too late in the year, we did not succeed in gathering haws, but we had tolerable success in scratching up hickory nuts from under a light snow. After our return the hunters came in. They had killed only two small turkeys, which were but little among twenty-one persons. But all was divided with the greatest justice—everyone got their equal share.

The next day the hunters turned out again, and killed one deer and three bears. One of the bears was very large and remarkably fat. The hunters carried in meat sufficient to give us all a hearty supper and breakfast.

The squaws and all that could carry turned out to bring in meat. Everyone had their share assigned them. My load was among the least, but I was not accustomed to carrying in this way. I got exceedingly weary.

"My load is too heavy," I told them. "I must leave part of it and come for it again."

They made a halt and only laughed at me. Taking part of my load, they added it to a young squaw's, who had had as much before as I carried.

This kind of reproof had a greater tendency to excite me to exert myself in carrying without complaining than if they had whipped me for laziness. . . .

A Lesson About Generosity

After about two weeks we moved on to Lake Erie and encamped again. While we were here, Tontileaugo went out to hunt. When he was gone, a Wyandot came to our camp. I gave him a well-roasted shoulder of venison which I had by the fire and he received it gladly.

When Tontileaugo came home, I told him about the Wyandot and the roasted venison.

"That was very well," he said. "And I suppose you also gave him sugar and bear's oil to eat with his venison?"

"I did not. The sugar and bear's oil were down in the canoe and I didn't want to go for them."

"You have behaved just like a Dutchman. Don't you know that when strangers come to our camp we ought always to give them the best that we have?"

I acknowledged that I was wrong. He said that he could excuse this as I was but young, but I must learn to behave like a warrior and do great things, and never be guilty of such selfish behavior.

It was not far to Sunyendeand, the Wyandot town to which the other members of our party had gone. In this town there were French traders who purchased our skins and fur, and we all got new clothes, paint, tobacco, etc.

After I had got my new clothes, and my head done off like a redheaded woodpecker, I, in company with a number of young Indians, went down to the cornfield to see the squaws at work. They asked me to take a hoe. I did, and hoed for some time. The squaws applauded me as a good hand at the business.

When I returned to the town, the old men, hearing of what I had done, chided me and said that I was adopted in the place of a great man, and must not hoe corn like a squaw. They never had occasion to reprove me for anything like this again, as I never was extremely fond of work. . . .

Stealing Unknown

While we remained here I went with a young Caughnawaga about fifteen or seventeen years of age, Chinnohete by name, to gather cranberries. . . .

At the forks of the Cuyahoga we found that the skins we had scaffolded were all safe. Though this was a public place and Indians frequently had passed, there was nothing stolen. It is seldom that Indians do steal anything from one another. They say they never did until the white people came among them and taught some of them to lie, cheat, steal, and swear.

I remember that Tecaughretanego, when something displeased him, said, "God damn it!"

"Do you know what you have said?" I asked him once.

"I do"—and he mentioned one of their degrading expressions which he supposed to have the same meaning.

"That doesn't bear the least resemblance to it—what you said was calling upon the Great Spirit to punish the object you were displeased with."

He stood for some time amazed. "If this be the meaning of these words, what sort of people are the whites? When the traders were among us these words seemed to be intermixed with all their discourse. You must be mistaken. If you are not, the traders applied these words not only wickedly, but oftentimes very foolishly.

"I remember once a trader accidentally broke his gun lock and called out aloud, 'God damn it!' Surely the gun lock was not an object worthy of punishment by Owaneeyo, the Great Spirit."

We took up our birch-bark canoes which we had buried here, and found that they were not damaged by the winter. Then we all embarked, and arrived safely at the Wyandot town, nearly opposite Fort Detroit, on the north side of the river. Here we found a number of French traders, every one very willing to deal with us for our beaver. We bought ourselves fine clothes, ammunition, paint, tobacco, etc., and, according to promise, the Indians purchased me a new gun. . . .

"Brother," Tecaughretanego said, "as you have lived with the white people, who have stocks of cattle and barns filled with grain, you have not had the same advantage as we Indians of knowing that the Great Being above feeds his people in due season. We are often out of provisions and yet are wonderfully supplied—so frequently that it is evidently the hand of the great Owaneeyo that doth this.

"I know you are now afraid we will all perish with hunger, but you have no reason to fear this. Owaneeyo sometimes suffers us to be in want in order to teach us our dependence upon him, and to let us know that we are to love and serve him.

"Brother, be assured that you will be supplied with food just in the right time, but you must go to sleep and rise early in the morning and go hunting. Be strong and exert yourself like a man, and the Great Spirit will direct your way."

Shaving

The notion formerly entertained that the Indians are beardless by nature and have no hair on their bodies, appears now to be exploded and entirely laid aside. I cannot conceive how it is possible for any person to pass three weeks only among those people, without seeing them pluck out their beards, with tweezers made expressly for that purpose. Before the Europeans came into the country, their apparatus for performing this work, consisted of a pair of muscle [sic] shells, sharpened on a gritty stone, which answered very well, being somewhat like pincers; but since they can obtain wire, of which that of brass is preferred, they make themselves tweezers, which they always carry with them in their tobacco-pouch, wherever they go, and when at leisure, they pluck out their beards or the hair above their foreheads. This they do in a very quick manner, much like the plucking of a fowl, and the oftener they pluck out their hair, the finer it grows afterwards, so that at last there appears hardly any, the whole having been rooted out. The principal reasons which they give for this plucking out their beards and the hair next to their foreheads, are that they may have a clean skin to lay the paint on, when they dress for their festivals or dances, and to facilitate the *tattooing* themselves, a custom formerly much in use among them, especially with those who had distinguished themselves by their valour, and acquired celebrity. They say that either painting or tattooing on a hairy face or body would have a disgusting appearance.

Abraham Steiner, *Thirty Thousand Miles with John Heckewelder*, 1958.

Such speeches from an Indian may be thought altogether incredible by those who are unacquainted with them. But when we reflect on the Indian war, we may readily conclude that they are not as ignorant or stupid sort of people, or they would not have been such fatal enemies. Besides, Tecaughretanego was no common person, but was among the Indians as Socrates in the ancient heathen world—equal to him, if not in wisdom and learning, yet perhaps in patience and fortitude. . . .

Early in 1760 I came home to Conococheague, and found that my people could never ascertain whether I was killed or taken, until my return. They received me with great joy, but were surprised to see me so much like an Indian both in my gait and gesture.

"I now began to realize that I would have to learn the ways of the white man."

An Indian Learns About White Culture

Luther Standing Bear

Luther Standing Bear, an Oglala Sioux, became part of the first class at the Carlisle Indian School. The Carlisle Indian School was established in 1879 as part of the government plan to improve the treatment of the Indians. The school was intentionally designed as a nonreservation boarding school, the more effectively to separate students from their native cultures as they were schooled to fit into white society. Carlisle, which flourished from 1879-1918, offered essentially an eighth-grade education, emphasizing skilled trades, farming, and home economics. In the following viewpoint, Luther Standing Bear describes his first days at Carlisle.

As you read, consider the following questions:

1. How did young Standing Bear interpret his purpose in going away with the white people?
2. What was the educational purpose of each event Luther Standing Bear describes?
3. In retrospect, how does the author evaluate his first days at Carlisle?

At last the train arrived at a junction where we were told we were at the end of our journey. Here we left the train and walked about two miles to the Carlisle Barracks. Soon we came to a big gate in a great high wall. The gate was locked, but after quite a long wait, it was unlocked and we marched in through it. I was the first boy inside. At that time I thought nothing of it, but now I realize that I was the first Indian boy to step inside the Carlisle Indian School grounds.

Here the girls were all called to one side by Louise McCoz, the girls' interpreter. She took them into one of the big buildings, which was very brilliantly lighted, and it looked good to us from the outside.

When our interpreter told us to go to a certain building which he pointed out to us, we ran very fast, expecting to find nice little beds like those the white people had. We were so tired and worn out from the long trip that we wanted a good long sleep. From Springfield, Dakota, to Carlisle, Pennsylvania, riding in day coaches all the way, with no chance to sleep, is an exhausting journey for a bunch of little Indians.

But the first room we entered was empty. A cast-iron stove stood in the middle of the room, on which was placed a coal-oil lamp. There was no fire in the stove. We ran through all the rooms, but they were all the same—no fire, no beds. This was a two-story building, but we were all herded into two rooms on the upper floor.

Well, we had to make the best of the situation, so we took off our leggins and rolled them up for a pillow. All the covering we had was the blanket which each had brought. We went to sleep on the hard floor, and it was so cold! We had been used to sleeping on the ground, but the floor was so much colder.

Next morning we were called downstairs for breakfast. All we were given was bread and water. How disappointed we were! At noon we had some meat, bread, and coffee, so we felt a little better. But how lonesome the big boys and girls were for their far-away Dakota homes where there was plenty to eat! The big boys seemed to take it worse than we smaller chaps did. I guess we little fellows did not know any better. The big boys would sing brave songs, and that would start the girls to crying. They did this for several nights. The girls' quarters were about a hundred and fifty yards from ours, so we could hear them crying. After some time the food began to get better, but it was far from being what we had been used to receiving back home. . . .

Becoming "Luther"

Although we were yet wearing our Indian clothes, the interpreter came to us and told us we must go to school. We were marched into a schoolroom, where we were each given a pencil and slate. We were seated at single desks. We soon discovered that the pencils made marks on the slates. So we covered our heads with our blankets, holding the slate inside so the other fellow would not know what we were doing. Here we would draw a man on a pony chasing buffalo, or a boy shooting birds in a tree, or it might be one of our Indian games, or anything that suited our fancy to try and portray.

When we had all finished, we dropped our blankets down on the seat and marched up to the teacher with our slates to show what we had drawn. Our teacher was a woman. She bowed her head as she examined the slates and smiled, indicating that we were doing pretty well—at least we interpreted it that way.

One day when we came to school there was a lot of writing on one of the blackboards. We did not know what it meant, but our interpreter came into the room and said, 'Do you see all these marks on the blackboard? Well, each word is a white man's name. They are going to give each one of you one of these names by which you will hereafter be known.' None of the names were read or explained to us, so of course we did not know the sound or meaning of any of them.

The teacher had a long pointed stick in her hand, and the interpreter told the boy in the front seat to come up. The teacher handed the stick to him, and the interpreter then told him to pick out any name he wanted. The boy had gone up with his blanket on. When the long stick was handed to him, he turned to us as much as to say, 'Shall I—or will you help me to take one of these names? Is it right for me to take a white man's name?' He did not know what to do for a time, not uttering a single word—but he acted a lot and was doing a lot of thinking.

Finally he pointed out one of the names written on the blackboard. Then the teacher took a piece of white tape and wrote the name on it. Then she cut off a length of the tape and sewed it on the back of the boy's shirt. Then that name was erased from the board. There was no duplication of names in the first class at Carlisle School!

Then the next boy took the pointer and selected a name. He was also labeled in the same manner as Number One. When my turn came, I took the pointer and acted as if I were about to touch an enemy. Soon we all had the names of white men sewed on our backs. When we went to school, we knew enough to take our proper places in the class, but that was all. When the teacher called the roll, no one answered his name. Then she would walk around and look at the back of the boys' shirts. When she had the right name located, she made the boy stand up and say 'Present.' She kept this up for about a week before we knew what the sound of our new names was.

I was one of the 'bright fellows' to learn my name quickly. How proud I was to answer when the teacher called the roll! I would put my blanket down and half raise myself in my seat, all ready to answer to my new name. I had selected the name 'Luther'—not 'Lutheran' as many people call me. 'Lutheran' is the name of a church denomination, not a person.

First Lessons

Next we had to learn to write our names. Our good teacher had a lot of patience with us. She is now living in Los Angeles, California, and I still like to go and ask her any question which may come up in my mind. She first wrote my name on the slate for me, and then, by motions, indicated that I was to write it just like that. She held the pencil in her hand just so, then made first one stroke, then another, and by signs I was given to understand that I was to follow in exactly the same way.

The first few times I wrote my new name, it was scratched so deeply into the slate that I was never able to erase it. But I copied my name all over both sides of the slate until there was no more room to write. Then I took my slate up to show it to the teacher, and she indicated, by the expression of her face, that it was very good. I soon learned to write it very well; then I took a piece of chalk downstairs and wrote 'Luther' all over everything I could copy it on. . . .

A few days later, she wrote the alphabet on the blackboard, then brought the interpreter into the room. Through him she told us to repeat each letter after her, calling out 'A,' and we all said 'A'; then 'B,' and so on. This was our real beginning. The first day we learned the first three letters of the alphabet, both the pronunciation and the reading of them.

I had not determined to learn anything yet. All I could think of was my free life at home. How long would these people keep us here? When were we going home? At home we could eat any time we wished, but here we had to watch the sun all the time. On cloudy days the waits between meals seemed terribly long. . . .

First Haircut

One day we had a strange experience. We were all called together by the interpreter and told that we were to have our hair cut off. We listened to what he had to say, but we did not reply. This was something that would require some thought, so that evening the big boys held a council, and I recall very distinctly that Nakpa Kesela, or Robert American Horse, made a serious speech. Said he, 'If I am to learn the ways of the white people, I can do it just as well with my hair on.' To this we all exclaimed 'Hau!' — meaning that we agreed with him.

In spite of this meeting, a few days later we saw some white

252

men come inside the school grounds carrying big chairs. The interpreter told us these were the men who had come to cut our hair. We did not watch to see where the chairs were carried, as it was school time, and we went to our classroom. One of the big boys named Ya Slo, or Whistler, was missing. In a short time he came in with his hair cut off. Then they called another boy out, and when he returned, he also wore short hair. In this way we were called out one by one. . . .

Right here I must state how this hair-cutting affected me in various ways. I have recounted that I always wanted to please my father in every way possible. All his instructions to me had been along this line: 'Son, be brave and get killed.' This expression had been moulded into my brain to such an extent that I knew nothing else.

But my father had made a mistake. He should have told me, upon leaving home, to go and learn all I could of the white man's ways, and be like them. That would have given a new idea from a different slant; but Father did not advise me along that line. I had come away from home with the intention of never returning alive unless I had done something very brave.

Now, after having had my haircut, a new thought came into my head. I felt that I was no more Indian, but would be an imitation of a white man. And we are still imitations of white men, and the white men are imitations of the Americans.

We all looked so funny with short hair. It had been cut with a machine and cropped very close. We still had our Indian clothes, but were all 'bald-headed.' None of us slept well that night; we felt so queer. I wanted to feel of my head all the time. But in a short time I became anxious to learn all I could.

White Men's Clothes

Next, we heard that we were soon to have white men's clothes. We were all very excited and anxious when this was announced to us. One day some wagons came in, loaded with big boxes, which were unloaded in front of the office. Of course we were all very curious, and gathered around to watch the proceedings and see all we could.

Here, one at a time, we were 'sized up' and a whole suit handed to each of us. The clothes were some sort of dark heavy gray goods, consisting of coat, pants, and vest. We were also given a dark woolen shirt, a cap, a pair of suspenders, socks, and heavy farmer's boots. . . .

How proud we were with clothes that had pockets and with boots that squeaked! We walked the floor nearly all that night. Many of the boys even went to bed with their clothes all on. But in the morning, the boys who had taken off their pants had a

This Navajo outwardly adapted to the white culture that overwhelmed his own. Whether his heart followed suit is unknown.

most terrible time. They did not know whether they were to button up in front or behind. Some of the boys said the open part went in front; others said, 'No, it goes at the back.' There is where the boys who had kept all their clothes on came in handy to look at. They showed the others that the pants buttoned up in front and not at the back. So here we learned something again. . . .

I now began to realize that I would have to learn the ways of the white man. With that idea in mind, the thought also came to me that I must please my father as well. So my little brain began to work hard. I thought that some day I might be able to become an interpreter for my father, as he could not speak English. Or I thought I might be able to keep books for him if he again started a store. So I worked very hard.

Learning a Trade

One day they selected a few boys and told us we were to learn trades. I was to be a tinsmith. I did not care for this, but I tried my best to learn this trade. Mr. Walker was our instructor. I was getting along very well. I made hundreds of tin cups, coffee pots, and buckets. These were sent away and issued to the Indians on various reservations.

After I had left the school and returned home, this trade did not benefit me any, as the Indians had plenty of tinware that I had made at school.

Mornings I went to the tin shop, and in the afternoon attended school. I tried several times to drop this trade and go to school the entire day, but Captain Pratt said, 'No, you must go to the tin shop—that is all there is to it,' so I had to go. Half school and half work took away a great deal of study time. I figure that I spent only about a year and a half in school, while the rest of the time was wasted, as the school was not started properly to begin with. Possibly you wonder why I did not remain longer, but the Government had made an agreement with our parents as to the length of time we were to be away. . . .

My Father Visits

One Sunday morning we were all busy getting ready to go to Sunday School in town. Suddenly there was great excitement among some of the boys on the floor below. One of the boys came running upstairs shouting, 'Luther Standing Bear's father is here!' Everybody ran downstairs to see my father. We had several tribes at the school now, many of whom had heard of my father, and they were anxious to see him.

When I got downstairs, my father was in the center of a large crowd of the boys, who were all shaking hands with him. I had to fight my way through to reach him. He was so glad to see me, and I was so delighted to see him. But our rules were that we were not to speak the Indian language under any consideration. And here was my father, and he could not talk English!

My first act was to write a note to Captain Pratt, asking if he would permit me to speak to my father in the Sioux tongue. I said, 'My father is here. Please allow me to speak to him in Indian.' Captain Pratt answered, 'Yes, my boy; bring your father over to my house.'

This was another happy day for me. I took my father over to meet Captain Pratt, who was so glad to see him and was very respectful to him. Father was so well dressed. He wore a gray suit, nice shoes, and a derby hat. But he wore his hair long. He looked very nice in white men's clothes. He even sported a gold watch and chain. Captain Pratt gave father a room with Robert American Horse, in the boys' quarters. He allowed the boys to talk to him in the Indian tongue, and that pleased the boys very much. Here Father remained for a time with us.

Chapter 6

How Should Columbus Be Viewed in the Twentieth Century?

Chapter Preface

Much is made of anniversaries, whether the commemoration is somber or silly. Recently the 50th anniversary of the bombing of Pearl Harbor elicited TV commentaries, personal recollections, and retrospectives. The 100th anniversary of the invention of the game of basketball merited a commemorative U.S. postage stamp. The 200th anniversary of the birth of our nation resulted not only in speeches, editorials, and prayers, but in tall ships, T-shirts, a fiesta of fireworks, and a resurgence of Sousa. The 500th anniversary of Christopher Columbus's arrival in the Americas has produced a similar frenzy of activity. In part it has become a merchandising extravaganza; in part, an opportunity for taking stock of where we are and where we hope to go.

Although some potential corporate sponsors of quincentennial events may have been scared off by threats of criticism from all segments of the political spectrum, many American marketers saw the anniversary as an extraordinary opportunity. Rice Chex, for example, emblazoned the back of its cereal box with a "Voyage of Columbus 500th Anniversary Map," complete with cartoon portraits of the explorer and Ferdinand and Isabella. Ads starring an archeologist excavating possible Columbus landing sites announced the discovery of Christopher Columbus glass mugs, etched with likenesses of the three ships, which could be had free with a meal at participating Long John Silver restaurants. A bonanza of novels was published, such as *1492* by Homero Aridjis and *The Crown of Columbus* by Michael Dorris and Louise Erdrich, Peter Lis's charming children's book *Follow the Dream: The Story of Christopher Columbus*, the *Guinness Book of Records, 1492* and even *Garfield Discovers America*. Model shipbuilding kits with which one could construct the *Niña, Pinta,* and *Santa Maria* hit the toy stores. Pierce Puzzle Company of Hutchinson, Kansas, offered a 500-piece jigsaw puzzle "Departure of Columbus from Palos in 1492, painted in 1855 by Emmanuel Leutze." Two movies, *Christopher Columbus: The Discovery* with Tom Selleck, Rachel Ward, George Corraface, and Marlon Brando and *1492: Conquest of Paradise* with Gerard Depardieu, Sigourney Weaver, and Armand Assante, were released in time to commemorate the anniversary. The Smithsonian Institution offered a transatlantic crossing under sail; Columbus, Ohio, the largest city named for the explorer, floated a replica of the *Santa Maria* on the Olentangy River and was the site of the quincentennial garden extravaganza, Ameriflora.

Despite all the commercial tie-ins for sale, the Quincentennial also offers, as do most anniversaries, a time for reflection and resolutions. Few in 1992 are so sanguine as in centuries past in assessing the legacy of Columbus. Yet there is little agreement; the commentators, like those in this chapter, are polarized over what deserves celebration or condemnation. Was the major demographic consequence the virtual annihilation of the native American population, or the creation of a new people, the Latinos? Was the conquest the first illustration of impoverished Europeans making a fresh start—or of the economic exploitation of two continents? Did Columbus lead an invasion resulting in genocide, or an exploration creating over a dozen new countries? The evaluations of Columbus's legacy included in this chapter reflect the varying ethnic, political, and philosophical biases of their authors.

In 1992 it is certain that, as many have claimed, Columbus has become a metaphor. But for what? On this few would agree. This very disagreement may be Columbus's current legacy: the stimulus to reassess ourselves and our ideas, and to formulate new solutions to today's problems.

Viewpoint 1

"The indisputable consequences of Columbus's achievement . . . would seem to be worthy of appreciation by even our most skeptical contemporaries."

Modern Attacks on Columbus Are Unwarranted

Mark Falcoff

Mark Falcoff, a resident scholar at the American Enterprise Institute, writes on Latin American politics, U.S. foreign policy, and intelligence policy. In the following viewpoint, Falcoff argues that the vicious attacks on Columbus, which include blaming him for a host of ills, are for the most part historically inaccurate and unfounded.

As you read, consider the following questions:

1. According to Falcoff, is the resistance to *celebrating* the quincentenary a result of new discoveries about Columbus, his life and works?
2. How does Falcoff use recent research to undermine the "noble savage" concept?
3. According to the author, what is the logical conclusion to be reached if one accepts the revisionists' arguments?
4. What does Falcoff think is the real agenda of the Columbus critics?

Until quite recently, Columbus's arrival in what is now the Dominican Republic on October 12, 1492, was unambiguously regarded as one of the most important—and fortuitous—events in history. And Columbus himself, part mystic and dreamer, part man of science, part arbitrageur, has long embodied qualities particularly attractive to Americans. "The pioneer of progress and enlightenment" was the way President Benjamin Harrison described Columbus when he opened the celebrations marking the fourth century since the voyage. What followed in 1892 was a vast orgy of self-congratulation that lasted a full year, punctuated by brass bands, the Columbian Exposition in Chicago, even the commissioning of Dvorak's New World Symphony.

Every age tends to rewrite history according to its own needs and prejudices, so a repetition of the 1892 commemoration was unlikely. Given the temper of our times and the particular drift that elite culture has taken in the United States, uncritical accolades were hardly to be expected. Even so, some of the indisputable consequences of Columbus's achievement—the sudden, radical enlargement of geographical knowledge, the transcontinental exchange of plants and animals, the incorporation of a huge portion of the earth into a larger economic system, the birth of new nations and cultures, even the widening of the political and moral horizons of humanity—would seem to be worthy of appreciation by even our most skeptical contemporaries. In fact, . . . Columbus and his legacy have come under an attack from a coalition of religious, cultural, and racial groups.

The struggle over historical meaning began with words. The term "discovery" has suddenly become suspect because it seems to indicate that the indigenous peoples of this hemisphere existed only after Europeans became aware of them. Stated that way, who could disagree? But finding another word to substitute for "discovery" proved to be surprisingly difficult. Only after extensive negotiations was the Columbus Quincentenary Commission in the United States able to convince its critics to accept a compromise: we are now to regard what happened in 1492 not as a "discovery" at all but as an "encounter." Encounter sounds agreeably neutral since it places both the discoverer and the discovered on an apparent plane of cultural equality. But it fails to convey the full richness of the event; clearly, something is missing. Columnist John Leo recently quipped, "'Encounter'—as in, 'My car has encountered a large truck going 80 miles an hour.'"

The struggle over terms masks deeper emotions. After all, those who are trying to consign the word "discovery" to oblivion have not set out to merely establish cultural parity between two worlds; rather, they hope to advance a more radical social and historical vision. The United Nations discovered this as long ago as 1986 when, after four years of impassioned debate, it abandoned altogether any attempt to celebrate the event. Here in the United States, the lead has been taken by the National Council of Churches, which refers to 1492 and all of the events that followed as "an invasion and colonization . . . with genocide, economic exploitation, and a deep level of institutional racism and moral decadence."

Columbus Started Democratic System

In my family, Columbus has always been viewed as a hero, as in many other Italian homes. [Columbus was born in Italy.] Having October 12 as a national holiday has given many Italian immigrants great pride.

I think we all should recognize, though, that not all groups are going to feel the same way about Columbus. But I think it is also unfair to conclude that . . . Columbus is unworthy of being hailed as a great explorer, as a man who introduced an old world to a new one. He started a democratic system that we still hold on to today, even though it wasn't and still isn't perfect.

Mario Cuomo, *Scholastic Update*, September 20, 1991.

With an even broader brush, the American Library Association classifies the entire period of the European discovery and colonization of the Western hemisphere as the "Native American Holocaust" and urges its members to approach the Columbus celebrations "from an authentic Native American perspective, dealing directly with topics like cultural imperialism [and] colonialism." Author Kirkpatrick Sale, whose new book about Columbus, *The Conquest of Paradise*, has appeared just in time to benefit from the new "revisionist" wave, prefers to condemn the Great Mariner for "ecocide"—the destruction of the delicate balance between man and nature that presumably existed before his arrival.

Not surprisingly, leaders of indigenous communities in the United States have contributed much to this discussion. According to Russell Means of the American Indian Movement (AIM), Columbus "makes Hitler look like a juvenile delinquent." Suzan Shoan Haijo [*sic*: Shown Harjo] of the Morningstar Foundation, a member of the Cheyenne and Arapaho Indian nations, urges us to commemorate instead the five-hundredth anniversary of *1491*, which she calls "the last *good* year." As Garry Wills recently put it, "A funny thing happened on the way to the quincentennial celebration of America's discovery . . . Columbus got mugged. This time the Indians were waiting for him." A headline summarizes the situation telegraphically: "Columbus, a Ruthless Racist Now, Sails Toward Public Relations Reef."

Columbus's Early Critics

The sudden tidal wave of resistance to the Columbus celebrations might be the product of new information about the man, his life, and his works, but in fact it is not. Most of what we know today was known by earlier generations 100, possibly even 200, years ago. There have always been arguments about Columbus's ancestry as well as whether he really was the first European mariner to discover this hemisphere. (Lately, there have been assertions that not Columbus but African sailors first established the translantic link between the two hemispheres.) But the circumstances of Columbus's voyages as well as the short- and longer-term impacts have never been in doubt, including all of the unlovely aspects: the virtual obliteration of some Indian populations, the enslavement of others, and the subsequent decision to import African chattels to supplement the colonial labor force.

The controversy over the moral dimension of the European conquest is likewise not new. It was initiated more than 400 years ago by a Spaniard, Bartolomé de las Casas. A soldier and settler in Cuba and Hispaniola before taking Dominican orders, Las Casas was the first person in Western history to clearly raise the issue of the rights of the conquered indigenous peoples. As a demographer, he left something to be desired, but as a propagandist he displayed uncommon imagination, verve, and what today we would call public relations sense. He managed to get a hearing at the special levee of the Spanish court specifically convoked in Valladolid in 1550 to resolve the most controversial issue of the day: whether the Indians of the newly discovered lands possessed immortal souls and therefore deserved the same treatment as other men. There Las Casas took on Juan Ginés de Sepúlveda, one of the most learned advocates in Europe, who had been retained by the Spanish-settler community in America. Though the great debate ended in a draw, the Spanish monarchy, influenced by Las Casas's arguments, finally abolished Indian servitude in its overseas provinces—a command that was unenforced and also, unfortunately, ultimately unenforceable.

Las Casas's real contribution, however, was not legal but ideological and historiographic. His *Brief History of the Destruction of the Indies*, published in 1550-1551, was the first human rights report in history. It recounted in exquisite detail incidents of torture, murder, and mistreatment of the native populations by ruthless Spanish adventurers. In effect, Las Casas accused his fellow countrymen of nothing less than genocide. Translated almost

262

immediately into the major European languages and published under the new title *Tears of the Indies*, his book became an international best-seller. Outside the Iberian peninsula, it generated an entire literature of indictment of Spain and all things Spanish. In fact, it became the cornerstone of the Black Legend, the enduring notion—particularly in Northern European countries but also in the United States and to some degree even in Latin America— that Spaniards are uniquely cruel, bigoted, tyrannical, obscurantist, lazy, fanatical, greedy, and treacherous. Las Casas's work thus marks the point of departure for another, singularly Western phenomenon: the penchant for certain strains of national self-criticism to pass, sometimes imperceptibly, over into national self-hatred.

Nor is the notion of pre-Columbian America as Paradise Lost something only now being discovered by our environmentalists. Columbus's own journals make reference to the innocence and primitive charm of the Indians who approached his caravels ("naked as their mothers bore them") and to the abundance of their natural environment. The concept of the "noble savage" dominates Las Casas's work. Even Spaniards who actually participated in the conquests of Mexico and Peru thought much the same at first; fascinated by the complexity and sophistication of the societies they encountered, some found themselves grasping for metaphors drawn from the Spanish books of chivalry, the closest thing they possessed to utopian literature. . . .

What We Know Now

It is easier to forgive eighteenth-century Europeans for playing loose with the facts about pre-Columbian America than it is to excuse some of our contemporaries. After all, the former did not have the benefit of the modern disciplines of history, anthropology, and archaeology. In his *Brief History*, Las Casas claimed that the Spaniards had killed 20 million Indians in the process of settling Hispaniola and the other islands of the archipelago. Today, we know that Columbus and his men could not have done this even if they had tried. As historian John Tate Lanning pointed out some years ago, "If each Spaniard listed in Bermúdez Plata's *Passengers to the Indies*" for a half century after the discovery "had killed an Indian every day and three on Sunday, it would have taken a generation to do the job."

The issue, of course, is not just one of numbers, although perhaps it bears repeating here that exterminating Indians was decidedly not the purpose of the conquest. The Spaniards had no interest whatever in reducing the numbers of their potential labor force or, for that matter, the number of potential converts to Catholic Christianity. In arriving at his figures, Las Casas and many others who followed in his tradition did not allow for the diminution of the Indian populations by simple circumstance: their lack of immunity to European diseases, warfare with other tribes, culture shock, and even miscegenation—that is, the gradual integration into the newer and larger racially mixed communities created by Spanish settlements in the late sixteenth and early seventeenth centuries.

Nor is what we now know about some of the more important Indian societies particularly reassuring, at least for those who claim to hold in high regard such things as harmony with nature or respect for cultural and political pluralism. The Aztecs were a people of remarkable attainments—authors of a civilization that merits our admiration even now, nearly four centuries after its extinction—but they were an imperial race that had conquered and subordinated most of the other peoples of the Valley of Mexico and waged relentless war upon their neighbors to extract victims for human sacrifice to continually appease the gods.

By the time the Spaniards reached what is now Central America, the Mayan civilization there had been in decline for several hundred years. Until very recently, archaeologists were mystified by the apparent sudden disappearance of a federation of Mayan temple-cities around 900 A.D., since they believed that the Mayans had been a peaceful and philosophical people—accomplished artists, poets, and astronomers. But now, the first commemorative stones have been deciphered, and we know otherwise. There was no federation in the first place, nor could there have been one, because the Mayans were every bit as aggressive and warlike as the Aztecs. But at some point, things veered out of control, and stylized warfare between kings degenerated into large-scale attacks on each other's cities, devastation of agricultural fields, and the wholesale murder of innocent civilians.

In North America, the Indians were far less sophisticated than the Aztecs or the Mayans. Human sacrifice did not play a role in their religious life, but it cannot be said that they were particularly respectful of the environment, except insofar as their small numbers and their primitive level of technology made it difficult to leave much of a mark on the lands they occupied. Many lived a seminomadic existence as hunter-gatherers, moving on after the most obvious and immediate natural resources were becoming depleted. Nor were they, by and large, respectful of other Indian peoples, whom they considered as alien as the white man. From what we know about these societies—and we know quite a lot—ideas like minority rights and pluralism played no role in their political, or rather prepolitical, organization.

Despite this, we hear that the Indian peoples of the Americas—past and present—constitute a peerless repository of virtues. When examined more carefully, however, these turn out to be

Western virtues, and uniquely Western virtues at that. This, surely, is the message of Kevin Costner's updated horse opera, *Dances with Wolves*. The question is indiscreet, but the "revisionists" do not allow us to avoid it: Are indigenous peoples better practitioners of Western values than the West? Alas, there is not much evidence that they are or were. And it is as unfair to them as it is to us to pretend otherwise.

With the best will in the world, it is simply not possible to be historically honest and at the same time credit them with achievements that parallel those of our Founding Fathers in Philadelphia.

The Central Paradox

Nothing we know and nothing we are likely to learn will ever justify to our contemporaries the conquest of other peoples—no matter how primitive or brutal those people were. That is the point first made by Father Las Casas, and it is crucial to the development of the modern Western sensibility. But to debate these issues as if they are part of ongoing events completely upsets the applecart of context. Las Casas wrote at a time when there was still some hope of shaping native policy in the Spanish colonies. Today, the Columbus controversy is not about what to do but (at least by indirection) about what should have been done. In so doing, the revisionists force the rest of us to follow their argument to its "logical" conclusion. If the European discovery of America was indeed "an invasion of colonization . . . with genocide, economic exploitation, and a deep level of institutional racism and moral decadence," then there can be only one historical conclusion: 1492 was a mistake. Columbus went too far. And to this there can be only one solution—we must all mount our boats and return from whence we came.

There is another troubling contradiction in the critics' bill of indictment: How seriously can we take accusations of genocide, ecocide, and other disasters nothing less than cosmic when the remedies counseled are at best meliorative and incremental? The best that the more serious-minded can manage is a year-long program of reflection and repentance. In this spirit, Professor Franklin B. Knight of Johns Hopkins University instructs us to "educate ourselves about a brave new world devoid of the arrogance and ethnocentrism of the past, in which all people are taken on their own terms and accorded dignity and respect—the rich as well as the poor, the developed as well as the underdeveloped, the mighty and the weak, the large and the small."

Today's Focus

These and other incongruities do not trouble Columbus's contemporary critics because they are really not much interested in what happened in 1492 or even the centuries thereafter. Theirs is a distemper with the world in which we live today. Having failed thus far to sell on the open market their political agenda—slow-growth or no-growth, an incomes policy based on imagined grievances rather than productivity, and redistribution of resources based on racial spoils—they are now trying to bludgeon it home on the cultural battlefield. The Columbus controversy is merely the latest engagement in this war.

By selecting this particular issue, the revisionists and their allies have shown a certain panache. They have already managed to turn what might have been a rather dull, pro forma observance into something more controversial and even newsworthy, and before the quincentennial year is over, they will doubtless have done still more: by leveraging the machinery of our sensitive political system; by intimidating university administrators, museum directors, and librarians; by threatening unseemly public demonstrations; and by straining this country's apparently inexhaustible fund of patience, tolerance, and basic decency. But will they succeed in what after all is their large objective—to change the way we feel about ourselves, our country, and the larger civilization of which we are a part? Not likely.

But even without intending to do so, they have raised some questions that are entirely appropriate to the quincentennial year and also to the ongoing cultural debate in our own country. According to what standards can the West be held accountable for the actions that accompanied its discovery and settlement of the Americas? The only possible answer would seem to be—its own. Do we know today something we did not know yesterday that puts in a morally inferior light the spread of European culture to the Western hemisphere? We do not. In a larger sense, has the spread of European civilization around the globe, not just in this hemisphere, been on balance a positive factor in world history? There can be no doubt that it has.

In its particulars, the Iberian conquest of the Americas in no way differed from the course of other empires in world history, replete with murder, exploitation, forced relocation of populations, and the destruction of whole cultures. But its moral framework was radically dissimilar. Yes, it was Spaniards who committed the abuses and crimes of the conquest, but it was also Spaniards, as the distinguished Peruvian novelist Mario Vargas Llosa has reminded us, who were the first to condemn those abuses and demand that they be brought to an end, "abandon[ing] the ranks in order to collaborate with the vanquished.". . .

For even the harshest critics of our societies in this hemisphere cannot deny that over these past 500 years—and particularly the last 200—we have not exactly wallowed in complacency and self-satisfaction. After all, the Americas were the birthplace of the revolutionary ideas of political self-determination and the economic autonomy of the individual. Those who imagine that these are antiquated nineteenth-century notions that have outlived their relevance must face the fact that today they are now spreading around the world, even to such unlikely corners as Albania and China. Admittedly, this is not what Columbus had in mind when he set sail from Huelva thinking he would eventually drop anchor in the harbors of the Great Khan, but without his journey in the first place, the history of humanity might have been very different—and very much darker.

Nor is this merely a matter of historical speculation. We can, in fact, test the proposition. The entire period since 1945 has been one long orgy of anticolonialism throughout much of Africa and Asia and of milder forms of anti-Western sentiment in much of Latin America. What we have learned from recent experience in these places is that where Western ideas and values have declined or been expelled, there is less freedom, not more; less human dignity; less food; less education; poorer health—in short, regression, not progress.

The failure of anti-Western ideologies in Cuba and Angola, in Vietnam and Mozambique, in Algeria, Syria, and Iraq, ought to give greater pause to the critics of Western civilization currently trying to hitch a free ride home on Columbus's caravels.

On one point, the critics of Columbus are not wrong: his voyage is indeed a proper metaphor for the spread of Western influence throughout the world. That influence is once again on the rise, this time not inadvertently but by the sheer force of its ideas. As Western civilization approaches a universal ideal, the distinction between discoverers and the discovered will become meaningless. And 100 years from now, the Columbus controversy will seem even more bizarre and incomprehensible than it does today.

VIEWPOINT 2

"We have no reason to celebrate an invasion."

Modern Attacks on Columbus Are Justified

Suzan Shown Harjo, interviewed by Barbara Miner; and Michael Dorris

Suzan Shown Harjo, a Cheyenne-Creek, is president and director of the Morning Star Foundation in Washington, D.C. The foundation sponsored the 1992 Alliance, a vehicle for "indigenous peoples' response to the Columbus Quincentenary." In Part I of the following viewpoint, Harjo explains why modern attacks on Columbus are necessary to eradicate injustice. In Part II, Michael Dorris cites and condemns several examples of how modern society uses Indians as symbols. Dorris is a well-known author whose works include *The Broken Cord*.

As you read, consider the following questions:

1. Examine the questions Ms. Miner asks Suzan Harjo. Would you answer any of them differently? Why or why not?
2. How are Michael Dorris's ideas similar to Harjo's? How are they different? Does the difference in format (editorial vs. interview) account for the differences? If so, why?

I

Why aren't you joining in the celebrations of the Columbus quincentenary?

As Native American peoples in this red quarter of Mother Earth, we have no reason to celebrate an invasion that caused the demise of so many of our people and is still causing destruction today. The Europeans stole our land and killed our people.

But because the quincentenary is a cause celebre, it provides an opportunity to put forth Native American perspectives on the next 500 years.

Columbus was just "a man of his times." Why are you so critical of him? Why not look at the positive aspects of his legacy?

For people who are in survival mode, it's very difficult to look at the positive aspects of death and destruction, especially when it is carried through to our present. There is a reason we are the poorest people in America. There is a reason we have the highest teen suicide rate. There is a reason why our people are ill-housed and in poor health, and we do not live as long as the majority population.

That reason has to do with the fact that we were in the way of Western civilization and we were in the way of westward expansion. We suffered the "excesses" of civilization such as murder, pillage, rape, destruction of the major waterways, destruction of land, the destruction and pollution of the air.

What are those "positive" aspects of the Columbus legacy? If we're talking about the horse, yeah, that's good. We like the horse. Indians raised the use of the horse to high military art, especially among the Cheyenne people and the tribes of the plains states.

Was that a good result of that invasion? Yes. Is it something we would have traded for the many Indian peoples who are no longer here because of that invasion? No.

We also like the beads that came from Europe, and again we raised their use to a high art. Would we have traded those beads for the massacres of our people, such as the Sand Creek massacre [in which U.S. soldiers massacred hundreds of Native American men, women, and children at Sand Creek, Colorado, in 1864]? No.

Why do we focus on Columbus rather than any number of U.S. presidents who were also responsible for the death and destruction of Indian people? Because it's his 500 years; it's his quincentenary.

Isn't criticism of Columbus a form of picking on the Spaniards? Were they any worse than other Europeans who came to America?

In my estimation, the Spaniards were no worse than any number of other Europeans. The economy of slavery and serfdom that existed in northern Europe—how do you measure that in cruelty and in long-term effects against the Spanish Inquisition?

I view the issue more as the oppressive nature and arrogance of the Christian religions. And that continues today.

Our Indian religions are not missionary religions. We are taught to respect other religions. It was a shock when we were met with proselytizing zealots, especially those who thought that if your

soul can't be saved, you're better off dead—or if your soul can be saved, you should be dead so you can go to heaven. And that's the history of that original encounter.
How does that arrogance and ignorance manifest itself today?

Native Americans See Worshipping Columbus as an Insult

It's a tragedy that no one seems to really care what Native Americans think about all of this. The majority of the groups that are planning events for the quincentenary haven't reached out to our communities to hear what they have to say.

People have to realize that many Native Americans view America's worshiping Columbus as an insult. Even though the comparison may seem strange to some, many see him as a pre-Colonial-day Hitler. He not only stripped Native Americans of their land, but their culture and livelihood.

Wilma Mankiller, *Scholastic Update*, September 20, 1991.

How? Well, for example, the Catholic Church has said that 1992 is a time to enter into a period of grace and healing and to celebrate the evangelization of the Americas. My word, how can you be graceful and healing about the tens of thousands of native people who were killed because they would not convert to a religion they didn't understand, or because they didn't understand the language of those making the request?

It's difficult to take seriously an apology that is not coupled with atonement. It's as if they're saying, "I'm sorry, oops, and we'll be better in the next hemisphere." That doesn't cut it. We've had empty platitudes before.

The combination of arrogance and ignorance also results in making mascots of Indian people, of dehumanizing and stereotyping them—in the sports world, in advertising, and in society at large. The Washington Redskins football team is an excellent example.

There is no more derogatory name in English for Indian people than the name Redskins. And the Redskins is a prominent image right here in the nation's capital that goes by unnoticed. Because we are an invisible population, the racism against us is also invisible for the most part.

You don't see sports teams called the White Trash, the Black Chicks, the Jew Boys, or the Jack Mormons. And if we did see that, it wouldn't be for long, you can be sure of that.

Why can't we use the Columbus quincentenary to celebrate American diversity and the contributions of all, Europeans and Native Americans alike?

270

There will be lots of people who will be putting forth the perspective of rah rah Columbus, rah rah Western Civilization. Our perspective is putting forth native peoples' views on our past and present. We also want to get into the public consciousness the notion that we actually have a future on this planet. This is something missed by even what is hailed as the most progressive of American movies, *Dances with Wolves*.

We're more interested in the 500 years before Columbus and what will go on in the next 500 years. The truth of the intervening 500 years is really known in the hearts of people worldwide, even though the particulars have been obscured by a cotton-candy version of history.

Aren't some of the criticisms of Columbus just substituting Native-centrism for Euro-centrism?

Oppressed people need to be centered within themselves. Racism and centrism become a problem if you are in the dominant society and are subjugating other people as a result of your centrism. I don't accept the question. I think it's an empty argument.

Aren't criticisms of Columbus just another form of insuring "political correctness"?

The Eurocentric view, having been exposed for its underlying falsehood, now wishes to oppose any other view as either equally false or simply the flip side of reality: a secondary or dual reality.

Feelings are usually dual realities; perspectives are dual realities. But there are some things that don't have a dual reality. For example, if we look at who has polluted all of our water, causing a whole lot of death and whole lot of illness in this country alone, then we have a bit of a clue where the problem might rest. We have a clue whose reality might expose the truth and whose reality might obscure the truth.

It's about time for the people who are the true historic revisionists, who are on the far right side of this whole political correctness debate, to stop lying to themselves, to their readership and to their students. They must stop their silly ivory tower kinds of debates about whether multiculturalism should be used, and so forth.

What is the true history? Just start dealing with some undisputable realities. The world is a mess. This country is a mess. The people who fare the worst in this country are poor, non-white children and poor, non-white old people. Societies who do not care for their young people and old people are decadent, decaying societies.

I think there are a lot of good minds that are reflecting that decadence and decay when they choose to spend their time on these kinds of ivory tower debates. There are things about which they can do much, and they are doing nothing.

What are the key struggles that native people face today?

We need, in the first instance, basic human rights such as religious freedom. Or how about life, liberty and the pursuit of happiness, and other things that many people in the United States view as standard fare but are out of reach for Indian people?

There is also the issue of land and treaty rights. We have property that we don't own and we should, and we have property that we own that we don't control and we should.

We have treaties with the United States that are characterized in the U.S. Constitution as the supreme law of the land. Yet every one, without exception, of nearly 400 treaties signed between native peoples and the U.S. government has been broken. Every one of them.

A good place to start would be for the United States to live up to every treaty agreement. It's also the way you get at resolving some of the problems of poverty, alcoholism, unemployment, and poor health.

If we don't handle the big things, we can't get to the manifestations of the problem. We have to go to the basic human rights issues, the basic treaty rights issues.

If we don't resolve these issues, then all people in this country are going to be complicit in the continuing effort to wipe out our Indian people. It's as simple as that.

II

People of proclaimed good will have the oddest ways of honoring American Indians. Sometimes they dress themselves up in turkey feathers and paint—"cultural drag," my friend Duane Bird Bear calls it—and boogie on 50-yard lines.

Presumably they hope this exuberant if ethnographically questionable display will do their teams more good against opponents than those rituals they imitate and mock did for 19th century Cheyenne and Nez Percé men and women who tried, with desperation and ultimate futility, to defend their homelands from invasion.

Sometimes otherwise impeccably credentialed liberals get so swept up into honoring Indians that they beat fake tom-toms or fashion their forearms and hands into facsimiles of the axes European traders used for barter and attempt, unsuccessfully, to chop their way to victory.

Everywhere you look such respects are paid: the street names in woodsy, affluent subdivisions; mumbo-jumbo in ersatz male-bonding weekends and boy Scout jamborees; geometric fashion statements, weepy anti-littering public service announcements. In the ever popular noble-savage spectrum, red is the hot, safe color. For centuries, flesh and blood Indians have been assigned the role of a popular-culture metaphor for generations. Today, their evocation instantly connotes fuzzy images of Nature, the Past, Plight or Summer Camp. Warbonneted apparitions pasted to football helmets or baseball caps act as opaque, impermeable curtains, solid walls of white noise that for many citizens block or distort all vision of the nearly two million native Americans today.

And why not? Such honoring relegates Indians to the long-ago and thus makes them magically disappear from public consciousness and conscience. What do the 300 federally recognized tribes, with their various complicated treaties governing land rights and protections, their crippling unemployment, infant mortality and teen-age suicide rates, their manifold health problems have in common with jolly (or menacing) cartoon caricatures, wistful braves or raven-tressed Mazola girls?

Perhaps we should ask the Hornell Brewing Company of Baltimore, manufacturers of the Original Crazy Horse Malt Liquor, a product currently distributed in New York with packaging inspired by, according to the text on the back, "the Black Hills of Dakota, *steeped* [my italics] in the History of the American West, home of Proud Indian Nations, a land where imagination conjures up images of blue clad Pony Soldiers and magnificent Native American Warriors."

Whose imagination? Were these the same blue-clad lads who perpetrated the 1890 massacre of 200 captured, freezing Dakota at Wounded Knee? Are Pine Ridge and Rosebud, the two reservations closest to the Black Hills and, coincidentally, the two counties in the United States with the lowest per capita incomes, the Proud Nations?

Is the "steeping" a bald allusion to the fact that alcohol has long constituted the No. 1 health hazard to Indians? Virtually every other social ill plaguing native Americans—from disproportionately frequent traffic fatalities to arrest statistics—is related in some tragic respect to ethanol, and many tribes, from Alaska to New Mexico, record the highest percentage in the world of babies born disabled by fetal alcohol syndrome and effect. One need look no further than the congressionally mandated warning to pregnant women printed in capital letters on every Crazy Horse label to make the connection.

The facts of history are not hard to ascertain: the Black Hills, the "paha sapa," the traditional holy place of the Dakota, were illegally seized by the Government, systematically stripped of their mineral wealth—and have still not been returned to their rightful owners. Crazy Horse, in addition to being a patriot to his Oglala people, was a mystic and a religious leader murdered after he voluntarily gave himself up in 1887 to Pony Soldiers at Fort Robinson, Neb. What, then, is the pairing of his name with 40 ounces of malt liquor supposed to signify?

The Hornell brewers helpfully supply a clue. The detail of the logo is focused on the headdress and not the face; it's pomp without circumstance, form without content. Wear the hat, the illustration seems to offer, and in the process fantasize yourself more interesting (or potent or tough or noble) than you are. Play at being a "warrior" from the "land that truly speaks of the spirit that is America."

And if some humorless Indians object, just set them straight. Remind them what an honor it is to be used.

VIEWPOINT 3

"The latest converts to the trash-Columbus cause are the politically correct editors on the news desks of our major media."

History Should Continue to Acknowledge Columbus as a Discoverer

Reed Irvine and Joe Goulden

Reed Irvine is chairman and Joe Goulden is the director of media analysis for Accuracy in Media, a conservative organization that attempts to correct and publicize media errors. In the following viewpoint the authors argue that oversensitivity to minority rights corrupts language and skews the interpretation of history.

As you read, consider the following questions:

1. How do the authors move from the specific (the issue of the quincentennial and the media coverage of it) to the general? In a broad sense, what are the authors arguing?
2. According to Irvine and Goulden, is the sensitivity to language encouraged in *Winners & Sinners* widespread?

Poor Christopher Columbus. Five hundred years after the fact, the explorer is being stripped of recognition as the man who "discovered" America and the New World. The latest converts to the trash-Columbus cause are the politically correct editors on the news desks of our major media.

"Discover America: Find a Way Around It," admonished a headline in a recent issue of *Copy Editor*, a newsletter for newspaper and magazine copy editors. The article signals how newspapers will cover the 500th anniversary of Columbus' historic 1492 voyage. (Copy editors are the people who check stories for errors, grammar and style, and write the headlines.)

The reasoning for banning "discover" was spelled out in *Winners & Sinners*, a *New York Times* staff newsletter. The paper ordered editors not to use the "d" word in references to Columbus' voyage. "It's offensive to readers who remember that there were people in this hemisphere long before he was," *Winners & Sinners* counseled. Approved substitutes were listed as "he landed, reached, made his voyage—the sensitive possibilities are endless."

What the editors are doing, of course, is pre-emptive self-defense against Native Americans (Indians in pre-PC terminology) who argue that their prior occupancy of the New World means that Columbus was little more than an Italian sailor who happened to travel further than his predecessors.

We admit to sympathy for poor Christopher. Rather than have his 500th anniversary celebrated with pomp and style, he is under attack by the American left and the usual assemblage of hemorrhaging hearts for bringing Western civilization to the North American Continent. The U.S. and Spanish governments are collaborating on events leading up to the actual anniversary in October 1992. But our media are giving advance storm signs that much rain will drum down on the festivities.

Rather than emphasizing the courage of a man who braved an uncharted ocean, the advance stories are billing Columbus as a seagoing Ghengis Khan. Everything evil that has happened on the continent since his arrival is laid on Columbus' gangplank. A book published last year by a socialist writer accused Columbus of introducing racism, genocide, economic exploitation, disease and heavens knows what other ills to the land he . . . Oops! We almost wrote "discovered." Make that sentence conclude "to the land he reached."

The National Council of Churches, whose preachers boom out their nonsense from the left side of the pulpit, resolved in mid-1990 that the 500th anniversary of Columbus' "landing" should be marked not by a celebration, but by "repentance" for crimes committed against native inhabitants and black slaves. *New York Times* op-ed writer Hans Konig charged that the explorer set into motion a sequence of greed, cruelty, slavery and genocide with few parallels in the bloody history of mankind.

The leftists, insofar as we can tell, would prefer that the North American Continent remain the exclusive domain of the 600,000 Native Americans living here in 1492. We suppose that the rest of us—including the leftists, surely?—have a moral obligation to go back where we came from.

In a strict dictionary sense, the PC purists have a semblance of an argument. We consulted Webster's New World Dictionary (New College Edition), which suffices for Accuracy in Media office use. We found these definitions for discover: "to discover, reveal; to be the first to find out, see or know about; to find out; learn the existence of; realize."

But how far will the "discover" nonsense go? One of Hollywood's enduring legends was the "discovery" of the actress Lana Turner as she perched on a soda stool at Schwab's Drug Store in Los Angeles. Now surely the theatrical agent who spotted Lana Turner was not the first person to recognize her physical presence. But he certainly was the first to realize her theatrical potential—so isn't "discover" the right word to describe his decision to take her to a studio? Similarly, the "presence" of the North American Continent had been known to the persons living there for centuries before arrival. But Columbus, and those who followed him, recognized the significance of the New World; in this sense, they certainly deserve credit for having "discovered" America.

There is a significance in the copy editors' decision to blacklist "discovery." Our media are becoming sensitive to a fault in their

277

use of language, to the point that the very fear of what pressure groups might do inhibits them. An aggressive language-police brigade is fielded by the Gay and Lesbian Alliance Against Defamation (GLAAD), which distributes a lengthy list of "no-no" words and phrases to the media. Oddly, one of the more militant homosexual groups calls itself "Queer Nation," incorporating a word that the mainstream media would use at the risk of having angry homosexuals do war dances on their news desks.

For the sake of journalistic history, we're happy that the PC Police were not on patrol at the *Baltimore Sun* in 1948, when H.L. Mencken wrote from the Democratic National Convention that some women delegates were so gaudy that they resembled "British tramp steamers dressed for the king's birthday."

VIEWPOINT 4

"To accept a mountain of lies as historical fact under-
mines the humanity of people of color and destroys
any possibility of genuine multicultural dialogue."

History Should Acknowledge Columbus as a Ruthless Exploiter

Manning Marable

Manning Marable is a political science and history professor at the University of Colorado at Boulder. His most recent book is *The Crisis of Color and Democracy*, published in 1991. Currently he is completing a political biography of Malcolm X. In the following viewpoint Marable condemns anyone, especially white Americans, who continue to view Columbus as a hero.

As you read, consider the following questions:

1. What, according to the author, was the real legacy of Columbus?
2. How does Marable shape his summary of history to support his thesis?

For much of white America, the mythology surrounding Columbus is a central part of their racial identity. But to accept a mountain of lies as historical fact undermines the humanity of people of color and destroys any possibility of genuine multicultural dialogue.

For generations, white history books have related the tale about the supposedly humble son of a Genovese weaver. The Italian sea captain was convinced that the world was round, and persuaded Queen Isabella of Spain to finance an expedition to the west. After a difficult and dangerous journey, the brave navigator and his intrepid crew landed on the island of San Salvador on October 12, 1492. Because he believed that he was only miles from the Asian mainland, Columbus called the people whom he met along the shore "Indians." Thus, we are told, white western civilization finally arrived to what would become America.

The myth of Columbus' "discovery" is also based on the erroneous idea that fifteenth century Europeans believed that the world was flat. But the historical fact is that nearly all learned Europeans of the 1400s knew that the world was indeed round, and that uncharted lands were located to the west. Columbus' chief pilot and business partner, Martin Alonzo Pinzón, had found documents in the library of Pope Innocent VIII which confirmed territories west of the Atlantic Ocean.

What motivated Columbus and the Spanish conquistadors was the lure of gold and the possibility of exploiting the people and resources of these new lands. Within several decades, the Spanish initiated a series of repressive laws which in effect enslaved millions of Native Americans in a system of forced labor. "Civilization" meant the destruction of indigenous cultures and societies. When the Indians resisted, the Europeans showed no mercy. In the Mayan revolt in the Yucatan in the 1520s, Indian chiefs were burned alive; the arms and legs of captured warriors were cut off; Indian women by the thousands were raped and lynched. In one century, Mexico's total population of 25 million declined to one million.

The exploitation of the Americas required a large labor force, so Europeans turned to Africa. As early as the 1460s, about 1,000 Africans were imported annually into the Iberian peninsula as slaves. The Catholic Church was prepared to sanction the expansion of the slave trade to the Americas. In 1488, Pope Innocent VIII accepted 100 Moors as his own personal slaves as a gift from the Spanish King Ferdinand. In 1517, Bishop Bartholomeo de las Casas urged the importation of 12 African slaves for every white Spanish settler.

Over the next three centuries, between 10 and 15 million Africans were involuntarily shipped to the New World. This figure does not include the millions who perished in the transatlantic crossing, the notorious "Middle Passage," in which their bodies were hurled overboard. Nor does it account for the millions of families which were divided, the children torn away from their parents, the daughters sexually molested before their mothers and fathers.

Destructive Myths

The legacy of Columbus lives on in the hearts of many white people. There is still a belief that any meager gains achieved by people of color are acquired at the expense of white people. The myths of discovery, civilization and racism are the direct consequence of Columbus' encounter with the Americas and the Caribbean. The essential cultural justification for all three myths was white Christianity. The image of the humble carpenter of Nazareth was manipulated to rationalize rape, torture, and the seizure of gold. In his ship's diary, on 22 December 1492, Columbus wrote: "Our Lord in his piety, guide me that I may find the gold, I mean their mine, as I have many here who profess to know it." The quest for power and profits demanded the obedience of nonwhites to the icons and idols of Europe.

Europe's dream of economic power, racial privilege and Christian paternalism, which comes together under the quincentennial, has become the historical nightmare of millions of Latinos, Africans, and Native American people. Yet ironically, the quincentennial provides us with a rare opportunity to reconstruct the distortions of cultural history. By liberating ourselves from the historical truths of the violent encounter between Europe and people of color, we might begin to write a new type of history, freed from the half-truths, racism and terror.

By recognizing the genocide which occurred in the wake of Columbus' occupation of the Americas, we might appreciate the struggles for self-determination and dignity of Native American people. And by learning from the errors of the past, we might create the foundations of genuine multicultural and interracial dialogue and understanding. In saying goodbye to the myths of Columbus, we may yet discover a common humanity.

Manning Marable, *The Witness*, January 1992.

Slavery required the development of an ideology of domination. It was inevitable that Africans ceased to be described by their languages or cultures and only by the most superficial distinction which separated them from most Europeans—their skin color. "Blacks" were defined by the boundaries of their skin. Conversely, the Europeans began to call themselves "whites," a racist term, rooted in power, privilege and violence.

By recognizing the genocide and slavery which was the real legacy of Columbus, we might begin to appreciate the dignity of Native American cultures and the history of African people. And by learning from the truths of the past, we might begin to forge the basis for honest interaction and dialogue across racial lines today.

For Discussion

Chapter One

Giraudon/Art Resource, NY

Library of Congress

The Bettmann Archive

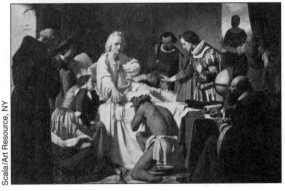

Scala/Art Resource, NY

Examine this portfolio of art that portrays Columbus. Consider the following questions:

a) How do the portrayals differ? Try to apply a single adjective to each portrait that would sum up the character presented.

b) When Columbus is one of a group of figures, how do the other people in the picture help define his character?

283

Chapter Two

1. Debate whether the conquistadors were heroes or villains. Consider point of view as you debate this question. How does each writer in this chapter reveal his point of view? Does each author paint his side as heroic and the other as villainous? Why or why not?

2. James Michener wrote in his *Iberia: Spanish Travels and Reflections* (1968): "The New World was won for Spain not by gentlemen from Toledo and Sevilla but by a group of uneducated village louts who, realizing they had no future in their homeland, had volunteered for service overseas, where their Extramaduran courage proved the most valuable commodity carried westward by the Spanish galleons." Based on the viewpoints of this chapter, do you agree with this interpretation? Why or why not?

3. In his essay "The Significance of the Frontier in American History" Frederick Jackson Turner argued in part that the American character, as we know it, is the product of repeated moves west, away from Europe. Examine these selections to determine whether any "American" traits were brought from Spain by the conquistadors. Were any indigenous to the native Americans? Are any a combination of the two?

4. What were the fundamental differences between the Spaniards and the native Americans when they first met? Did the two cultures have anything in common, or were their differences so great that conquest and its corollary, subjugation, were inevitable? Can you imagine any circumstances in which an alternate history could have been written?

5. Assume a character and write your analysis of the conquest. For example, you might choose to be the soldier who rescued Cortés when he was knocked from his horse in Tenochtitlan, the Aztec priest of the temple there, a messenger returning from the coast with news for Montezuma of the arrival of a strange people, Emperor Charles V, or a twentieth-century mestizo.

Chapter Three

1. Choose a particular case history involving Indians and whites in conflict over land use. (Examples might include the removal of the Cherokees, Wisconsin spearfishing controversies, or reallocation of lands between the Hopis and the Navajos by the Bureau of Indian Affairs.) Divide into two opposing groups and, using principles presented by de Vitoria and von Vattel, argue the case in a mock trial.

2. Compare and contrast all the authors' viewpoints concerning individuals' relationship to their society. Do any of these authors recognize individual virtue apart from the society's collective goals?

3. Do you think there are any circumstances in which it is proper to deny a person his property? Explain.

4. What ironies are present in the inserts by Crawford and Marshall in von Vattel's viewpoint? How do other viewpoints and inserts in this chapter reflect or contradict these ironies?

5. List as many bases for ownership of land or other property as you can think of. Indeed, consider what may be owned. Have these notions of property and ownership changed over the years?

6. Theodore Roosevelt writes, "On the border each man was a law unto himself." How would each of the authors in this chapter respond to this assertion?

7. In 1879 Chief Joseph said, "The earth is the mother of all people, and all people should have equal rights upon it." Is this possible today? Was it ever possible? What might be the consequences if the principle were applied? If it were to be denied?

Chapter Four

1. If possible, invite a non-native speaker of English to address your group. Ask that person to speak for at least 10-15 minutes, without using English and without responding to questions asked in English. At the end of this time, write down your emotional responses. Then attempt to summarize what you think the lecturer told you. What does this exercise reveal about the emotional and intellectual processes involved in exchanges between cultures?

2. Consider Montaigne's observation "everyone gives the title of barbarian to everything that is not according to his usage." What contemporary examples illustrate this point? If you think that the comment is valid, what hope is there for international or even cross-cultural understanding?

3. Examine popular culture—TV, movies, novels, and perhaps even brand names for automobiles or names for athletic teams. How has the American Indian been portrayed? Do these portrayals reflect the positions of Montaigne and Mather and polarize into the Noble Savage and the Beast? Are they more subtly varied? Do you believe that the objection by some native Americans to the Atlanta Braves' Tomahawk Chop, for example, is justified? Why or why not?

4. Several of the selections in this chapter describe the difficulty of feeling comfortable with the social customs of another society. Yet all the authors seem to recognize that adopting these conventions—learning good manners, if you will—is necessary to be an accepted member of any society. Have you personally experienced this component of acculturation? If so, how?

5. Lewis Cass and Nelson A. Miles wrote almost exactly fifty years apart. What events separated the publication of their articles? How might these events affect each man's arguments? For each historical event (the building of the transcontinental railroad, for example), build a chain of cause-effect relationships which might explain the differences in policies proposed by the two men.

6. Differences help define us but can also destroy us. (As this book goes to press, the varied ethnic populations of what used to be Yugoslavia are involved in a bitter bloodbath echoing the atrocities of World War II.) Is it possible to maintain our identity—personal, ethnic, or national—and still live in peace with each other? Or is homogenization, subjugation, or extermination inevitable when two cultures meet?

Chapter Five

1. Unlike Lewis Cass, T.J. Morgan and Nelson A. Miles argue that Indians should be assimilated. Are their proposed methods similar? How have their respective backgrounds influenced their philosophies?

2. T.J. Morgan writes, "Modern studies [late nineteenth century] in ethnology have made us acquainted with the depth to which distinctions of civilization penetrate." Consider all the viewpoints in this chapter to determine the major factors which define a culture and make it distinct from others.

3. Most of the viewpoints in this chapter deal with education, whether formal or informal. How do the writers' philosophies on education differ? What are their educational goals and methods of instruction? What, according to each author, should be the result of the educational process? What would each author consider an "educated" person?

4. Benjamin Franklin, like Michel de Montaigne, makes use of many of the satirist's techniques. Identify some of these devices. Although he ostensibly is writing about the Indians, many of his observations are really about white, "civilized" society. Are any of his comments borne out by other viewpoints in this chapter?

5. In the last line of his poem "The Jesuits in North America,"

Donald Davie writes of Christian missionaries that they are "Savages [who] convert the savages." Based on the viewpoints in this book, do you agree with Davie?

6. By what right may one person undertake to change another? This question, underlying many of the viewpoints in this chapter, persists to the present—in politics, religion, criminology, economics, art, and literature, for example. How would you answer the question?

7. At various stages in American history acculturation of large numbers of people was a major concern: when boarding schools were established for native Americans, when big-city public schools sought to Americanize waves of European immigrants, and after the Vietnam War when new waves of immigrants arrived. At all of these times the question was raised as to whether education should be bilingual. What is your opinion of the issue? Some readers may have undergone the process firsthand and can share their experiences. Others may want to research the issue.

8. Imagine a conversation between Abraham Steiner and Charles Eastman on the subject of religion. Are there any points on which they would agree? On which points would they strongly disagree?

Chapter Six

1. At each centennial of Columbus's arrival in the Americas, his career is reexamined. Do you agree that Columbus should be blamed for the decimation of the native American population, for destruction of the environment, and for the economic exploitation of two hemispheres? Or, conversely, should he be praised for bringing religion to heathens, for introducing the notion of the importance of the individual, and for integrating the world into one economic system?

2. How has the trend toward political correctness impinged upon the evaluation of Columbus's career?

3. Make a list of all the words the authors in this chapter and elsewhere employ to avoid saying "Columbus *discovered* America." In each instance, examine the nuances of meaning.

4. How has Columbus become a vehicle for broader arguments between political liberals and political conservatives?

5. It has been said that those who do not understand history are doomed to repeat it. How would the authors in this chapter respond to that comment?

6. Several of the viewpoints in this chapter suggest that "by

learning from the errors of the past, we might create the foundations of genuine multicultural and interracial dialogue and understanding." Do you agree?

7. Should the church—or religious figures individually—be held more responsible for correcting perceived past errors than are secular organizations and individuals?

8. In your opinion, *was* 1492 a mistake?

Bibliography

Books

James Axtell, *The European and the Indian: Essays in the Ethnohistory of Colonial North America*. New York: Oxford Univ. Press, 1991.

James Axtell, *The Invasion Within: The Contest of Cultures in Colonial North America*. New York: Oxford Univ. Press, 1985.

John Francis Bannon, ed., *The Spanish Conquistadors: Men or Devils?* New York: Holt, Rinehart and Winston, 1960.

William Barrows, *The Indian's Side of the Indian Question*, 1887. Reprint, Freeport, NY: Books for Libraries Press, 1972.

Fernando Benitez, *The Century After Cortés*. Translated by Joan MacLean. Chicago: Univ. of Chicago Press, 1965.

John Bierhorst, ed., *In the Trail of the Wind: American Indian Poems and Ritual Orations*. New York: Farrar, Straus and Giroux, 1971.

Leonardo Boff and Virgil Elizondo, eds., *1492-1992: The Voice of the Victims*. London: SCM Press, 1990.

Daniel J. Boorstin, *The Exploring Spirit: America and the World, Then and Now*. New York: Random House, 1976.

David Brainerd, *The Life and Diary of David Brainerd*. Edited by Jonathan Edwards. Newly edited by Philip E. Howard Jr. Chicago: Moody Press, 1957.

Gordon Brotherston, *Image of the New World: The American Continent Portrayed in Native Texts*. London: Thames and Hudson, 1979.

Roger Burlingame, *The American Conscience*. New York: Alfred A. Knopf, 1957.

Robert Burnette, *The Tortured Americans*. Englewood Cliffs, NJ: Prentice-Hall, 1971.

Joseph H. Cash and Herbert T. Hoover, eds., *To Be an Indian: An Oral History*. New York: Holt, Rinehart and Winston, 1971.

George Catlin, *Letters and Notes on the Manners, Customs, and Conditions of the North American Indians Written During Eight Years' Travel (1832-1839) Amongst the Wildest Tribes of Indians in North America*. 2 vols. London: 1844. Reprint, New York: Dover, 1973.

J. E. Chamberlin, *The Harrowing of Eden: White Attitudes Toward Native Americans*. New York: Seabury Press, 1975.

Christopher Columbus, *The Log of Christopher Columbus*. Translated by Robert H. Fuson. Camden, ME: International Marine Publishing, 1987.

J. Hector St. John de Crèvecoeur, *Journey into Northern Pennsylvania and the State of New York*. Ann Arbor: Univ. of Michigan Press, 1964.

J. Hector St. John de Crèvecoeur, *Letters from an American Farmer*. New York: Dutton, 1957.

J. Hector St. John de Crèvecoeur, *Sketches of Eighteenth Century America*. New Haven: Yale Univ. Press, 1925.

Alfred W. Crosby Jr., *The Columbian Exchange: Biological and Cultural Consequences of 1492*. Westport, CT: Greenwood Press, 1972.

Robert Cushman, "Reasons for Emigration from England to America" in *Chronicles of the Pilgrim Fathers of the Colony of Plymouth from 1602 to 1625*. Edited by Alexander Young. Boston: Charles Little and James Brown, 1844.

Donald Davie, *Collected Poems, 1950-1970*. London: Routledge & Kegan Paul, 1972.

Nigel Davies, *The Ancient Kingdoms of Mexico*. London: Penguin, 1982.

Vine Deloria Jr., *God Is Red*. New York: Grosset & Dunlap, 1973.

Jean Descola, *The Conquistadors*. Translated by Malcolm Barnes. New York: Viking, 1957.

Bernal Díaz del Castillo, *The Conquest of New Spain*. Translated by J. M. Cohen. New York: Penguin, 1963.

J. M. Dickey, ed., *Christopher Columbus and His Monument Columbia*. Chicago: Rand McNally, 1892.

Zvi Dor-Ner, *Columbus and the Age of Discovery*. New York: William Morrow, 1991.

Michael Dorris, *The Broken Cord*. New York: Harper & Row, 1989.

Michael Dorris and Louis Erdrich, *The Crown of Columbus*. New York: HarperCollins, 1991.

Clifford Drury, *Nine Years with the Spokane Indians: The Diary, 1838-1848, of Elkanah Walker*. Glendale, CA: Arthur H. Clark, 1976.

John Dyson, *Columbus: For Gold, God, and Glory*. New York: Simon & Schuster, 1991.

Charles Alexander Eastman [Ohiyesa], *The Soul of the Indian*. Boston: Houghton Mifflin, 1911. Reprint, Johnson Reprint Co., 1971.

Elaine Goodale Eastman, *Pratt: The Red Man's Moses*. Norman: Univ. of Oklahoma Press, 1935.

J. H. Elliott, *The Old World and the New: 1492-1650*. Cambridge: Cambridge Univ. Press, 1970.

John C. Ewers, *The Blackfeet: Raiders on the Northwestern Plains.* Norman: Univ. of Oklahoma Press, 1958.

Brian Fagan, *Kingdoms of Gold, Kingdoms of Jade: The Americas Before Columbus.* London: Thames and Hudson, 1991.

William M. Ferguson and Arthur H. Rohn, *Mesoamerica's Ancient Cities.* Niwot, CO: Univ. of Colorado Press, 1990.

Benjamin Franklin, *Letters and Papers of Benjamin Franklin and Richard Jackson, 1753-1785.* Edited by Carl Van Doren. Philadelphia: The American Philosophical Society, 1947.

Patricia de Fuentes, ed., *The Conquistadors: First-Person Accounts of the Conquest of Mexico.* New York: Orion Press, 1963.

J. Galloway, *The Sugar Cane Industry.* Cambridge: Cambridge Univ. Press, 1989.

Paul Wallace Gates, ed., *The Rape of Indian Lands.* New York: Arno Press, 1979.

Antonello Gerbi, *Nature in the New World from Christopher Columbus to Gonzalo Fernandez de Oviedo.* Pittsburgh: Univ. of Pittsburgh Press, 1985.

Stephen Greenblatt, *Marvelous Possessions: The Wonder of the New World.* Chicago: Univ. of Chicago Press, 1991.

Francis F. Guest, "The Franciscan World View," in *New Directions in California History.* Edited by James J. Rawls. New York: McGraw Hill, 1988.

A. B. Guthrie Jr., *The Big Sky.* Boston: Houghton Mifflin, 1947.

John Heckewelder, *Account of the History, Manners and Customs of the Indian Nations, Who Once Inhabited Pennsylvania and the Neighboring States.* Philadelphia: American Philosophical Society, 1819.

John Hemming, *The Conquest of the Incas.* San Diego: Harcourt Brace Jovanovich, 1970.

Henry Hobhouse, *Seeds of Change: Five Plants That Transformed Mankind.* New York: Harper & Row, 1986.

Peter Charles Hoffer, ed., *Indians and Europeans: Selected Articles on Indian-White Relations in Colonial North America.* New York: Garland Publishing, 1988.

Peter Charles Hoffer, ed., *Planters and Yeoman: Selected Articles on the Southern Colonies.* New York: Garland Publishing, 1988.

Washington Irving, *A History of the Life and Voyages of Christopher Columbus.* New York: G & C Carvill, 1828.

Cecil Jane, ed., *Select Documents Illustrating the Four Voyages of Columbus.* New York: Dover, 1988.

Francis Jennings, *The Invasion of America: Indians, Colonialism, and the Cant of Conquest.* New York: Norton, 1976.

Basil H. Johnston, *Indian School Days*. Norman: Univ. of Oklahoma Press, 1989.

Howard Mumford Jones, *O Strange New World: American Culture, the Formative Years*. New York: Viking, 1964.

Alvin Josephy Jr., *Red Power*. New York: American Heritage Press, 1971.

Peter Kalm, *The America of 1750: Peter Kalm's Travels in North America*. 2 Vols. Edited by Adolph B. Benson. New York: Dover, 1964.

Benjamin Keen, ed., *The Life of the Admiral Christopher Columbus by His Son Ferdinand*. New Brunswick, NJ: Rutgers Univ. Press, 1959.

J. P. Kinney, *A Continent Lost—A Civilization Won: Indian Land Tenure in America*. New York: Octagon Press, 1975.

Hans Konig, *Columbus: His Enterprise, Exploding the Myth*. New York: Monthly Review Press, 1991.

Theodora Kroeber, *Ishi in Two Worlds: A Biography of the Last Wild Indian in North America*. Berkeley: Univ. of California Press, 1961.

Oliver La Farge, ed., *The Changing Indian*. Norman: Univ. of Oklahoma Press, 1942.

Father Joseph Francis Lafitau, *Customs of the American Indians Compared with the Customs of Primitive Times*. Toronto: Champlain Society, 1974.

Bartolomé de las Casas, *The Devastation of the Indies: A Brief Account*. Translated by Herma Briffault. New York: Seabury Press, 1974.

Bartolomé de las Casas, *In Defense of the Indians*. Translated by Stafford Poole. DeKalb, IL: Northern Illinois Univ. Press, 1974.

Miguel Leon-Portilla, *Pre-Columbian Literatures of Mexico*. Norman: Univ. of Oklahoma Press, 1969.

Miguel Leon-Portilla, ed., *The Broken Spears: The Aztec Account of the Conquest of Mexico*. Boston: Beacon Press, 1962.

Robert H. Lowie, *The Crow Indians*. New York: Rinehart, 1935.

T. C. McLuhan, ed., *We Touch the Earth: A Self Portrait of Indian Existence*. New York: Outerbridge & Dienstfrey, 1971.

William Hardy McNeill, *Plagues and Peoples*. New York: Doubleday, Anchor Books, 1976.

Salvador de Madariaga, *Christopher Columbus*. London: Hollis & Carter, 1949.

R. H. Major, *Select Letters of Christopher Columbus, with Other Original Documents Relating to His First Four Voyages to the New World*. London: The Hakluyt Society, 1847. Reprinted 1961.

Alice Marriott and Carol K. Rachlin, *Plains Indian Mythology*. New York: Thomas Y. Crowell, 1975.

James A. Michener, *Iberia: Spanish Travels and Reflections*. Greenwich, CT: Fawcett, Crest Publications, 1968.

James E. Miller Jr., with the assistance of Kathleen Fargey, *Heritage of American Literature*. San Diego: Harcourt Brace Jovanovich, 1991.

Michel Eyquem de Montaigne, "Of Cannibals," in *Montaigne: Selected Essays*. Translated by Charles Cotton and W. Haslitt. New York: Random House, Modern Library, 1949.

T. J. Morgan, *Indian Education*. Bureau of Education Bulletin No. 1, 1889. Washington: Government Printing Office, 1890.

Samuel Eliot Morison, *Admiral of the Ocean Sea: A Life of Christopher Columbus*. Boston: Little, Brown, 1942.

Samuel Eliot Morison, *Christopher Columbus, Mariner*. Boston: Little, Brown, 1955.

Toribio Motolinia, *Motolinia's History of the Indians of New Spain*. Translated and edited by Elizabeth Andros Foster. Westport, CT: Greenwood Press, 1973.

Peter Nabokov, ed., *Native American Testimony: A Chronicle of Indian-White Relations from Prophecy to the Present, 1492-1992*. New York: Viking, 1991.

Alvar Nunez Cabeza de Vaca, *Relation of Nunez Cabeza de Vaca*. Ann Arbor, MI: University Microfilms, 1966.

Stephen B. Oates, *Portrait of America*. Vol. 1. Boston: Houghton Mifflin, 1991.

Michael Paiewonsky, *Conquest of Eden: 1493-1515: Other Voyages of Columbus*. Rome: MAPes MONDe Editore, 1991.

Roy Harvey Pearce, *Savagism and Civilization: A Study of the Indian and the American Mind*. Berkeley: Univ. of California Press, 1988.

George Perkins, Sculley Bradley, Richmond Croom Beatty, and E. Hudson Long, *The American Tradition in Literature*, 7th ed. New York: McGraw Hill, 1990.

William D. Phillips Jr. and Carla Rhan Phillips, *The Worlds of Christopher Columbus*. Cambridge: Cambridge Univ. Press, 1992.

Francis Paul Prucha, *The Great Father: The United States Government and the American Indians*, abridged edition. Lincoln: Univ. of Nebraska Press, 1986.

Kenneth Roberts, *Northwest Passage*. Greenwich, CT: Fawcett, 1937.

Theodore Roosevelt, *The Winning of the West*, Vol. I. New York: G.P. Putnam's Sons, Knickerbocker Press, 1903.

Annette Rosenstiel, ed., *Red and White: Indian Views of the White Man. 1492-1982*. New York: Universe Books, 1983.

Jean-Jacques Rousseau, *The First and Second Discourses*. Edited by Roger D. Masters. New York: St. Martin's Press, 1964.

Nancy Rubin, *Isabella of Castille: The First Renaissance Queen*. New York: St. Martin's Press, 1991.

Benjamin Rush, *The Autobiography of Benjamin Rush: His "Travels Through Life" Together with His* Commonplace Book *for 1789-1813*. Edited by George W. Croner. Princeton, NJ: Princeton Univ. Press, 1948.

Kirkpatrick Sale, *The Conquest of Paradise: Christopher Columbus and the Columbian Legacy*. New York: Alfred A. Knopf, 1990.

Thomas E. Sanders and Walter W. Peek, eds., *Literature of the American Indian*. Beverly Hills: Glencoe Press, 1973.

Henry Nash Smith, *Virgin Land: The American West as Symbol and Myth*. Cambridge, MA: Harvard Univ. Press, 1978.

James Smith, "Prisoner of the Caughnawagas," in *Captured by the Indians: Fifteen Firsthand Accounts, 1759-1870*. Edited by Frederick Drimmer. New York: Dover, 1961.

James Morton Smith, ed., *Seventeenth Century America: Essays in Colonial History*. Chapel Hill: Univ. of North Carolina Press, 1959.

William Smith, *An Historical Account of the Expedition Against the Ohio Indians, in the Year 1764, Under the Command of Henry Bouquet, 1765*. Ann Arbor, MI: University Microfilms, 1966.

Luther Standing Bear, *Land of the Spotted Eagle*. Boston: Houghton Mifflin, 1933.

Luther Standing Bear, *My People the Sioux*. Edited by E.A. Brininstool. Lincoln: Univ. of Nebraska Press, 1975.

[Abraham Steiner], *Thirty Thousand Miles with John Heckewelder*. Edited by Paul A.W. Wallace. Pittsburgh: Univ. of Pittsburgh Press, 1958.

Brian Swann and Arnold Krupat, eds., *I Tell You Now: Autobiographical Essays by Native American Writers*. Lincoln: Univ. of Nebraska Press, 1987.

Paolo Emilio Taviani, *Christopher Columbus: The Grand Design*. London: Orbis, 1985.

Paolo Emilio Taviani, *Columbus: The Great Adventure*. Translated by Luciano F. Farina and Marc A. Beckwith. New York: Orion Books, 1991.

Frederick Jackson Turner, "The Significance of the Frontier in American History," in *The Turner Thesis: Concerning the Role of the Frontier in American History*. 3rd ed. Edited by George Rogers Taylor. Lexington, MA: D.C. Heath, 1972.

Katharine C. Turner, *Red Men Calling on the Great White Father*. Norman: Univ. of Oklahoma Press, 1951.

S. Lyman Tyler, *A History of Indian Policy*. Washington: U.S. Dept. of the Interior, Bureau of Indian Affairs, 1973.

S. Lyman Tyler, ed., *Two Worlds: The Indian Encounters with the Europeans, 1492-1509*. Salt Lake City: Univ. of Utah Press, 1988.

Richard Van Der Beets, *The Indian Captivity Narrative: An American Genre*. Lanham, MD: University Press of America, 1984.

W. C. Vanderweth, *Indian Oratory: Famous Speeches by Noted Indian Chieftains*. Norman: Univ. of Oklahoma Press, 1971.

Emmerich von Vattel, *The Law of Nations; or Principles of the Law of Nature, Applied to the Conduct and Affairs of Nations and Sovereigns*. Translated by Joseph Chitty. Philadelphia: T. & J. W. Johnson & Co., 1876.

Alden T. Vaughan and Edward W. Clark, eds. *Puritans Among the Indians: Accounts of Captivity and Redemption, 1676-1724*. Cambridge, MA: Harvard University Press, Belknap Press, 1981.

Herman J. Viola, *After Columbus: The Smithsonian Chronicle of the North American Indians*. New York: Orion Press, 1990.

Herman J. Viola, *Diplomats in Buckskins: A History of Indian Delegations in Washington City*. Washington: Smithsonian Institution Press, 1981.

Herman J. Viola, *Exploring the West*. Washington: Smithsonian Books, 1987.

Herman J. Viola and Carolyn Margolis, eds., *Seeds of Change: A Quincentennial Commemoration*. Washington: Smithsonian Institution Press, 1991.

Francisco de Vitoria, *Political Writings*. Edited by Anthony Pagden and Jeremy Lawrance. Cambridge: Cambridge Univ. Press, 1991.

Wilcomb E. Washburn, ed., *The Indian and the White Man*. Garden City, NY: Doubleday, Anchor Books, 1964.

Frank Waters, *Book of the Hopi*. New York: Viking, 1963.

Frank Waters, *Pumpkin Seed Point*. Chicago: Swallow Press, 1969.

Jack Weatherford, *Indian Givers: How the Indians of the Americas Transformed the World*. New York: Crown Publishers, 1988.

Henry Wheaton, *Elements of International Law*. Oxford, England: Clarendon Press, 1936.

Jon Manchip White, *Cortés and the Downfall of the Aztec Empire*. New York: Carroll & Graf, 1971.

Simon Wiesenthal, *Sails of Hope: The Secret Mission of Christopher Columbus*. New York: Macmillan, 1973.

John Noble Wilford, *The Mysterious History of Columbus: An Exploration of the Man, the Myth, the Legacy*. New York: Alfred A. Knopf, 1991.

John Williams, *The Redeemed Captive Returning to Zion*. Ann Arbor, MI: University Microfilms, 1966.

Justin Winsor, *Christopher Columbus and How He Received and Imparted the Spirit of Discovery*. Boston: Houghton Mifflin, 1892.

Periodicals

Joel Achenbach, "Debating Columbus in a New World: Is This About Defining the Past or the Future?" *The Washington Post National Weekly Edition*, October 7-13, 1991.

John Andrew, "Educating the Heathen: The Foreign Mission School Controversy and American Ideals," *American Studies* 12:3 (1978).

Dave Barry, "Blame It on Columbus," *Reader's Digest*, February 1990.

Jacob Bernstein, "Quincentenary: U.S. Commission Adrift," *Report on the Americas*. December 1991.

Bill Bigelow, "Two Myths Are Not Better than One," *Monthly Review*, July/August 1992.

Kay Brigham, "The Columbus Nobody Knows," interview with David Neff, *Christianity Today*, October 7, 1991.

Peter Burnham, "500 Years in North America as Native People Saw Them," *Insight*, January 6, 1992.

Warren H. Carroll, "The Historical Truth About Christopher Columbus," *Fidelity*, April 1992.

Lewis Cass, "Removal of the Indians," *North Amerian Review*, xxx (1830).

Rae Corelli, "To Celebrate or Repent? Critics Assail the Columbus Myth," *Maclean's*, August 5, 1991.

Paula DiPerna, "Was Columbus' Wife His Inspiration?" *USA Today*, February 19, 1992.

Michael Dorris, "Native Savages? We'll Drink to That," *The New York Times*, April 21, 1992.

Wayne Ellwood, "Hidden History: Columbus and the Colonial Legacy," *New Internationalist*, December 1991.

Brian Fagan, "A Clash of Cultures," *Archaeology*, January/February 1990.

Mark Falcoff, "Was 1492 a Mistake? Did Columbus Go Too Far?" *The American Enterprise*, January/February 1992.

Friends Committee on National Legislation, "We Have All Been Here Before," *Washington Newsletter*, November 1991.

Jo-Ellen Darling Gerhard, "Do You Know What Your Children Are Learning About Columbus?" *Human Events*, November 30, 1991.

Stephen Goode, "Debunking Columbus," *Insight*, October 21, 1991.

David T. Haberly, "Women and Indians: *The Last of the Mohicans* and the Captivity Tradition," *American Quarterly*, Fall 1976.

Suzan Shown Harjo, "We Have No Reason to Celebrate an Invasion," an interview with Barbara Miner. *Rethinking Schools*, October/November 1991.

Jeffrey Hart, "Discovering Columbus," *National Review*, October 15, 1990.

Jeffrey Hart, "The World Is Moving in a Western Direction," *Conservative Chronicle*, October 23, 1991.

Barbara Holland, "Vespucci Could Have Been Wrong, Right?" *Smithsonian*, March 1990.

James H. Howard, "The Native Image in Western Europe," *American Indian Quarterly*, February 1978.

Frederick E. Hoxie, "Red Man's Burden," *The Antioch Review*, Summer 1979.

Reed Irvine and Joe Goulden, "Taking the Discovery Detour," *The Washington Times*, October 1991.

Chief Joseph, "An Indian's View of Indian Affairs," *North American Review* CXXVIII (1879).

Louis C. Kleber, "Religion Among the American Indians," *History Today*, February 1978.

Peter Kovler, "Native American Land Rights," *Current*, July/August 1978.

Charles Krauthammer, "Hail Columbus, Dead White Male," *Time*, May 27, 1991.

Oliver La Farge, "Myths That Hide the American Indian," *American Heritage*, October 1956.

Janet Karsten Larson, "Redeeming the Time and the Land: Epilogue to '1776,'" *The Christian Century*, April 13, 1977.

Gary MacEoin, "Genocide Continues as Beneficiaries of Spanish Conquest Prepare Celebration," *National Catholic Reporter*, August 16, 1991.

James R. McGraw, "God Is Also Red: An Interview with Vine Deloria Jr.," *Christianity and Crisis*, September 15, 1975.

Robert McLaughlin, "Giving It Back to the Indians," *The Atlantic*, February 1977.

Robert McLaughlin, "Who Owns the Land? A Native American Challenge," *Juris Doctor*, September 1976.

Manning Marable, "1492: A Personal Perspective," *The Witness*, January 1992.

Manning Marable, "Myths of Columbus Cloud Our Past and Present," *People's Weekly World*, November 30, 1991.

Martin E. Marty, "Discovering Columbus: A Quincentennial Reading," *The Christian Century*, November 20-27, 1991.

Nelson A. Miles, "The Indian Problem," *North American Review* CXXVIII (1879).

Peter Montgomery, "Holy Columbus!" *Common Cause Magazine*, November/December 1989.

James Muldoon, "The Columbus Quincentennial: Should Christians Celebrate It?" *America*, October 27, 1990.

Newsweek, "Columbus, Stay Home! The Bitter Debate over His 500th Anniversary," June 24, 1991.

Frederick A. Norwood, "Two Contrasting Views of the Indians: Methodist Involvement in the Indian Troubles in Oregon and Washington," *Church History*, June 1980.

Charles W. Polzer, "Reflections on the Quincentenary," *America*, November 16, 1991.

Stephen Robinson, "1492 and All That," *The Spectator*, November 9, 1991.

W. Stitt Robinson Jr., "Indian Education and Missions in Colonial Virginia," *The Journal of Southern History* 18 (1952).

James P. Ronda, "'We are Well as We Are': An Indian Critique of Seventeenth Century Christian Missions," *The William and Mary Quarterly*, January 1977.

Robert Royal, "Columbus as a Dead White European Male: The Ideological Underpinnings of the Controversy over 1492," *The World & I*, December 1991.

Robert Royal, "Consequences of Columbus," *First Things*, February 1992.

Jeffrey Russel, "Inventing the Flat Earth," *History Today*, August 1971.

Ernesto Sabato, "The 'Nina,' the 'Pinta,' and the Debate They Started: A Latin American Writer Defends Christopher Columbus," *World Press Review*, October 1991.

Kirkpatrick Sale, "Columbus on the Couch," *New Internationalist*, December 1991.

Simon Schama, "They All Laughed at Columbus," *The New Republic*, January 6 & 13, 1992.

Senior Scholastic, "Indians Take to the Courts," February 9, 1978.

Thyme S. Siegel, "The Jewish Connections to the Voyages of Columbus," *Creation Spirituality*, September/October 1991.

Albert J. Snow, "The American Indian Knew a Better Way," *The American Biology Teacher*, January 1973.

Luther Standing Bear, "The Tragedy of the Sioux," *The American Mercury*, November 1931.

Carl Starkloff, "The Church Between Cultures: Missions on Indian Reservations," *The Christian Century*, November 3, 1976.

Rennard Strickland, "The Idea of the Environment and the Ideal of the Indian," *Journal of American Indian Education*, October 1970.

E. G. R. Taylor, "Idée Fixe: The Mind of Christopher Columbus," *The Hispanic American Historical Review*, August 1931.

USA Today, "Misdiagnosed Patient Freed After Two Years," June 17, 1992.

Aileen Vincent-Barwood, "Columbus: What If?" *Aramco World*, January/February 1992.

Herman J. Viola, "How *Did* an Indian Chief Really Look?" *Smithsonian*, June 1977.

Robert Allen Warrior, "Columbus Quincentennial Is Nothing to Celebrate," *Utne Reader*, November/December 1991.

Wilcomb E. Washburn, ed., "A Moral History of Indian-White Relations: Needs and Opportunities for Study," *Ethnohistory: The Bulletin of the Ohio Valley Historic Indian Conference* 4 (1957).

Frank Waters, "Two Views of Nature: White and Indian," *South Dakota Review*, May 1964.

Delbo C. West and August Kling, "Columbus and Columbia: A Brief Survey of the Early Creation of the Columbus Symbol in American History," *Studies in Popular Culture* 12:2 (1989).

Chilton Williamson Jr., "Flat-Earth Theories," *Chronicles*, October 1991.

Garry Wills, "Goodbye, Columbus," *The New York Review of Books*, November 22, 1990.

Samuel M. Wilson, "The Admiral and the Chief," *Natural History*, March 1991.

Samuel M. Wilson, "Columbus, My Enemy," *Natural History*, December 1990.

Jack Wintz, "500 Years of Evangelization: A 'Teaching Moment' for the Americas," *St. Anthony Messenger*, April 1992.

Jack Wintz, "Respect Our Indian Values," *St. Anthony Messenger*, July 1975.

Jamil S. Zainaldin, "The Scholarly Benefits of the Columbus Quincentenary Will Reach Far Beyond 1992," *The Chronicle of Higher Education*, April 12, 1989.

Index

Acknowledgments

The following material from copyrighted works has been included in the present volume:

Chapter 1: From *Admiral of the Ocean Sea* by Samuel Eliot Morison. Copyright 1942 by Samuel Eliot Morison, © renewed 1970 by Samuel Eliot Morison. Reprinted by permission of Little, Brown and Company; p. 18. From Jack Wintz, "500 Years of Evangelization: A Teaching Moment," *St. Anthony Messenger*, April 1992. Reprinted with permission; p. 39.

Chapter 2: From *The Conquistadors* by Jean Descola, translated by Malcolm Barnes, translation copyright © 1957 by the Viking Press. Copyright renewed © 1985 by Viking Penguin, Inc. Used by permission of Viking Penguin, a division of Penguin Books USA Inc.; p. 51. From *The Devastation of the Indies: A Brief Account* by Bartolomé de las Casas, translated by Herma Briffault. New York: Seabury Press, 1974; p. 61. From *The Conquest of New Spain* by Bernal Díaz del Castillo, translated by J.M. Cohen (Penguin Classics, 1963), pp. 378-88, copyright © J.M. Cohen, 1963. Reproduced by permission of Penguin Books Ltd.; p. 70. From *Broken Spears* by Miguel Leon-Portilla. Copyright © 1962 by Miguel Leon-Portilla. Reprinted by permission of Beacon Press; p. 80.

Chapter 3: From *Political Writings* by Francisco de Vitoria, edited by Anthony Pagden and Jeremy Lawrance. Cambridge: Cambridge University Press, 1991. Reprinted with permission; p. 103.

Chapter 4: From *Selected Essays of Montaigne* by Michel Montaigne, translated by C. Cotton, W.C. Hazlitt, B. Bate. Copyright 1949 by Random House, Inc. Reprinted by permission of Random House, Inc.; p. 147. From *Puritans Among the Indians: Accounts of Captivity and Redemption, 1676-1724*, edited by Alden T. Vaughan and Edward W. Clark. Cambridge, MA: The Belknap Press of Harvard University Press, © 1981 by the President and Fellows of Harvard College. Reprinted by permission of the publishers; p. 156.

Chapter 6: From "Was 1492 a Mistake? Did Columbus Go Too Far?" by Mark Falcoff, *The American Enterprise*, January/February 1992, © 1992, The American Enterprise. Distributed by The New York Times Special Features. Reprinted with permission; p. 259. From "We Have No Reason to Celebrate an Invasion," by Suzan Shown Harjo, interviewed by Barbara Miner in *Rethinking Schools*, October/November 1991. Reprinted with permission; p. 268. From

About the Editor

Mary Ellen Jones received her A.B. and M.A. from Duke University and her Ph.D. from the Union Graduate School. From her early emphasis on American literature and fiction, she began teaching courses in the literature of the American frontier. At a summer institute on northern Plains Indians at the Buffalo Bill Historical Institute in Cody, Wyoming, she met Dr. Herman J. Viola, director of the Seeds of Change Quincentennial programs at the Smithsonian Institution. He encouraged Jones in work that led to the publication of her book, *Seeds of Change: Readings on Cultural Exchange After 1492* (1993), a joint project of the Museum of National History, the Smithsonian Institution, and the National Council for the Social Studies.

Dr. Jones is currently associate professor of English at Wittenberg University where, in addition to frontier literature, she teaches courses in Hemingway, Steinbeck, war literature, and the literature of the Mediterranean. Jones previously taught at Bakersfield College, California, and as a Fulbright teacher in Corfu, Greece.

CHRISTOPHER
COLUMBUS
AND HIS LEGACY
OPPOSING VIEWPOINTS®

David L. Bender & Bruno Leone, *Series Editors*

Mary Ellen Jones, Associate Professor of
English, Wittenberg University,
Springfield, Ohio, *Book Editor*

OPPOSING
VIEWPOINTS
SERIES®

Greenhaven Press, Inc.   PO Box 289009 San Diego,   CA 92198-9009

Other Books of Related Interest in the Opposing Viewpoints Series:

American Values
Constructing a Life Philosophy
The Environmental Crisis
Global Resources
Immigration
Racism in America
Religion in America
Social Justice

Library of Congress Cataloging-in-Publication Data

Christopher Columbus and his legacy : opposing viewpoints / Mary Ellen
Jones, editor.
    p. cm. — (Opposing viewpoints series)
    Includes bibliographical references and index.
    Summary: Articles present opposing viewpoints on such Columbus-related issues as the motives of the conquistadors, treatment of the Indians, and twentieth-century views of Columbus.
    ISBN 0-89908-196-7 (lib.: alk. paper) — ISBN 0-89908-171-1 (pbk.: alk. paper)
    1. Columbus, Christopher. 2. America—Discovery and exploration— Spanish. 3. Latin America—History—To 1830. 4. Indians, Treatment of—Latin America. [1. Columbus, Christopher. 2. America—Discovery and exploration—Spanish. 3. Indians—Treatment.] I. Jones, Mary Ellen. II. Series.
E111.C554 1992
970.01'5—dc20   92-18160
                                                            CIP
                                                            AC